D1367450

Working Dazed

Why Drugs Pervade the
Workplace and What
Can Be Done About It

Working Dazed

Why Drugs Pervade the Workplace and What Can Be Done About It

Angela Browne Miller, M.P.H., Ph.D.

Kensington, California

INSIGHT BOOKS
Plenum Press • New York and London

Library of Congress Cataloging-in-Publication Data

Browne Miller, Angela, 1952–
    Working dazed : why drugs pervade the workplace and what can be
  done about it / Angela Browne Miller.
        p.   cm.
    "Insight books."
    Includes bibliographical references and index.
    ISBN 0-306-43765-1
    1. Drugs and employment.   I. Title.
  HF5549.5.D7B76   1991
  658.3'822--dc20   91-7247
                                                                            CIP

ISBN 0-306-43765-1

© 1991 Plenum Press, New York
A Division of Plenum Publishing Corporation
233 Spring Street, New York, N.Y. 10013

An Insight Book

Printed in the United States of America

To the men in my family
Cary, Lee, George
and my husband, Richard

Preface

Working Dazed grew out of my long-term fascination with work-places and workplace mental health. At work, we are confronted with pressures to produce, to earn, to cooperate, to achieve, and to obey. Economic survival and cultural reward drive us to work. One's ability to work well determines one's ability to compete. The workplace is thus one of the key arenas in human evolution.

Because the majority of us spend a significant portion of our lives "at work," the destiny of the individual human adult is, in large part, being shaped in the workplace. So often we hear ourselves saying, "My life is my work." Individuals' identities are overwhelmingly determined by the work that they do. Yet how much of what we do to "earn a living" is what we would choose to do with the time of our lives were earning a living not at stake?

And once we are "at work," how much autonomy do we really have? Even those who think that they have a relatively high degree of decision-making power may have succumbed to the daze of progress. There is something pervasive but subtle about this daze. Perhaps it is so difficult to recognize because we are so deeply enmeshed in it.

Working Dazed also grew out of my concern regarding the narcoticization of the workforce. The influence of drugs is pervasive in the workplace. It is far too often that employees work under the influence of illegal and legal drugs. They either use these drugs during the working day or they arrive at work on the drugs, withdrawing from the drugs or craving the drugs. Whatever the case may be, they are working under the influence. They are working dazed. Their daze is a drug daze. While the greatest uproar in the 1970s and 1980s was around the use of illegal drugs by employees, it is clear that the effects of alcohol, prescription drugs, and over-the-counter drugs are taking their tolls on workplace productivity, product and service quality, and employee and consumer safety. Drugs are much more pervasive in the workforce than they appear to be if we focus entirely on the very present but more sensational problems of employee cocaine, crack, amphetamine (speed), and marijuana use. It is time that we scrutinize the effects of "acceptable" drugs such as pain killers, muscle relaxants, tranquilizers, and diet pills on employees' fine and gross motor coordination, judgment, morale, and job performance. It is also time that we investigate the effects of nicotine and caffeine upon these and other indicators of employee productivity.

We must recognize employee drug use as a signal. When a portion of the workforce works under the influence of drugs, it is making perceptible a bit of the daze to which we may all have succumbed. What is it that those who use drugs are drugging? Pain? Stress? Frustration? Anger? Powerlessness? Role strain? Competition? Alienation? Disenchantment? Failure? Boredom? To the extent that these ingredients of the human condition are generated in the workplace, the workplace must be refashioned to alleviate these detractors from employee satisfaction, job performance, and consumer safety.

Every working person must understand that she or he is a player in the processes of social and biological change. Are we adapting the human species to a work orientation which will bring us to the brink of mindless droneship? Or will we manage to snap out of the daze and become highly conscious of the choices we make as individuals, as businesses, and as societies?

Going to work armed with information about employee drug use and its implications is a beginning. Every working person has a right to know what motivates working people to drug themselves, what the effects and symptoms of drug use in the workplace are, what a company drug policy is and how it is made, how drug tests work and what the legal implications of testing are. Every working person has a right to know how drug use by co-workers threatens her or his safety.

Every consumer of goods and services must also be armed with information about employee drug use and its dangers. Consumers must know enough about employee drug use to demand answers to critical questions: Is my surgeon on drugs? Is my child care worker experiencing a hangover? Were the tires put back on my car by an employee in an altered state of mind? Is my bus driver or airline pilot under the influence? Do I have a right to demand answers to these questions?

Consumers *do* have rights. They must become educated about employee drug use in order to exercise their rights. Consumers must demand answers to these questions as they select doctors, babysitters, schoolteachers, auto servicers, airlines, etc. Ask and ask loudly what drugs, if any, have been used during the past seven days by the doctor about to perform surgery on you or a member of your family. Ask and ask regularly if any of the people in your child care center use drugs, including pills and alcohol, at any time. Ask and ask insistently to speak to the pilots of the plane you are about to fly: Will you be flying under the influence of a drug today? Know and be able to explain what the definition of "drug" is and what "under the influence of a drug" means. If you are told that you have no right to ask such questions, let every other consumer at the ticket window, or patient in the hospital, or parent at the child care center know that information is being withheld. Make some noise about this. Make yourself an involved consumer.

I have written *Working Dazed* in an effort to inform readers of these and other important issues regarding employee drug use as well as to connect this information to the larger philosophical matters with which we must be concerned. Where is worklife taking us? Is this where we want to go? What can we do to stop, take measure, and take action?

ANGELA BROWNE MILLER

Tiburon, California

Acknowledgments

I wish to thank the many people who have inspired and aided in the development of this book. Among them are my husband, psychologist Richard Louis Miller, who has shared his profound clinical expertise in the area of addiction; my father, Lee Winston Browne, whose knowledge of corporate management dynamics and general wisdom has been invaluable to me; Cindy Bilbrey, who has been my long-term, unfailing, and dedicated research and manuscript production assistant and who offered many spirited and intelligent comments on my work; Don Lucas of the Lucas Dealership Group in San Jose, California, for his commitment to developing an improved workplace; Don Carlson of the Ark Foundation in Moraga, California, for his efforts to build a healthier world; and the many employers and employees who have shared their stories with me and opened their organizations and their hearts to my inquiring eyes.

Contents

Working Dazed

Why Drugs Pervade the
Workplace and What
Can Be Done About It

Working-Class Heroes
Drugged Drones

We are working-class heroes. We wake up to our blaring alarms, barking dogs, calling children. We dress in clothing that makes us look similar to other people: coveralls, aprons, suits, uniforms to make us appear uniform. We quickly search the newsprint of our morning papers for a little meaning. We sit in long lines on freeways, passing the time of our lives, breathing in exhaust fumes, and listening to deceptively alert voices pour out of our radios. We arrive at work with our public faces and take our positions in our public places, poised to get ahead or at least to save our faces, barely keeping up with the Joneses.

On payday we are paid money which we either must spend or have already spent on our blaring alarms, barking dogs, calling children, morning papers, uniforms, and automobiles, either keeping up with the Joneses or simply trying to stay alive. We go to work. We get paid. We spend the money, and then, heroically, we return again for more. We are, indeed, working-class heroes.

We are fortunate that worklife is not always experienced as being this grim. Many of us depend upon work for more than money. We develop a sense of identity and meaning in our jobs. We make friends at work. We learn about ourselves and others. We have something to focus on beyond ourselves and our families. We have what appears to be a productive way to spend our time. We feel important, necessary, even essential. Some of us become so very dependent upon the feelings that working gives us that we actually become addicted to our work.

Work is a strange activity. It brings out a wide range of explicit and implicit feelings and behaviors among those who are compelled to do it. Even when a working person finds work-life to be a highly positive experience, he or she is under some degree of stress. The stress is usually a combination of healthy and unhealthy stress. Even when the working person is very conscious of the stress that he or she is under, he or she is detecting only the tip of the iceberg. Work is so very much a part of our reality that we are unaware of its deepest effects upon our souls.

Much of the stress that working people experience is either undetected or unadmitted stress: We either don't recognize it or don't want to recognize it. The effects of fluorescent lights, continuous noises, commuter traffic, workplace pollution, personality conflicts, competition, deadline pressure, taking orders, alienation from one's labor, boredom, and other common work-life experiences are all too often registered only on the subconscious level.

It is not surprising that drugs have entered the workplace. Even when working people are only vaguely aware of the presence of stress, they need a way to diminish the insidious stress of continuous physical irritation, psychological pressure, boredom, and identity confusion. Unfortunately, the effects of repeated on- or off-the-job alcohol and drug use are, in themselves, stressful and tend to be registered only in the subconscious until it is too late. Most of the time, working people do not know what it is about their occasional or regular drug use that they must watch out for, and they do not have the time to watch out for it. Sadly, when it comes to employee drug and alcohol[1] use, a high degree

---

[1]Alcohol itself is a drug. I include alcohol whenever I refer to drugs unless otherwise specified.

of denial—ignoring, not seeing, and denying the situation—actually precludes the desire to watch out.

And we are all engaged in this denial. The individual working-class hero is responsible for this predicament no more than are the society and the company in which he or she works. We have created the world we live in. We perpetuate its idiosyncrasies. We serve quite willingly in the direction of societal evolution; we all help create the mirage of progress.

Moreover, we must refrain from scrutinizing only drug-using and drug-addicted employees. The "problem" extends far past these people. The "problem" is not really drug use and drug addiction; it is drugged minds, regardless of how they come to be drugged. Try telling Joe Smith that his two very innocent cups of black coffee before leaving for work, followed by one little cigarette in the car on the way and another cup of coffee with a sugar-coated danish when he gets to work, are putting him under physiological stress and rendering him more vulnerable to the other stresses of worklife. Try telling Jane Doe that her overeating at lunch causes her to feel tired after lunch and to want large amounts of caffeine and sugar to stay awake all afternoon. Try telling either Joe or Jane that their job performance is affected by caffeine, nicotine, sugar, and heavy eating. Then inform them that the "few" drinks that they have on the way home place them or someone else in danger because they are driving under the influence.

At this point, their employer may comment that this last point is relevant only if they are driving a company car. However, what mind- and physiology-altering chemicals Joe and Jane use after work, in whatever amounts they use them, will in some way influence their attitude, morale, and performance at work the next day. This is difficult and even threatening information to accept, for both employees and employers. Yet this understanding is essential in our fight against the "more pressing" problems of employee drug abuse and addiction.

Employers can make a positive contribution to the job performance and well-being of their employees. More important, they can help improve the performance and well-being of all society. Employers must come to understand that their companies have become chemically dependent. Employees are working-dazed. Sometimes chemical dependence takes the form of an outright addiction. Other times, all too often, it is a much more subtle and pervasive problem. Better living through chemistry and through technology may be a euphemism for less living, less awareness, less presence of mind and being.

The vitality of the self is threatened. It is not only the quality of worklife but the quality of human existence that is strained. We must respond to the diminishment of the self by helping to heal workers across the nation and around the world. Try spreading this message. There is a good chance that employers and employees will begin to listen, because the time has come for us all to change. It will cost us too much not to.

We must bring the hidden but very present trend toward increasing mental and spiritual submission, dehumanization, and mechanization to everyone's attention. This book is, therefore, about a hidden epidemic. However, it calls for beginning with what is most visible, most tangible about the problem: recognizing and then trying to heal the chemically dependent corporation. Of course, chemical dependence is evidenced by news-shaking and heartbreaking stories of drug abuse, drug addiction, and drug-related accidents, but chemical dependence does not stop there. Chemical dependence is pervasive. It affects us all in our daily lives. It is a way of life. It is a state of mind.

It is important that we stop the invasion of drugs into the workplace. A drugged workforce is dangerous. A drugged workforce is unproductive. But more important, a drugged workforce is too numb to keep a watchful eye on the evolution of worklife. Workers must stay aware of their role in production. We are more than machines. We must be more than drones. We must not allow ourselves to become drugged drones who cannot see what is happening to our selves, our souls.

Fighting drugs in the workplace is a major undertaking, but

it can be done. Such an endeavor is an excellent launching pad for broader social change. If we, as a society, can take an honest look at the states of mind of people in their workplaces, then we can critically examine the evolution of the human mind. Then we can confront the perils to our minds and souls that we, as a society and as a species, face.

We have the political, analytical, organizational, and clinical tools to engage in this effort. In fact, public policy is, perhaps unbeknownst to itself, leading the way into a deeper examination of ourselves at work. With the enactment of the federal Drug Free Workplace (DFWP) Act of 1988, many employers have had additional incentive to take action. This forward-looking piece of legislation made the prevention of substance abuse the responsibility of all employers who had $25,000 or more in government contracts. These employers were required by law (as of March 1989) to:

- Notify employees that the possession, manufacture, sale, or use of alcohol or illegal drugs in the workplace is prohibited and that disciplinary action will be taken in cases of breach of this regulation;
- Inform the designated federal agency whenever an employee is convicted of a drug-related offense; and
- Impose disciplinary action upon employees who are convicted of drug offenses in the workplace, the employers' options for discipline being requirements such as mandatory participation in an addiction treatment or rehabilitation program, compensatory action such as suspension without pay, or complete discharge from the job. [1]

In support of this mandate, employers have also been required to:

- Provide educational programs regarding the general hazards of drug and alcohol abuse and the specific hazards of this abuse in the workplace; and

- Provide information on services that counsel and treat employees having trouble with alcohol and drugs. [2]

The implications of the Drug Free Workplace Act are numerous. Some of the implications are readily apparent. Those employers who have been or will be affected by this legislation and who do not already have clearly stated policies which prohibit the use, possession, distribution, and/or sale of alcohol and illegal drugs in the workplace must formulate these policies. Employers entering into government contracts for the first time must meet the requirements of this act in order to maintain the contract. Massive efforts must be made along educational lines. The workplace can become one of the key sites in the dissemination of public health information.

As treatment becomes one of the legislated forms of "disciplinary action," which it does in this act, there is increased pressure upon employers to make treatment available to their employees. With this pressure comes a mounting emphasis upon the cost-effectiveness of chemical dependence treatment. This emphasis does not necessarily ensure improvements in the quality of the treatment available to working people. Furthermore, it does not ensure that treatment will always be available to all employees. When employers feel that treatment is either too costly or too ineffective to remedy an employee's chemical dependence problem, the DFWP legislation says employees should lose their jobs. Addiction is then cycled back into society, and eventually, into another workplace.

Some of the most profound implications of the Drug Free Workplace Act are less apparent. In order to bring these implications to your attention, I share, in the following chapters, what I have learned in my work with organizations seeking to solve the problems of employee drug and alcohol abuse: Chemical dependence will become a way—the dominant way—of life if we do not remain alert to its expanding presence. Chemical dependence is much bigger than drug addiction. It is a way of being in the world. It may not look like addictive behavior. It may not even appear to be a problem. We have the opportunity to open our eyes and admit that we have arrived at a major choice point in human evolution. We can make and act upon a decision about the future of our species rather than let the future happen to us. Do we or do we not want to be as mentally, physically, and spiritually alert as possible? Do we or do we not want to avoid treating ourselves and being treated like machines? Like drugged drones? Are we ready to examine critically the role of work and workers in modern cultures?

Drug-addicted minds become robotic, cloudy, mindless, and self-destructive. We know this by watching the course of untreated alcohol and cocaine addictions. Yet, we do not necessarily recognize to what degree all of our minds are drugged and drug-addicted—drugged not only by the so-called "hard" drugs, but also by the many seemingly harmless "soft" drugs which are becoming part of our daily lives. These soft drugs are socially acceptable. They are over-the-counter medications, "soft" drinks, cups of caffeinated coffee, and cigarettes. We also drug ourselves "softly" with other more subtle mind alterers such as noise, television, commercialism, competition, and obedience. We do not yet understand how easily we working-class heroes can be drugged and/or drug ourselves to ease the stress of work-life and how simply we can become acquiescent drones. Join me as we uncover the hidden epidemic, the spread of mechanical mindlessness. Join me as we find ourselves behind the benign mask of our societal denial. Join me as we recognize and stop the many ways we cloud our minds, bodies, and souls. Let us ward off the encroaching daze by admitting to its symptoms.

The Ailing Company
Chemicals to Cope?

We have unwittingly catapulted through light-years of drug history in a few short decades. The 1950s and 1960s images of the heroin addict lying alone in the distant gutter and the destitute alcoholic hidden in the back room in somebody else's run-down house are fading. The "All-American" imagery of two parents in every home, two cars in every garage, and a chicken in every pot has matured and wearied. It now includes Valium or some other stress and or pain killer behind every bathroom mirror and a dose of caffeine, nicotine, or some other mind and body booster every day or maybe even every hour. Experimentation with drugs is almost taken for granted. Kids will be kids. Young adults will be young adults. In fact, some researchers are now claiming that adolescents who engage in some experimentation with drugs may be better adjusted than those who completely abstain. [1] New drugs, designed to create new experiences, new highs, new emotions, new insights, and new abilities, are emerging. These "designer drugs" are created in clandestine laboratories and are designed to stay one step ahead of the law, altering illegalized molecular compounds into legal forms.

"Drug lords" and "crack babies" have become household words, almost archetypal symbols in the mythology of chemical dependence. Modern-day crusades, "drug wars," have been waged against the "drug barons," leaders of the cocaine crack cartels, with a political and almost a religious fervor. Reverence and irreverence for human rights have been scrambled: We say that addiction is an illness but drug abuse is a crime although their symptoms are frequently indistinguishable. We seek to improve the quality of addiction treatment while we fortify police power to quell the rise of drug abuse.

We may be confused, but we are no longer naive. The world is getting smaller. Addiction can strike closer to home. It can strike home. By the end of the 1980s, the media were citing federal research which concluded that "alcoholism and dependence on other chemicals is the most common psychiatric problem" in the United States and that it "can be expected to strike 16.4% of all adults over 18 at some time during their lives." [2] That is about one in six of us. And this estimate does not include chemical dependences on the "lesser drugs" such as caffeine and nicotine. We have now incorporated chemical dependence into our social imagery. A significant proportion of American individuals, families, and workplaces are or will be afflicted with this problem.

If the current prevalence rates for alcohol abuse and dependence continue, the number of Americans who abuse and/or are addicted to alcohol will continue to rise to at least 15.5 million by the year 2000. [3] While the number of nonaddicted alcohol abusers is expected to remain stable (at about 6 million), the number of addicted users is expected to increase. [4] Data on nonaddicted alcohol abuse are difficult to obtain because nonaddicted alcohol use takes a wide variety of forms. We are uncertain as to when social use of alcohol becomes abuse of alcohol. Driving drunk after a party or doing brain surgery with a hangover may both be called "social use of alcohol" even though abuse of alcohol is present. This ambiguity results in profound underestimation of the "alcohol problem."

Cocaine use is another, equally difficult problem to measure, but for different reasons. Cocaine use is undergoing regional shifts in prevalence. When the cocaine problem was once greatest on the Southeast and West Coasts of the United States, it appeared to have shifted to the Northeast by the end of the 1980s. This shift is indicated in data such as those obtained by drug tests of arrested males. In the northeastern United States, 68% of all those arrested (males tested) tested positive for cocaine in 1988, compared with 44% in the West, 43% in the Midwest, and 48% in the South. [5] However, the same type of statistical measurement reveals that the West and Northeast are closer when it comes to multiple drug use, with 82% of all arrested in the Northeast testing positive for one or more drugs and 74% testing positive in the West. [6] Cocaine use has also shifted in method of ingestion, with "crack" smoking and injecting increasing. And with these changes have evolved age, race, and economic class differences in the methods of use and the related risks of contracting AIDS. All of these shifts make estimates of the usage level of cocaine and crack (smoked cocaine) debatable. [7]

New drugs and new forms of old drugs will continue to emerge. Some observers claim that the 1990s signal the beginning of an American "ice wave." This is the advent and spread of the abuse of and addiction to smoked speed. [8] Other observers predict that "synthetic" or "lab" drugs and "designer" drugs will be the dominant drugs of abuse in coming years. These drugs will offer users new highs in new domains of human experience and will often be incorrectly touted as safe, legal, nonaddictive, and inexpensive.

Although they tend to appear intractable, these and other drug "problems" can be attacked on an incremental basis in specific target areas. One of the most important target areas is the workplace. Employers are increasingly aware of the subtle but inextricable relationship between employee health (mental and physical) and employee productivity. This awareness has been stimulated indirectly by the media's focus on the problem of alcohol and drug addiction and directly by the soaring costs of employee alcohol and drug abuse and addiction. In the 1970s and 1980s, employers watched cocaine and marijuana join alcohol as substances commonly used and abused by employees. [9] Prescription drugs, over-the-counter drugs, and even tobacco have also become mental and physical health concerns for employers. [10]

Although it continues to seem to be a problem among a statistical minority of the total workforce, drug and alcohol abuse among employees is extensive enough to warrant serious concern. Few industries, if any, have been spared the costly and counterproductive effects of this malaise. Ten to twenty-five percent of the American population is sometimes on the job under the influence of alcohol, cocaine, or some other drug. [11] It has been estimated that 5% to 10% of all those now employed in the United States have already progressed to a state in which their use of alcohol and drugs requires treatment. [12] Countless other employee drug and alcohol problems are as yet and may remain untreated. And future chemical dependence problems are waiting in the wings. Research indicates that today's younger members of the workforce actually use greater amounts of drugs with more frequency than do their older counterparts. [13]

The estimated cost to workplaces of employee alcohol and drug abuse is now some $100 billion a year. [14] Employees who use drugs are far less productive, are responsible for more work slowdowns, and miss ten times more workdays than employees who do not use drugs. They are also three times as likely to injure themselves or someone else. [15]

Empirical studies conducted during the 1970s and 1980s indicate that drug use among employees has extended and continues to extend across occupational categories throughout the United States. [16] The transportation industry has found employee drug abuse to be very costly in both lives and dollars. Over fifty train accidents have definitely been related to drug-impaired workers. One such accident, involving a Conrail train, killed two people and caused $467,500 worth of damages. The employee at the controls missed a stop signal when he was high on marijuana. [17] Marijuana, cocaine, and alcohol use have been involved in many train, bus, and air accidents. In some cases it appears pilots have actually used their drugs while flying. [18] Even the aerospace industry has not remained untouched. In a three-year period, an estimated 20% to 25% of the workers at the Palmdale, California, space shuttle assembly plant were under the influence on the job. Their drugs included alcohol, cocaine, marijuana, phencyclidine (PCP or angel dust), and heroin. [19] This is not surprising. Drug use and abuse are not restricted to only a few workplaces. They are relatively evenly distributed across all occupations.

THE USE OF ILLEGAL DRUGS BY EMPLOYEES

A sharp but artificial division exists in our thinking about employee alcohol use as opposed to employee illegal drug use. Somehow, a legal drug such as alcohol is viewed as being more acceptable, more forgivable, and safer for employees to use. Although this perception may not be correct, the use of illegal drugs brings with it the added problem of criminality.

In a mid-1980s survey of Silicon Valley (Santa Clara County, home of high technology in California) electronics industry employees, 35% of those interviewed stated that they used marijuana or cocaine *on the job*. [20] This finding suggested that at least one-third of that workforce had worked under the influence of a drug during a period of one year. There is a great probability that the productivity of such a workforce is severely compromised. Consider marijuana. The effects of marijuana on job performance are difficult to identify and controversial. Indications are that short-term memory is affected. The employee who is a habitual marijuana smoker may be unable to recall information that is important and sometimes critical on the job. Additional research indicates that sensory-motor functions are impaired by marijuana; the result is slowed reaction times and misjudged distances by employees who operate equipment (including forklifts, automobiles, airplanes, computers, and typewriters). [21] Consider cocaine. Estimates of on-the-job cocaine (including crack) use range from 10% to 50% of all employees. Employed individuals who are addicted to cocaine frequently report high rates of cocaine use among their co-workers. [22] Cocaine can have severe physiological effects. Cocaine use can result in cardiac arrhythmia and death and in serious psychological effects such as depression and suicide. Prior to reaching physical and psychological extremes, employees who use cocaine on and/or off the job, even "just" socially, usually believe that they are performing well while they are performing poorly, inaccurately, sloppily, and dangerously. An employee who is severely addicted to cocaine (in any of its forms) may feel the "economic pinch," the need for money to support an expensive habit, and may be tempted to respond by selling drugs to fellow employees and to customers or, in some circumstances, by selling company property. (I will further detail signs and symptoms of employee drug abuse in Chapter 3.)

Whether it be cocaine, speed, or an innocuous drug like caffeine, stimulants are popular among employees. As I noted earlier, amphetamine (speed) use appears to be on the increase and is popular among employees who do not want to risk cocaine use or cannot find or afford it. In its current form, smoked speed (ice) is highly addictive and extremely difficult to detect. [23]

Estimates of employees' use of illegal drugs are minimal estimates, because employees are understandably reluctant to discuss illegal behavior. The illegal behavior that employees are hesitant to discuss includes but is not restricted to the use of illegal drugs. Many employees understand that the use of a mind-altering substance while on the job, even when it is a *legal* drug such as alcohol or a prescription drug, may be illegal or against policy at work. Thus, employees' reports about their legal drug use may also be underestimates of the problem.

THE LEGAL USE OF DRUGS BY EMPLOYEES

Alcohol is one of the most popular of all legal drugs. Because it is so easy to get and is legal to use, it may present an even more difficult challenge to advocates of the drug-free workplace. The study in Silicon Valley (mentioned earlier) found that 43% of all employed persons interviewed admitted to some use of alcohol while at work. Prescription drugs are also popular "legal" drugs. Barbiturates (central nervous system depressants), relaxants, and minor tranquilizers are often unwittingly used *on the job.*

Caffeine is also a physiology- and mood-altering chemical. We rarely describe this chemical as a "drug," yet it is addictive and can cause withdrawal symptoms as do many other compounds which are commonly called drugs. Because it takes 50 to 100 milligrams to produce the pharmacological action of caffeine, many employees consume enough caffeine to produce symptoms of "caffeinism" without realizing that they are doing so. One or two cups of caffeinated coffee, tea, or cans of soda on a daily basis are enough to produce headaches, irritability, insomnia, and other disturbing symptoms. [24] Of all adults in the United States, 60% drink more than two cups of caffeinated coffee per day, 25% drink five or more cups per day, and 10% drink seven or more cups per day. [25] Other sources of caffeine include black tea; several popular sodas; and numerous nonprescription drugs, including some stimulants, some pain relievers, some diuretics, some cold remedies, and some weight-control aids. [26]

Another legal drug, nicotine, is so commonly used that its psychoactive effects may be overlooked. Smokers, just as other drug users, can overdose. The symptoms of nicotine overdoses are burning in the chest, dizziness, loss of appetite, and sometimes, vomiting. Smokers can also experience intense withdrawal symptoms such as extreme irritability, jitters, intense craving, sleeplessness, and distractibility. [27] The use of nicotine, in the form of cigarette smoking, in the workplace has become a controversial issue and an expensive habit. Workplace absenteeism is 57% higher for male smokers and 45% higher for female smokers than it is for nonsmokers. Smokers miss more days of work, use more health care benefits, and probably affect the morale, job performance, and health of other employees more than nonsmokers and more than any other group of drug users. Nonsmokers are seriously endangered by passive inhalation of cigarette smoke. [28] Do employees have a right to expose other employees to the costly psychoactive and health hazard effects of cigarette smoking?

In addition to caffeine and nicotine, refined sugar is a highly addictive legal drug which is so common that its users are often unaware of the amounts they use or the effects of use. Moreover, sugar is not viewed as a drug. This type of protective thinking about caffeine, nicotine, and sugar may explain the presence of coffee, cigarette, and candy machines in workplaces.

DEFINING THE PROBLEM

With even a fraction of the labor force using drugs off *and* on the job, workplace productivity is seriously threatened. It is evident that employee drug use, whether it is legal or illegal, whether it is of recognized or unrecognized drugs, and whether it is on or off the job, affects employee behavior, health, performance, and safety. Alcohol use, when separated from other drug use, is still costly. The employee having trouble with alcohol is said to operate at 50% efficiency, to average twenty-two days in lost working time, and to cost a minimum of $1,500 to $4,000 each year. [29]

As suggested earlier, estimates of rates and costs of drug use among employees may be low because of the underreporting of drug- and alcohol-related problems by employees in order to avoid social stigma, legal complications, and being fired. There are additional reasons for the underestimation of the extent of drug problems. Employers themselves may be underreporting employee drug use because of the lack of information about it. To add to employers' difficulties in reporting, from a philosophical standpoint it is difficult to define the problem. Which chemicals are we willing to call psychoactive drugs and which chemicals are protected from this often damaging label? And why do we draw a boundary around our definition of the things that drug us? Perhaps paint fumes, television, electromagnetic rays, work, and other things that are "not drugs" can drug us. To add to the problem of definition, the effects of what we typically call drug and alcohol abuse are indirect and difficult to quantify. For example, the spouse of an alcoholic may not use or abuse alcohol or drugs but may have a difficult home life that affects his or her performance on the job and attendance at work. The parent whose teenager is having trouble with drugs may be so emotionally and financially affected that her or his concentration and morale at work reach serious lows. These are not direct instances of drug abuse among employees; they are instead cases of drug use among employees' family members.

Employers are increasingly motivated to take action against drug and alcohol abuse by their employees and sometimes by employees' families. However, the treatment of the problem is based upon its definition. When one hears the word *drug,* two categories of chemicals come to mind: the first one includes illegal drugs such as cocaine, speed, heroin, lab drugs, angel dust, and marijuana; the second one is legal drugs, including over-the-counter (or OTC) drugs such as Tylenol and aspirin and prescription drugs such as Valium, Soma, Darvon, and Dilaudid. Whether or not they immediately come to mind, alcohol, nicotine, caffeine, and perhaps even sugar are legal OTC "drugs" in that they act on the brain and body chemistry to produce marked mood and energy swings and other mental and physical effects. Moreover, alcohol, nicotine, caffeine, and sugar are chemicals with high potentials for user addiction. Note that these days alcohol is more frequently included when we speak of "drugs," but caffeine, nicotine, and sugar are still rarely perceived this way.

These legal drugs are supported by the economic system. The free-market system has developed around the national and international production and trade of essential or nearly essential commodities. Alcohol, coffee, tobacco, and sugar are in high demand. They are virtually essential. Massive sums are spent on advertising to keep consumers buying these drugs. Powerful lobbies sponsored by the alcohol, coffee, tobacco, and sugar industries influence legislators with direct and indirect financial support of their campaigns.

These legal drugs are also supported by an elaborate and largely implicit belief system. We have faith in the concept of the *controlled use* of selected drugs. While the controlled use of heroin or cocaine may appear to be next to impossible, the controlled use of alcohol, caffeine, nicotine, and sugar is usually viewed as quite possible. *Controlled use* means that most people can control their levels of use of these drugs without external pressure or authority. *Controlled use* also means that use in a controlled manner is not a problem. The concept of controlled use is essential in working with food addicts. We cannot ask a compulsive overeater to stop eating, even after that overeater has treated food as if it were a drug.

Clearly, we have to respond to the use of different drugs in different ways. Employers who want to stop employee drug abuse must first decide what drugs they are concerned about. They must be willing to interrogate themselves as to why they consider some drugs acceptable while others are not. Despite its utility, we must examine carefully our implicit controlled use policies. Are we lying to ourselves about the "drug problem?"

An understanding must also be reached about the meaning of *abuse*. The term *abuse* simply means to *ab* ("wrongly or improperly") *use*. This definition suggests that there may be a way to use drugs correctly, without abusing them. The very use of the phrase "drug abuse" is confusing. When individuals abuse a drug, they are actually abusing themselves with a drug (and are probably also abusing their friends and family members as a result of their drug use). Drug and alcohol "abuse" is, therefore, actually a shorthand for a particular form of self-abuse. This is a hazy area for all concerned with the treatment of drug and alcohol problems. Some drugs, such as heroin, are viewed as socially unacceptable to such a great degree that any use is deemed abuse. On the other hand, alcohol is a legal drug and moderate use is deemed acceptable. A case in point is the company executive who is addicted to cocaine and tells of being willing to drink "a few glasses" (of alcohol) at a company party, but of being unwilling to "snort" cocaine with his employees because it is illegal. The former is considered "use"; the latter, "abuse." If it is possible to use some drugs in a controlled fashion, or to return to controlled use from addictive use, then the applications of "use" and "abuse" are further confounded.

Various drugs are associated with particular subpopulations. For example, many suppose that only adolescents in some geographical regions smoke marijuana, that upwardly mobile young professionals snort cocaine or use particular lab drugs, that street people shoot heroin, and that adolescent boys and middle-aged men drink alcohol to excess. These are incorrect assumptions. If the problems were this readily attributed to special subgroups of society, prevention and treatment of the problems of drug abuse might be easier to target. However, the use and abuse of most types of drugs extend across the socioeconomic spectrum.

Drug use also spans the occupational gamut. Individuals coming into treatment for drug and alcohol addiction provide information regarding the prevalence of drug and alcohol abuse among fellow employees. Through their own reports, it is evident that the problem exists among food store employees, clerical and word-processing personnel, data-processing employees, child care and education employees, throughout the computer industry, in auto repair shops and auto dealerships, in the public and private transportation industries, in public utility settings including nuclear power plants, in the legal and medical professions, among professional athletes and media personnel, and in most other fields of occupation. [30] A 1989 survey I conducted of 300 employed individuals in treatment for alcohol and drug addiction revealed that employee drug use in and around some workplaces is extensive. The 300 respondents, representing a broad range of all occupations, reported that over half of all of their fellow employees used alcohol, pot, cocaine, or some other drug while at work. A checkout clerk in a large foodstore reported that 10% of his co-workers used cocaine at work and that 30% came to work under the influence of cocaine or crack or pot; a nurse reported that 10% of all hospital employees used cocaine and that 50% used pills at work; a nuclear-power-plant repair engineer reported that he did not know of anyone at work who did not use either cocaine, speed, pot, or pills at or around work; an airline pilot reported that 30% of his colleagues "flew high" on either alcohol, cocaine, pills, or speed; a stock broker claimed that one-eighth of the people in his office building used cocaine while at work and that over half drank at least one drink containing alcohol at lunch. [31]

Despite continuing reports about extensive drug use in so many different occupations, employers disagree about the prevalence of the problem. With respect to their reporting and analysis of the extent of the drug problem, employers are in a difficult position in several ways. Public exposure of the problem may be bad for business. Who will have a car serviced by a staff of mechanics on cocaine? Who will have her or his credit checked by someone viewed as being a drug addict? What company will be able to compete for and win a government contract if it admits that at least 10% of its employees are dependent upon cocaine or alcohol or both and that 30% more use one or more of the illegal drugs socially?

Other reasons employers disagree among themselves about

the prevalence of the problem are: (1) they have a difficult time reading the symptoms of drug problems; (2) their employees do not come to them for help; and (3) some employers themselves are having trouble with drugs and alcohol.

Whatever the actual prevalence of the problem, even if it is only *some* employers and employees who are having trouble with drugs, there are serious implications for businesses. Productivity and morale are threatened both directly and indirectly by even limited employee drug use: indirectly, there are marked increases in tardiness and absenteeism, more frequent leaves of absence, higher rates of turnover, and increases in theft and embezzlement; directly, performance is lowered in one or both of two ways: (1) the illusion of high performance is continued in the employee's mind long after his or her performance deteriorates, leading to dangerous accidents and costly mistakes and overall waste; and/or (2) the user denies his or her lowered performance to others when asked about it and continues to work while privately recognizing his or her own lowered performance, and the result is diminished quality and decreased output at a higher production cost to the company.

CLINICAL ISSUES

Employees who are having trouble with drugs and alcohol suffer from a number of elements which can be alleviated or ameliorated by education, prevention, and treatment programs. Among these elements are:

1. *Lack of information.* Persons who are new to drugs and those who have made drugs part of their lives frequently suffer from a lack of information about the dangers of drug use to their own physical and mental health and to that of their families and co-workers.
2. *Fear.* Employees who are having trouble with drugs fear

job loss, social stigma, other forms of reprisal, and, when they are using illegal drugs, arrest.

3. *Denial.* Employees experiencing fear develop patterns (sometimes very intricate patterns) of denial, in which they avoid admitting the truth about their drug problems to others and to themselves.

4. *Peer pressure.* Many employees socialize on and off the job with co-workers. The desire to "fit in" and be accepted by one's peers and fellow workers may result in drug use as a social tool—an employee may feel that other drug users will accept only a fellow drug user into their social circle and will exclude an employee who does not use drugs.

5. *Family coaddiction.* Employees who are having trouble with drugs may have developed long-term family-life patterns which resist change—even if the change is that the employee in trouble with drugs gets help and gets out of trouble.

6. *Resistance to treatment.* When the employee in trouble with drugs is offered or is required to take treatment, the employee or her or his family may actually resist this treatment.

ORGANIZATIONAL ISSUES

Employers are aware that individual-level problems affect entire organizations. Organizational drug abuse issues replicate the individual clinical issues listed above, as follows:

1. *Lack of information.* Employees at all levels of the organizational hierarchy lack information regarding the effects, symptoms, and treatment of drug abuse and dependence. Supervisors may not notice mood swings, per-

sonality changes, erratic performance, diminishing attention to grooming, and physical deterioration among employees, or they may observe one or several of these symptoms and may be uncertain as to when they indicate employee drug problems. Supervisors and other employees may also be generally unaware of the dangers that drug use poses to the health of the users, the safety of the co-workers, and, sometimes, the well-being of the consumer community.

2. *Fear.* The fear of discovery may extend beyond one employee who is abusing drugs to a group of employees who use drugs together or who "look the other way" while someone else uses drugs. Organizational morale and communication are threatened by this fear.

3. *Denial (and protection).* As a result of fear, massive organizational denial and protection arise. Employers as well as employees may deny their own drug use or their knowledge of drug use among their co-workers. Secret keeping (rather than production) may even become the primary goal of employees and, sometimes, employers. Company denial is not only a verbal process; it can also take the form of organizational "looking away" to avoid seeing the drug use of employees—to protect the company from the consequences of discovery. Companies with extensive employee-drug-abuse problems often feel that they will lose business, contracts, and customers and will hurt their public image when they admit that their ranks are plagued by drug abuse and chemical dependence.

4. *Peer pressure.* While it is felt by individuals, peer pressure is actually an organizational problem. Employees who pressure each other into using drugs are generating or perpetuating an organizational drug culture inside the company. Many employees may feel that social survival

in the workplace demands acculturation to drugs. Similarly, many employers find their workplaces acculturating to a society in which drug use is prevalent.

5. *Families' codependences.* When a company attempts to treat employee drug problems, the costs, and the commitments made by the decision to treat, are predictably larger than expected. One reason for this predicament is that most employees are engaged in social and familial relationships outside the company. Treating employees without treating their families and friends may jeopardize the treatment. A set of codependent families can interfere with a set of employees' decisions to break their drug habits. Companies must take the families of employees into account in planning drug abuse treatment and educational programs.

6. *Resistances to treatment.* Coaddicts are not the only sources of resistance to treatment. Employees, as noted earlier, may resist required changes in their behavior, just as their employing organizations may resist change, even if it is a change for the better. This resistance is, at least in part, a result of the organizational tendency to want to stay the same and to avoid transition, even transition for the better. [32]

POLICY ISSUES

Employers are confronted with the task of strategically selecting their definitions of drug abuse so that their treatments of employees' problems are cost-effective and appropriate. They must ask:

1. What is drug abuse?
2. Is there such a thing as recreational drug use?

3. Are caffeine, nicotine, and sugar drugs to be concerned about?
4. Which, if any, drugs are acceptable in the workplace? Why are some acceptable while others are not?
5. Are there drugs that some employees may use on their days or times off (including lunch hours) that affect job performance and safety in the workplace? Do employers have a right to develop policies that affect employees' behavior off the job? Can an employer tell an employee what not to do (what drugs not to take) during time off?
6. Is drug use among employees' family members of concern to employers? Does it affect employee productivity? Do employers have either a right or an obligation to concern themselves with their employees' family lives?
7. What is the best way to protect employees' rights as employers become more concerned about drug use? Are drug testing and drug searches justifiable under any circumstances?
8. Is education aimed at prevention more cost-effective than treatment? Can an employer make prevention-education programs mandatory for all employees?

In an effort to curb drug and alcohol abuse among employees, employers have experimented with numerous measures. One of these is preemployment screening. This can consist of an interview or a test conducted by a therapist or an evaluator; a medical laboratory test such as a saliva, urine, or blood test; or some combination of these. The logic of preemployment screening maintains that a proper evaluation process prior to hiring an employee can predict the future behavior of that employee. Unfortunately, although it is an important tool, preemployment screening methodology is not perfect, and more than a few persons who either have or will have trouble with drugs slip through the analysis. This slippage is not due entirely to the inabilities of this process to identify particular individuals. An individual who does not test out to have present or potential problems with drugs may develop them after being hired. These problems may be a result of the company acculturation process mentioned earlier.

Many new employees are hired onto workforces that are ridden with drug problems. In fact, it is not uncommon for young adults to report that they experienced their first and most intense social pressure to use drugs when they entered the workplace. Working adults of all ages in many occupations either use, see, or hear discussion of drugs at work. A regular drug-abuse prevention and education program, often described as "employee drug awareness training," mandatory for all employees, open to all employees' families, and sponsored by employers will help stop the spread of employee drug abuse.

Prevention is the best solution to the problem; however, prevention requires anticipation rather than an after-the-fact reaction. Once members of the workforce are in trouble with drugs, or are exhibiting symptoms of drug addiction, treatment is necessary. Despite the fact that many unknowns preside over current drug treatment efforts, certain truths about drug treatment are emerging. These are:

1. The longer former drug abusers are in formal treatment (i.e., eighteen months of outpatient care following a four-teen-day inpatient stay), the greater are their chances of becoming and remaining drug-free.
2. The longer former drug abusers go without using drugs, the greater are their chances of remaining drug-free.
3. The more extensive former drug abusers' support systems (the involvement of family, friends, employers, and fellow employees) are in their recovery rather than in their continued addiction, and the more involved the members of their support systems are in their treatment, the greater are their chances of remaining drug-free.

4. Former drug abusers who had marketable skills prior to using drugs and those who attain sound occupational skills during rehabilitation have a greater chance of success.

5. Former abusers who maintain legitimate and structured work roles significantly increase their chances of remaining drug-free. [33]

EMPLOYEE DRUG ABUSE IN A SOCIETAL CONTEXT

It is evident that the problem of drug and alcohol abuse by employees cannot be separated from the encompassing social problem of drug and alcohol abuse in nearly every facet of society: among employees, employers, and the unemployed, and among students, children, adolescents, parents, and the elderly. In short, employers who seek to understand workplace drug abuse and chemical dependence must look beyond the workplace to the world we live in. It is essential that employers take part in attacking the problem at the community level, in order to take an effective stand against drug abuse in the workplace.

The costs of drug and alcohol use to society are undeniable. This is especially apparent in traffic accident statistics. On a typical weekend night, 1 out of every 10 drivers on the road is drunk. [34] Alcohol-related traffic accidents kill over 20,000 and injure 750,000 more people each year. [35] The National Council on Alcoholism reports that alcoholics and problem drinkers alone (not including other drug users) cost society some $60 billion each year. [36] In 1980, $487 million (public and private) were spent on drug abuse treatment for some 260,000 persons in the United States. [37] Of every 6 or 7 drivers who were responsible for accidents in which 1 or more persons were killed, 1 was high on marijuana at the time of the accident. [38]

As employees fulfill the demanding obligations of their worklives, they are subjected to pressures to use drugs and alcohol both outside and inside their workplaces. Employees drive home past billboards advertising alcohol, arrive home to watch people drinking and drugging on television, and hear commercials saying, "Buy yourself a drink." At the dinner table, when their children are telling them about friends who are in trouble with drugs, these working-class heroes realize that their children may be trying to talk about themselves. If employees can sleep at night, they may awake rested the next morning only to go to work and experience the typical pressures of worklife (including deadlines and competition) as well as pressure to make it in the working world by partaking of the two-martini lunch, or to seal a deal by sharing in the use of an illegal drug. If the daze of worklife encroaches enough on employees' sensitivities, they may be conscious of very few of these pressures. They may be conscious of next to nothing.

3

Working Dazed
Signs and Symptoms of Substance Abuse, Addiction, and Other Grave Developments

So many of us are working dazed without realizing it. We are, somehow, not fully alert, not entirely present. We are under the influence of something which acts like a drug upon our psyches and somas. It is not what is commonly called "a drug." This something which influences us is so very subtle that we are rarely able to distinguish its presence.

Those who feel that they do not work under the influence of drugs are being taught an important lesson by those who are working under the influence of what are considered "real" drugs such as marijuana and alcohol. Users of real drugs are alerting all of us to the daze that we are slipping into, to the encroaching subservience and mechanization of our wills. This is a rather abstract and disturbing concept to absorb. I have found that it makes itself understood by inference. Drawing upon the lessons which can be learned from employee drug use, I refer throughout this book to the daze which is encroaching upon us.

Let's see what we can learn about the daze to which I refer by reviewing some of the signs and symptoms of employee use and abuse of what we like to call "real" drugs. Employers, managers, and co-workers may notice a range of unusual behaviors in employees who are "in trouble" with drugs. When an addiction to a drug or drugs is involved, there is often an increase in unusual and undesirable behaviors and a change over time in grooming, health, attitude, and other characteristics. There may also be abrupt mood swings. However, be warned that none of these symptoms and none of the other symptoms listed in this chapter constitute proof of drug use. You may see these symptoms alone or in combination, sporadically or regularly. You may find that some of these symptoms contradict each other. Close observation may help you distinguish between your own suspicions and the observed individual's actual behavior. Experience is the best teacher.

GENERAL CHARACTERISTICS ASSOCIATED WITH ONGOING DRUG USE

Appearance

- Physical appearance and grooming deteriorates.
- Cleanliness decreases.
- Neatness diminishes.
- Apparel such as sunglasses is worn at inappropriate times (hiding red eyes and/or dilated or constricted pupils).

Attitude

- Overall attitude changes.
- Temperament changes.
- Reluctance to accept the assignment of challenging tasks develops.
- Withdrawal from responsibility develops.
- Lack of patience develops.

- Daydreaming or inattentiveness develops.
- Lack of dependability develops.
- Surprizing outbreaks of temper and overreactions occur.
- Attention of co-workers and supervisors is avoided.
- Money is borrowed increasingly.

Association

- Family problems are observed.
- Peer associations change.
- Association with known drug users occurs.
- Dissociation from co-workers occurs.

Job Behavior

POOR JOB PERFORMANCE

- Abrupt changes in job performance, output, and work quality take place.
- Alternate periods of high and low productivity are observed.
- Morning productivity diminishes.
- Irregular work habits increase.
- Mistakes increase.
- Difficulty recalling instructions increases.
- Inattention and poor judgment appear.
- Disciplinary problems appear.
- Poor memory for new skills or assignments is evident.
- Missing of deadlines is apparent.
- Impairment of coordination (fine- and gross-motor) is evident.
- Stealing of small (and sometimes large) items from employer occurs.
- Secretive behavior, concealing action, conversation, or possession, occurs.

- Requests for paycheck advances increase in later stages of abuse.

INCREASED ABSENTEEISM

- Absenteeism increases.
- Leaving work early occurs more often.
- Multiple unauthorized absences occur.
- Rate of Monday morning absence is high and/or increases.
- Improbable excuses are offered for absences.
- Excessive sick days are taken for minor illnesses such as colds and flu.
- A particular pattern of absences becomes apparent.
- Tardiness in morning and after breaks and lunch increases.
- Frequent and unexplainable breaks and trips away from work area to bathroom, basement, or off grounds are observed.

POOR INTERPERSONAL RELATIONSHIPS ON THE JOB

- Arguments with co-workers increase.
- Excessive talking in workplace occurs.
- Irrational or illogical conversations take place.
- Trailing off during conversation or not responding in conversation occurs.
- Fellow workers complain.
- Customers complain.

The behavior and psychological changes that are associated with the use of drugs appear in varying amounts of time after the first use or abuse. For example, signs of alcohol abuse may emerge 6 months after adolescents begin habitual use but may take 15 years to appear in some adults. On the following pages, symptoms are listed according to drug or drug group. As in the above list, each of these symptoms may appear alone or in combination, or may not appear at all. Many of these symptoms become more regular and more obvious when the amount of the drug which is used increases and when use of the drug crosses over into abuse of and addiction to the drug. Caffeine and nicotine users will find their drugs listed with cocaine.

SUBSTANCE-SPECIFIC SIGNS AND SYMPTOMS

Alcohol

Appearance

- Gradual (or sudden in adolescents) and/or irregular deterioration in personal appearance and hygiene occurs.
- Odor of alcohol on the breath exists.
- Intoxication is apparent.
- Difficulty in focusing and a glazed appearance in the eyes are observed.
- Unexplained bruises appear.
- Unexplained accidents occur.
- Flushed skin is observed.

Attitude

- Combative and argumentative behavior is encountered.
- Irritability is observed.
- Uncharacteristically passive behavior is observed.

Association

- Changes in peer-group associations and friendships take place.

- Availability and consumption of alcohol become the focus of social or professional activities.
- Impaired interpersonal relationships (troubled marriage, unexplainable termination of deep relationships, alienation from close family members) develop.

Job Behavior

- Dysfunction in job performance develops gradually.
- Dysfunction in job performance appears abruptly.
- Absenteeism (particularly at the beginning of the week) occurs.

General Behavior

- Bouts of loudness are observed.
- Loss of memory (from minor lapses to blackouts) occur.
- Generally withdrawn behavior increases.

Paraphernalia

- Bottle in the brown bag may be noticed.

Caffeine, Nicotine, Cocaine, Crack, and Other Stimulants (Speed, Amphetamines, Uppers, Bennies)

Appearance

- Dilated pupils (when large amounts are taken) are observed in extreme cases.
- Dry mouth and nose and frequent lip licking are observed in extreme cases.
- Bad breath is apparent.
- In those who drink their drugs, indigestion, nausea, and vaguely upset stomach can be present.

- In those who snort their drugs in through their noses, runny nose, colds, chronic sinus or nasal problems, and nosebleeds can be apparent.
- In those who smoke their drugs, heavy coughing, a raspy voice, and trouble in breathing can be apparent.
- In those who inject their drugs, marks such as tracks and bruises can be found on arms and legs.

Attitude

- Attitude is irregular.
- Attitude is unpredictably irritable, argumentative, and nervous.
- Avoidance of eye contact is observed in extreme cases.

Association

- Associations with others who have similar physical appearances and behavior patterns increase as addiction to the drug increases.
- Changes in peer-group associations and friendships take place.
- Availability and consumption of the drug become the focus of social or professional activities.
- Impaired interpersonal relationships (co-worker conflict, troubled marriage, unexplainable termination of deep relationships, alienation from close family members) develop.

Job Behavior

- User can think that he or she is doing the job well when he or she is not.
- Workplace participation is uneven.
- Productivity is uneven and eventually decreases.
- Concentration is irregular.

General Behavior

- Complaints about headaches are common.
- Excessive activity and difficulty sitting still are observed.
- Lack of interest in food and in sleep can eventually develop.
- Talkativeness is observed (but conversation can lack continuity, and subject is changed rapidly).
- Jitteriness and irritability are observed when user is craving the drug—awaiting a coffee or smoking break or longing for the end of the workday in order to use the drug.

Paraphernalia

- Use or possession of paraphernalia, including coffee mugs, cigarette boxes, lighters, small spoons, razor blades, mirrors, little bottles of white powder, and plastic, glass, or metal straws, is observed.

Marijuana (Also Called Pot, Weed, Grass, Hash, etc.)

Appearance

- Sleepiness or stupor is observed.
- Inflammation in whites of eyes is observed.

Attitude

- Rapid and/or loud talking with bursts of laughter or giggles is heard in early stages of intoxication.
- Forgetfulness in conversation (asking, "What was I saying?" and simply trailing off) occurs.
- Distorted sense of time passage, with a tendency to overestimate time intervals, is apparent.

Association

- Associations with others who have similar physical appearance and behavior patterns increase.
- Changes in peer-group associations and friendships take place.
- Availability and consumption of marijuana become the focus of social or professional activities.
- Impaired interpersonal relationships (troubled marriage, unexplainable termination of deep relationships, alienation from close family members) develop.

Job Behavior

- Tardiness increases.
- Absenteeism, usually with vague explanation, increases.

General Behavior

- Stupor is apparent.
- Tendency to drive cars slowly, below speed limit, appears.

Paraphernalia

- Use or possession of paraphernalia, including "roach clips" for holding the cigarette, packs of cigarette papers, pipes, or "bongs," is observed.

Depressants (Barbiturates, "Ludes," Tranquilizers, "Downs")

Appearance

- Lack of facial expression or animation and flaccid appearance are visible.

- Slurred speech is heard.
- Symptoms of alcohol intoxication are apparent with no alcohol odor on the breath (remember, however, that depressants are frequently used along with alcohol).
- Pupils are unlikely to be dilated.
- Odor exists on clothing or breath.

Attitude

- Depressed, quiet, hang-low, "sunken" attitude is observed.
- Unusual variability in temperament is witnessed.

Association

- Few associations are observed.
- If associations occur, they may be with persons exhibiting similar behaviors and appearance.

Job Behavior

- Lackadaisical approach is observed.
- Low productivity is observed.
- Poor participation is observed.

General Behavior

- Slinking around and what appears to be moping may be observed.

Paraphernalia

- Pills, pill bottles, empty prescription bottles, and small bags and cases may be seen.

Narcotics (Heroin, Morphine)

Appearance

- Constricted pupils which fail to respond to light are observed.
- Lethargy and drowsiness are observed.
- Scars ("tracks") on inner arms or other parts of the body, from needle injections, may be observed.
- Redness and raw nostrils from inhaling heroin in powder form, possibly traces of white powder on nostrils, may be observed.

Attitude

- Depressed, quiet, hang-low, "sunken" attitude is observed.
- Unusual variability in temperament is witnessed.

Association

- Few associations are observed.
- If associations occur, they may be with persons exhibiting similar behaviors and appearances.

Job Behavior

- Lackadaisical approach is observed.
- Low productivity is observed.
- Poor participation is observed.

General Behavior

- Slinking around and what appears to be moping may be observed.

Paraphernalia

- Use, possession of, leaving around of, or hiding of para-phernalia, including syringes, bent spoons, bottle caps, eye droppers, rubber tubing, cotton, and needles, is observed.

Inhalants (Glue, Vapor-Producing Solvents, Propellants)

Appearance

- Substance odor on breath and clothes is observed.
- Runny nose and watering eyes are observed.
- Poor muscle control is apparent.
- Drowsiness or unconsciousness is observed.

Attitude

- Depressed, quiet, hang-low, "sunken" attitude is observed.
- Unusual variability in temperament is witnessed.

Association

- Few associations are observed.
- If associations occur, they may be with persons exhibiting similar behaviors and appearances.

Job Behavior

- Lackadaisical approach is observed.
- Low productivity is observed.
- Poor participation is observed.

General Behavior

- Slinking around and what appears to be moping may be observed.

Paraphernalia

- Presence of bags or rags containing dry plastic cement or other solvent at home, in locker at school, or at work is discovered.
- Discarded whipped-cream or similar chargers (for users of nitrous oxide) are found.
- Small bottles labeled "incense" (for users of butyl nitrite) are found.

Hallucinogens (LSD, Mescaline, MDA, MDM, Psilocybin, DMT, STP)

Appearance

- Extremely dilated pupils are observed.
- Warm skin and excessive perspiration are observed.
- Excessive body odor is observed.

Attitude

- Distorted image of self is expressed.
- Distorted perception of time is observed.
- Distorted sense of sight, hearing, and touch is observed.
- Mood and behavior changes, the extent depending on the emotional state of the user and the environmental conditions, are observed.
- Unpredictable flashback episodes, even long after withdrawal from LSD, are observed.

Association

- Loner characteristics emerge.
- Associations with others who have similar behavior patterns increase.

- Changes in peer-group associations and friendships take place.
- Availability and consumption of hallucinogens become the focus of social or professional activities.
- Impaired interpersonal relationships (troubled marriage, unexplainable termination of deep relationships, alienation from close family members) develop.

Job Behavior

- Tardiness increases.
- Absenteeism, usually with vague explanation, increases.

General Behavior

- Stupor is apparent.
- Tendency to drive cars slowly, below speed limit, appears.

Paraphernalia

- Paraphernalia are difficult to detect but include pill bottles, envelopes, capsules, powders, and plastic bags.

Dissociative Anesthetics ("Angel Dust" or Phencyclidine [PCP])

Appearance

- Symptoms of intoxication are observed.
- Dilated pupils are observed.
- Masklike facial appearance is observed.
- Rigid muscles and strange gait are observed.
- Floating pupils, appearing to follow a moving object (nystagmus), are observed.
- Deadened sensory perception (may experience severe injuries while appearing not to notice) is observed.

- If large amount is consumed, comatose appearance (unresponsiveness, eyes may be open or closed) occurs.

Attitude

- Unpredictable behavior and mood swings from passive to violent, for no apparent reason, appear.
- Disorientation, as well as agitation and violence if exposed to excessive sensory stimulation, occurs.
- Fear and terror are expressed.

Association

- Loner characteristics emerge.
- Associations with others who have similar physical appearance and behavior patterns increase.
- Changes in peer-group associations and friendships take place.
- Availability and consumption of dissociative anesthetics become the focus of social or professional activities.
- Impaired interpersonal relationships (troubled marriage, unexplainable termination of deep relationships, alienation from close family members) develop.

Job Behavior

- Tardiness increases.
- Absenteeism, usually with vague explanation, increases.

General Behavior

- Stupor is apparent.
- Profound detachment increases.

Paraphernalia

- Paraphernalia are difficult to detect but include powder, capsules, plastic bags, and small cases.

For the most part, these symptoms of what I call "worker daze" are more frequent, more obvious, and more extreme when the drug user is addicted to the drug. I have reviewed some of the basic psychological symptoms of addiction in Chapter 2 under the heading "Clinical Issues." Whether or not an employee is addicted, the use of one or more drugs may affect his or her job performance and overall attitude, as well as the safety of the workplace. It is important that all employees, front-line or managerial, learn to recognize the symptoms and para-phernalia of drug use. Waiting for proof of drug addiction while ignoring signs of drug use may be waiting too long.

BROADER IMPLICATIONS OF WORKING DAZED

All too often the discussion of employee drug use neglects some critical points:

- Alcohol is a drug and can impair an employee's judgment as much as other drugs.
- Even "small" amounts of drugs such as alcohol, mari-juana, cocaine, crack, and speed used on and off the job may affect job performance.
- Even "social use" of drugs such as alcohol, marijuana, cocaine, crack, and speed may affect job performance.
- Employees who never use their drugs at work can still come to work under the influence; they can be coming down from a high or undergoing withdrawal or may just have their senses slightly affected by the drug.
- Caffeine, nicotine, sugar, and even overeating have psy-choactive effects and should not be overlooked when we speak of the effect of drugs upon job performance. Many of the symptoms of "worker daze" listed in this chapter are visible in regular users of caffeine, nicotine, and sugar. We are fooling ourselves if we deny this.

- New compounds, new drugs, are being designed which may be more difficult to detect and which may have more subtle but still critical mind- and performance-altering effects. While new pharmacological experimentation and research are valuable, these new compounds should not enter the workplace.
- Alternative methods of mind numbing and mind alteration such as television watching and brain wave shift induction are increasingly popular and must be regarded as addictive and as affecting job performance.

The discussion of employee drug use also tends to overlook the broader implications of and questions about employee drug use and abuse. For example:

- Why are employees using drugs or electronic methods (also drugs) to drug themselves?
- Why do employees become addicted?
- How does one employee's drug use affect her or his co-workers?
- Is employee drug use an alarm system, signaling greater problems?

We may all be working very dazed, so dazed that we are unable to tell that we suffer from worker daze. You can start to halt the daze by answering these questions:

- How different are you and your behaviors from those of occasional and regular drug users?
- Are you aware of fluctuations in your ability to concentrate?
- Does your mind feel unexplainably numb or hypnotized at times?
- Do you feel as if you have very little choice in how, when,

where, for whom, with whom, why, and for how much money you work?

- Do you really love your job? Do you like it at all?
- Are you addicted to your work? Does it come before your physical and mental health and that of your family?
- How deep is your fatigue level? Are you aware of a core tiredness, an almost spiritual exhaustion, encroaching upon you?
- Is your work really fulfilling or do you just need to feel that way about it to do it?
- How much choice do you feel that you have in the way you use your time—the time of your life?
- Are you really doing what you want to do with your life?
- Do you want to ask these questions? Do you drug yourself or blank out in some way in order to avoid asking these questions?
- Do you feel that you control the thoughts, desires, and emotions that appear in your mind and the times that these appear in your mind? Do you feel too unaware of yourself to answer these questions?
- Are you working dazed, even ever so slightly? What is dazing you?

Keeping Company Lies
The Delicate Balance

Organizations are reluctant to change, even when the change may be for the better. This resistance to change within the organization gives rise to a host of behaviors that are designed to perpetuate the status quo. This is especially true in companies experiencing chemical dependence among their employees. There is a great deal of pressure to perpetuate company lies— lies that seek to cover up and "deny" the existence of minor and major addictive behaviors. These company lies are nourished by the atmosphere of denial in the surrounding society. We all partake in the increasing dependence of the human species upon chemicals. We have a pill for almost everything, a chemical answer to almost every physical and spiritual pain. Yet, we, as a society, deny our increasing level of chemical dependence.

Chemical dependence is here. And it does not always take the form of drug addiction. Still, it is drug addiction that has called us to attention, so, for now, let us focus on drug addiction as an indicator of a larger and more elusive dependence in which we are all engaged.

COINVOLVEMENT

Corporate culture is enmeshed in and mirrors the social culture in which it exists. For example, many of the behaviors which occur in families where there is a chemical dependence problem also occur in workplaces. Because co-workers are generally less intimate and more formal with each other than family members, their coinvolvement with an addicted employee may be even more difficult to pinpoint. Coinvolvement is, however, very present and very dangerous in the workplace. Coinvolvement assumes the following and many other forms.

Lies

Lies are so much a part of modern communication that they are largely indistinguishable from truths. Of course, some lies are more visible than others; these are obvious lies. However, the majority of lies are hidden neatly in our words and within our silences. Obvious and hidden lies take a variety of forms, which, when combined, lead to a condition of continuous lying.

Obvious Lies. Obvious lies are easy to spot. When John says, "I was late for work today because of the storm," when there was only a light drizzle and everyone knows this, John is not telling the truth. Watch out! Just because this is an obvious lie does not mean that it is easy to understand or to respond to. (And, of course, not all obvious lies are indications that there is a drug problem.) Many co-workers and managers need a great deal of practice in the confrontation of obvious lies. Managerial training programs would do well to include interpersonal skill training in this area. All too often, it is not knowing how to respond, or what the effects of the response will be in the workplace, that holds back the confrontation of even the most obvious lie.

This process of *holding back* is damaging to communications, to morale, and to productivity. When allowed to remain untouched, unquestioned, obvious lies set the stage for a workplace code of ethics which says, "Lying is OK, and confronting lies is dangerous." Responding directly, in words, to an obvious lie is healthier for everyone and, in the end, better for business. "John, there was no storm" must be said to clear the air. This response stops the spread of the message that lies are OK. It stops the damaging undermining of honesty by mutual consent.

Hidden Lies. However destructive they may be, obvious lies are the least insidious of all lies. By contrast, hidden lies are quite insidious; they do their damage—they produce their effects—without their presence being explicitly revealed. One of the most dangerous aspects of the hidden lie is that co-workers and managers may "allow" a lie to be hidden by not wanting to see that it is there at all. Sometimes they are concerned that if they call attention to someone else's lie, their own lies will be brought out. For example, if a manager knows that an employee regularly comes back from lunch "stoned" on marijuana and if that employee knows that the manager often arrives at work on Mondays with a hangover, they "have something" on each other.

Another type of *lie hiding* takes place when it is not clear what lie is being told, but it is clear that something is not "quite right" about what is being said. Perhaps Mary is experiencing a Valium withdrawal while she is word processing. She's dizzy and tense. "Do you feel all right Mary?" "Yes, I'm fine." The answer doesn't ring true, but co-workers do not touch it. People hearing such a subtle, indirect lie may look the other way. They may not know what it is that makes them uncomfortable about the communication; they may only feel a strange wordless question in the back of their minds. Wordless questions often remain unasked in the family setting, even in marriages; therefore it is not surprising that they are unexpressed in workplace relationships. There is a distance in workplace communication. The distance is not only acceptable, it is expected of the "serious" employee: "Don't get too close on the job. Don't spend paid time dealing with feelings."

And then, there are some hidden lies that are very hidden.

These lies do not become obvious until a crisis brings them out. Perhaps Bill only binge-drinks when he is away on fishing trips. By the time he goes back to work, he is "dried out" and his hangover is gone, or hardly detectable. He may not have any fish, but everyone chooses to think that this is because he is a terrible fisherman. Finally, Bill has a serious boating accident while he is drinking. When he finally returns to work, he is disabled. As a result of this crisis, the hidden lie about his alcohol problem is revealed.

All too often this type of hidden lie comes out as a result of a workplace accident in which co-workers and customers are victims. Recent transportation industry (airline, railroad, bus, and subway) accidents in which innocent citizens, customers, and consumers were injured and killed have alerted us to this sad reality. We now purchase tickets with the question still unasked but very present in our minds: Will my pilot, captain, or driver be drugged? Does anyone know for certain? And were we to voice this question, would we really expect an honest answer? The truth is, we never know for sure. We consumers shudder in silence, much the way co-workers of drug users shiver, feeling the nails of unasked questions scratching on their mental blackboards.

How can a company deal with unspoken truths? As much as possible must be spoken. Employees must be invited and urged to speak up. Regular group meetings (weekly is ideal) conducted by an unthreatening outsider, an unbiased person who is skilled at conducting group therapy, can open up closed minds and locked hearts. Hidden lies will wither when confronted with a desire for the truth about co-workers' feelings. Work must be a place where people are expected to connect with each other. Detachment is not the key to productivity. Open communications must be engendered in the workplace. Rather than an atmosphere of "Don't bother me with my own or anyone else's problems at work" or "I'm afraid I'll be found out and get fired," we must bring about a radical change in the workplace culture. Hidden lies hide in a world of detachment and fear. They die off when it becomes OK to really communicate.

Continuous Lies. In a workplace setting where there is a drug or alcohol problem (remember, alcohol is a drug), an array of obvious and hidden lies develops into a stream of continuous lies. The terrible confusion arising from continuous lies is that, over time, lies are built on lies that are added onto other lies; new lies are told to hide old lies. It becomes very hard to figure out what the truth is. Lies become so "normal" that they happen without a second thought. They are taken for granted. They are not only a part of the organizational culture, they are the overarching *modus operandi* of the organization.

It becomes difficult to stop lying in the workplace. It starts to feel wrong to tell the truth. When one or more people in the workplace are in trouble with drugs, a conscious and subconscious web of continuous lies is woven with the help of everyone in the company. Amidst this web, work goes on. Another day, another dollar. Yet, the work cannot be unaffected. There is no way of estimating how much workplace productivity is reduced by the expenditure of valuable energy to support wasteful but massive organizational denial. The "job" of such a work organization acquires a new dimension: the denial dimension. Production does not necessarily lose momentum, but it is necessarily distributed between the production of the company product and the production of company denial.

Excuses as Lies. A company with a drug problem will often find that one or more members are making excuses for themselves or someone else in the company on a regular basis. "Mark's intentions are good, he just gets overwhelmed easily," or "Jane's got a lot of problems at home right now but she'll be OK" are typical. These excuses help everyone look the other way. They are, in essence, lies. Many companies are grappling with the problem of excuse lies, whether or not they realize it, when they try to determine exactly what employee behaviors are excusable. Excused absences, tardiness, and accidents are essential. Human beings cannot work without having their human needs accommodated. But how much of what is excused is related to drug use?

Denial as Lies. Creeping denial invades a workplace that does not want to see the presence of chemical dependence. It is like an ivy, filling all the soil with its roots and creeping into everything. "Our employees do *not* use drugs, do you, Dick and Jane?" "Of course we don't, boss, and neither do you!" Although denial is a very obvious hidden lie, it is often the most difficult to expose. Moreover, when exposure is viewed as being "bad for business," denial is perversely justified. What a sorry "business expense"!

Communication Breakdown

Every single lie, whatever type it may be, results in a *non*-communication. At the same time, it is also true that every single lie is fostered within an atmosphere of *non*communication. Lies are thus both causes and effects of breakdowns in communication. Indeed, companies with chemical overuse, abuse, and other "drug problems" suffer from many forms of broken communication.

Lack of Communication. The typical scenario in many companies is "No time to talk, hello, goodbye, I'm busy, I'm over-committed, I have to meet this deadline, I'm late, I'm late, I'm late." Many working people rush around like Mad Hatters, rushing to get their work done on time and rushing away from real communications with their co-workers. Little or no effort is made to communicate and share feelings on a deep level, and even simple communications (such as "I really enjoy talking to you and would like to spend more time doing so") never occur.

Lack of communication in the workplace is so very common that most people have adjusted to it and do not find it at all unusual. After all, "You're here to work, not to chat." The implication is that "You are here to produce, not to have or express feelings."

   Inadequate Communication. Even when communication does occur, it can be inadequate. Consider the following conversation between a boss and an employee:

> "I told you we needed the report by the sixteenth."
> "I didn't hear you."
> "That's your problem. I can't vote in favor of your promotion now."
> "Who cares? I have applied for two other better paying jobs."
> "You didn't tell me you were looking."
> "Yes I did. Weeks ago."
> "Next time, let me know when you're telling me; maybe we can still accommodate you here."
> "If there is a next time."

   This kind of conversation is inadequate in that it does not clearly express the facts that the employee very much wants a promotion although he has applied for other better paying jobs and that the manager still wants to keep the employee in this department or workplace. The conversation is so inadequate that these important facts may be lost. Inadequate communication buries feelings and facts. While this problem is frequent in every human relationship, it is aggravated in the presence of chemical dependence and the lies which accompany it.

   Confused Communication. Reality is further distorted when communication becomes confused. Co-workers and managers who deal with other employees when they are craving a drink or drugs, when they are high on alcohol or drugs, or when they are going through hangovers or withdrawals, receive *and* send confusing messages. Employees with a drug problem may change their mind or mood or entire personality several times a day, week, or month. It becomes difficult to find any consistency in the drug user's behavior, except for consistent inconsistency. This is confusing and frightening. Confused communication can lead others to become confused communicators in order to "fit in." It can also plant and nurture the seed of deep emotional disturbance in workplace organizations.

It is all too easy to say that "We communicate well here in this company." The reason this is an easy statement to make is that so much of what goes on in the workplace is the essential but superficial sort of communication relayed in memos, phone calls, and business meetings. The exchange of information within and between business organizations is essential. However, there is another level of communication which is too frequently neglected—it is often described as unessential and overemotional communication. Granted, the bulk of time spent on the job should be dedicated to work itself. However, if a portion of that time is not connected to deeper communication, the time spent on the work is less productive. Employees must feel some degree of connection with each other and their superiors to develop organizational identity, to feel committed to their work.

Grudge Development

When they remain unattended, lies and broken communications lead to unexpressed, partially expressed, or indirectly expressed anxiety or pain. Grudges are then developed.

Private Grudges. A private "grudge" is a strange thing. It is a stuffed-away, unexpressed emotion that is always unstuffing itself and coming out in stiff, cold, or angry ways. Grudges develop slowly, when communication continues to fail and the lies, pains, and confusions compound. Many employees in troubled companies feel that their co-workers and even managers have grudges against them although "no one ever talks about it" and "nothing is ever really done that proves it."

Public Grudges. Some grudges become public in that they are obvious and out in the open. A least favored or always-blamed employee may be the subject of a public company grudge. This person often develops private grudges in response. Being unproductive, careless, wasteful, and damaging on the job is one way of expressing such a private grudge. Using drugs without telling anyone is another way of acting out a private grudge. But using drugs openly, despite the fact that "everyone knows and doesn't like it," is a public grudge-bearing act.

Hurts

Many people, ranging from co-workers to consumers, get hurt in companies with drug problems. In my own work with companies experiencing drug problems, I have found the mechanisms of fear and violence especially common around the use and sale of illegal drugs in or near the workplace. The fear that employees experience, which holds them back from reporting workplace drug sale and use to their employers, is often justified. Employees have reported to me that they have been threatened with property damage, violence, and even death if they "tell," and that they know of cases where the threats were carried out.

Obvious Hurt. Some of the hurt of the workplace drug problems is visible in forms such as accidents on the job, violence in the workplace, and frightening verbal injuries in the form of damaging threats and insults.

Blatant Hurt-Back. "You hurt me, so I hurt you." This eye-for-an-eye, tooth-for-a-tooth form of hurt can be very obvious and may continue to occur despite its visibility. Managers, who are usually promoted for organizational ability, are rarely trained to control this type of workplace warfare.

Buried Hurt. Unfortunately, much of the hurt is buried in the hearts and minds of employees who work in an organization with drug problems. The piercing pain is felt but denied. Work continues, business as usual, but with an undercurrent of resentment, anger, and fear.

Secret Hurt-Back. Many employees with buried hurt express it toward co-workers, manager, or the company as a whole via secret hurt-back. This involves private grudges, lies, gossip, and more direct but still invisible acts such as purposeful carelessness, neglect, theft, and damage. The most secret form of hurt-back is hidden self-destruction. Companies may not notice that one or more of their members are on self-destructive paths until the destruction is in crisis stage, as is often the case with addictive disorders.

COMPANY CODEPENDENCE

Eventually, the coinvolvement around chemical dependence becomes institutionalized. Companies that have drug problems begin to get used to their lies, broken communications, grudges, and hurts. In fact, they become dependent upon them. This is company codependence. Its characteristics are very similar to those found in families experiencing codependence.

Simple Codependence

No codependence is simple. However, for the sake of this discussion, we will call simple codependence a state in which an organization has only one or very few "identified patients" or one or a few persons who are drug-dependent. One characteristic of simple codependence in the workplace is confused feelings, in that co-workers who depend on the drug addict to have all of the problems become confused about their own problems and feelings. Another characteristic of simple codependence is enabling behavior, in which co-workers and managers seek to protect a drug-using employee for empathic reasons and, in the end, enable that employee to continue using drugs without getting help.

Compound Codependence

When more than one or very few employees are drug-addicted or have other undesirable habits, simple codependence is compounded. All the lies, broken communications, grudges, hurts, and confusions are then multiplied many times over. The characteristic of simple codependence listed above is increasingly complicated and exaggerated in companies where 10%, 20%, 30%, 40%, 50%, and even 75% of the employees are suffering from chemical dependence.

Over time, a company with chemical dependence problems experiences difficulties on the functional level. Minor problems eventually compound and have marked effects on job performance and overall productivity.

Practical problems of this sort can compound into major problems. Things can grind down even to a halt. *Destruction* is the process by which the structure of something, in this case an organization, falls apart; it moves away from structure, or *destroys*. Untreated company codependence undermines the structure of the organization.

Other issues may emerge when one or more employees are treated. Other members of the organization either change or try to stay the same. Those who change break out of the rigid holding patterns of their workplace roles. They transcend the unspoken company paradox of "We want you well but we want you sick (chemically dependent) because we need you to be well but we need you to be sick (chemically dependent) because the company must change and get well to survive but the company must stay the same and be sick to retain its identity. And if we change, we will not be us ever again—we will be different." Organizations, even small ones, tend to want to stay the same— to *preserve the status quo*—even if a change will be for the better. This is why so many companies with addiction problems cling to their holding patterns, which are fraught with paradox. This is why company employees often try to make themselves and their co-workers stay the same when an addicted co-worker attempts to break his or her addiction. For example, many managers inhibit a positive attitude toward breaking out of the holding pattern. They continue to deny that there is a drug problem in their department; they help to cover up the fact that a co-worker wants treatment; they influence other employees in belittling an employee who breaks out of the system, who refuses to work dazed any longer. The employee who attempts to break an addiction is viewed as a dark horse, an unknown quantity. He or she can no longer be blamed for all the problems and all the low performance. Moreover, he or she is considered disloyal. The delicate balance, no matter how troubled, is somehow preferred over healthy change, because the change is often frightening. The chemical dependence problems of the drug- or alcohol-addicted employee remind us all on a deep, unspoken level that we are increasingly chemicalized—dependent on chemicals.

When co-workers and managers of addicted persons claim that they want the addict to "get well," they must be ready to make the behavioral changes that will create a drug-free company. They must be willing to see all that they have done to contribute to chemical dependence in the workplace and in the world. Those of us who work with companies to help them heal their chemical dependence problems must educate the co-workers and managers of the addicted employees about the pervasiveness of chemical dependence, of mechanical thinking, and of all forms of automatic behavior. This is a major undertaking. The ramifications are profound. The responsibilities are great. We cannot stop at the narrowly defined boundaries of legislation such as the Drug Free Workplace Act. Although legislation can venture no further, organizations must. We cannot ask companies to end their old ways without offering something new. The beginning of something new in the workplace is improved communication, specifically aimed at shattering the pervasive web of lies, and at escaping the dimension of denial. Efforts to improve communication in the workplace must be driven by the goal of respecting, even applauding, the humanness of working people. This can lead the way to a new and healthier workplace culture. We will return to the new model for company change in Chapter 14.

5

Looking the Chemically Dependent Company in the Eye
Sighting the Hidden Epidemic

The following article appeared in the *Arizona Republic* in May of 1990. It hints at the difficulty of documenting the existence of a company drug problem. At this company, it was the complaints of employees and their family members that triggered an investigation:

---

38 at Magma lose jobs in internal drug probe

Miners, families sought action to end problems

Magma Copper Co. on Friday discharged 38 employees who allegedly used or sold drugs at the company's San Manuel mine.

An official of the mine, about 40 miles north of Tucson, said he knew of no action similar in scope at any other Arizona mining operation.

"This sort of thing has happened on a smaller scale here and at other mines some years ago, but in terms of the numbers involved now, I've never seen anything quite like it," said Marsh Campbell, vice president of human resources.

In February 1989, 27 workers at the fluid-system division of

Allied-Signal Aerospace Co. in Tempe were fired after an internal drug probe.

In the past two weeks, Magma had questioned 60 employees suspected of drug abuse and had suspended 58 of them with pay, Campbell said.

Magma told 38 workers Friday they had the option of quitting or being fired. Others agreed to participate in a company-paid rehabilitation program, Campbell said.

The employees who were terminated "were involved in something more than smoking a joint on the way to work," Campbell said. "It is a severe problem."

Some of those terminated were selling cocaine, marijuana or amphetamines on the job, he said, while others claimed they were only delivering the drugs, not selling them.

On Thursday, Magma met with leaders of Local 937 of the United Steelworkers of America, which represents about 1,300 of the company's 3,400 employees, and reviewed the evidence against the 38.

Don Shelton, president of the local, said, "As a worker, I want to work in a drug-free workplace. As a union official, I have to see that the rights of our members are respected."

Shelton said the union would represent any member who felt he was unfairly accused, but as of Friday none had requested union intervention.

"If they (Magma officials) have the evidence, and the people are guilty, the union isn't going to go out and spend money trying to defend the guy," he said.

Friday's action culminated an investigation of several months' duration conducted by Krout and Schneider, a private-detective agency based in San Francisco.

Campbell would not discuss the tactics used.

Informed sources said undercover agents from the agency had been working at the mine for several months and had identified workers suspected of drug use before formal interrogations began two weeks ago.

"The message to anyone on the workforce is that if they're using drugs, they're putting their jobs in jeopardy," Campbell said.

Campbell said the investigation was triggered by complaints from employees and some families because of concerns over working in the mine with individuals they claimed were using drugs on the job or coming to work under the influence of drugs. [1]

Family members of Magma employees were concerned, quite appropriately, about safety. They, as well as other citizens, employers, and employees have a right to an estimate of the extent of the drug problem in the companies that provide the jobs and manufacture the products. Citizens' safety as consumers and as employees may not be at odds with efforts to estimate the extent of workplace drug use; safety is critical in the workplace *and* in the marketplace. The irony is that these very efforts, designed to protect safety, can threaten civil rights.

It is natural for employers to want to estimate the extent of the drug problem in their companies. Often, they want to measure the level of drug and alcohol use in their organizations in order to develop or amend their employee assistance programs to better assist employees with alcohol and drug problems. Employers also measure the "size of the problem" to establish a baseline against which they can evaluate the effectiveness of any actions they may take. For example, an employee-crack-use estimate of 15% prior to employee-drug-awareness training or increased treatment benefits will be expected to drop by at least a few percentage points after expenditures for these benefits are made. Some employers have estimates of employee drug and alcohol use made regularly in order to evaluate the cost-effectiveness of their employee education and assistance programs. The basic expectation is that employee drug and alcohol use that causes problems will decrease over time when employer-sponsored programs are effective. When drug and alcohol use remains steady or increases in the face of increasing employee assistance expenditures, employers are inclined to conclude that

these expenditures are not cost-beneficial. Company budget
and policy decisions then reflect this thinking. Unfortunately,
employees who may be deriving great benefit from the employee assistance services deemed to be cost-detrimental lose
out when this is the conclusion. It is important, therefore, to
understand how these drug and alcohol use estimates are constructed and what are the practical, professional, personal, and
ethical issues which attend these estimations.

ESTIMATE METHODS

There are several common methods besides drug testing,
which I discuss in Chapter 6, of estimating the level of drug and
alcohol use in a company.

National Data

One method, the most obvious and readily accomplished, is
to apply national estimates of drug and alcohol use to the workplace. If 1 in 6 Americans is expected to suffer from an addiction,
then one might say that 1 in 10 employees will as well. Most
employers express the sentiment that this estimate tells them
very little about what is actually occurring in their plants and
offices. The national estimates can be broken down by age and
by socioeconomic and occupational status, and an estimate
which represents the demographics of the workforce being analyzed can be delivered. Even so, the employers with whom I
have worked tend to feel more comfortable with more specific
estimates of the extent of the problem in their own specific
workplace. The distrust of the national data seems to come from
two virtually opposed views of the drug reality. One, the most
typical, is "It can't be that bad here or I would know about it,"
and the other is "My group is worse off; we're higher than those
statistics indicate."

Undercover Investigation

Against the ominous backdrop of national data and usually in response to productivity or theft problems, some employers opt for the undercover approach to estimating the extent of the workplace drug problem. Outside agents, either from public law enforcement agencies (off-duty police officers are often available for such work) or private security firms are brought in to do undercover investigations. Outsiders tend to be more effective when this choice is made because most companies lack good undercover investigation capability. They have no trained detectives on staff and usually cannot afford to create an undercover department. The company brings in outside operatives to avoid disrupting ongoing business and to ensure anonymity of the investigators. Whether it be outside or inside investigation, undercover investigation hints of the Big Brother Is Watching scenario. The employee has no privacy and can be spied upon at any time.

Searches

Searches are conducted either undercover or in plain sight of everyone. Dogs have been trained to sniff out cocaine and marijuana. The legality of search and seizure comes into play. Both undercover investigation and search methods juxtapose the rights of the individual and the public welfare. This is a disturbing issue with which to have to contend inside the company.

Employee-Assistance-Program Utilization

A second method of estimation measures employee-assistance-service utilization. Employees in trouble with drugs and alcohol may seek confidential help from an employee assistance counselor. The number of such cases or the total number of visits to the employee assistance office per month can be recorded. This number can serve as an estimate of employees' needs for help in this area. However, many employees are reluctant to use employer-sponsored counseling and referral services even when the anonymity of the employee is guaranteed. This form of estimate may therefore be a gross underestimate. Moreover, many small- to medium-sized companies have no internal or external employee assistance programs and cannot collect this form of data.

Treatment Benefit Utilization

Treatment-benefit-utilization data will indicate the frequency and level of employee use of addiction treatment services without identifying the names of the employees who use the services. The shortcoming of this estimate method is that it counts only the number of employees getting employer-sponsored help for the problem and not the number of employees who receive help elsewhere or who have a chemical dependence problem and get no help. Those who are not getting help are as critical to workplace productivity and safety as those who are. Numbers produced via this estimate method are inherently deceiving.

Indirect Indicators

Another method of estimation is to establish indicators which reveal or imply that there exists a particular level of employee drug and alcohol abuse. For example, data suggest that employees who have trouble with alcohol or drugs are more often tardy or absent, utilize health benefits more frequently, and experience more accidents and injuries than other employees. Each of these employee behaviors can be measured and used as an indirect indicator of employee drug and alcohol use. Report 2 in this chapter provides an example of this type of estimate.

Organizational Indicator Map

Few companies are translating absenteeism, tardiness, benefit utilization, injury, and accident data into a composite picture of their organizations. These and other performance-related data can be regularly collected and then broken down by department. I developed *The Substance Abuse Organizational Indicator Map*© to provide a global analysis based upon these data. This map indicates which, if any, departments are experiencing unusually high indicator rates, and it compares indicator rates among departments as well as employee age, occupation, and gender groups. Indicators that are consistently high and grouped together (i.e., four continuous months of high absenteeism, tardiness, accidents, and injury) indicate a problem. Although this could be anything from a general morale condition to an environmental toxin problem, this type of finding often correlates highly with drug abuse and is an alert to the possibility of drug problems in a company. I have found this to be a powerful means of identifying problem areas within companies.

Direct Employee Reporting

Yet another method of estimation is employee reporting. This takes at least two general forms. The first is direct reporting, an inherently limited method in an environment of fear, denial, lies, and competition. From time to time, a few employees may report or "reveal" to a manager that there is a certain level of drug and alcohol use in the workplace. This kind of report is rare and therefore cannot be relied upon as an estimation method. Report 2 provides an application of this method.

Employee Reporting by Survey

More reliable is the questionnaire or survey which asks all employees questions about drug and alcohol use in the company. Report 1 in this chapter provides an example of this form of employee reporting. I have included a sample employee survey in the appendix to this chapter.

The indirect-indicator and employee-survey-estimate methods described above are the focus of this chapter because they can be and are being utilized by companies in many different industries whose workforces vary in size and composition. The following are two sample reports, each consisting of different estimate methods, most of which I have described above. The companies' and employees' names have been omitted to protect the anonymity of all involved. Both Report 1 and Report 2 were commissioned by the owners of auto dealerships whose services include auto sales, auto maintenance and repair, and related clerical and finance work. Both reports include some initial recommendations to the employers. One of the estimate reports, Report 1, is based on an employee survey distributed during an employee drug-and-alcohol-education program.

A final comment about the reports that follow: While they were delivered to the contracting employers in writing, they were also presented to them verbally. In both cases, the employers and their managers wanted to have several lengthy discussions regarding the contents and implications of these reports.

ESTIMATE REPORTS

1. Report to the "A" Corporation Regarding Employee Drug and Alcohol Abuse

Findings of Employee Survey. During a special and mandatory employee-drug-awareness seminar-program at this company, a questionnaire was distributed to all employees. Everyone was guaranteed complete confidentiality in answering the questionnaire (as well as in anything they might say during the seminars) by the seminar leader as well as the employer. The employer wrote the following letter to encourage discussion:

To: All Corporation "A" Employees

I am offering this two-part educational series on Drug and Alcohol Abuse Prevention as a service for you and your family—and as a personal contribution for the good of our community. Nothing said or discussed will be reported back to me or in any way affect your employment.

I hope you will feel free to ask any questions or otherwise participate in the discussions. I am confident that we will all benefit from experiencing these programs.

Sincerely,

B.N.

President

Employees filled out questionnaires with pencils that were provided. They were instructed not to put their names on the forms. They then were asked to leave the completed questionnaires in a carton by the door.

The questionnaire asked employees about their use of alcohol, marijuana, cocaine, crack (a form of cocaine), heroin, amphetamines (speed), and other legal and illegal drugs, both on and off the job. Because alcohol use is legal and socially approved of, this form of questionnaire can be expected to draw relatively accurate information about alcohol use. However, marijuana, cocaine, crack, heroin, and amphetamines are illegal drugs, and consequently, questionnaires can be expected to draw underestimates of their use. Alcohol *and* drug use on the job are viewed as being inappropriate, and therefore, on-the-job use data may also be underestimates.

Approximately 90% of all who responded to the questionnaire replied that they had tried alcohol, approximately 60%

reported having tried marijuana, 40% reported having tried cocaine or crack, and 10% reported having tried heroin, amphetamines, and other drugs.

Approximately 80% reported using alcohol at least once during the past month, approximately 40% reported using marijuana at least once during the past month, approximately 20% reported using cocaine or crack at least once during the past month, and 2% reported using heroin, amphetamines, and other drugs at least once during the past month.

Approximately 50% reported using alcohol at least once a week, approximately 30% reported using marijuana at least once a week, approximately 15% reported using cocaine or crack at least once a week, and approximately 2% reported using amphetamines at least once a week.

Approximately 5% reported that they were having trouble with alcohol; 2% reported having trouble with cocaine or crack.

Approximately 10% reported ever having used alcohol at work, with 2% regularly using it; approximately 5% reported ever having used marijuana at work, with none regularly using it; approximately 3% reported ever having used cocaine or crack at work, with 1% regularly using it.

Survey research is, of course, limited by the respondents' willingness to answer questions truthfully, even on anonymous questionnaires. The importance of these data is that they give some indication, and probably an underestimation, of drug use in your company workforce.

NOTE: Employees were also asked if they would benefit from more educational programs concerning drugs and alcohol at work. Approximately 50% responded "yes." Approximately 20% wrote in comments to the effect that they would benefit, but that they would not like the programs to be mandatory. (About 5% wrote in comments to the effect that "the boss" should be more concerned with exposure to toxic chemicals in the workplace than employee drug use.)

One seminar group, composed of forty-six employees, was

particularly agitated about the fact that attendance at the drug awareness seminars was mandatory. The majority of these persons were mechanics who work in the "shop." Many expressed anger about being made to do anything, about the amount of work they would be returning to, and about the fact that they would feel more pressured in their work now because they had missed time from it. A few suggested that this pressure would lead to drug use. When this presenter asked if they had learned anything during the seminar, two-thirds of them answered "yes." When asked if they would have attended had it been voluntary, all of them answered "no."

The data collected by the survey distributed at these seminars show that there is marked drug and alcohol use among employees at your company, "A" Corporation. Immediate and continuing action must be taken.

Recommendations. OPEN UP LINES OF COMMUNICATION BETWEEN MANAGEMENT AND FIRST-LINE EMPLOYEES, MAKE COUNSELING AVAILABLE, AND LET EMPLOYEES KNOW THAT MANAGEMENT AND THE BOSS CARE! ALSO, AND MOST IMPORTANT, DEVELOP A CLEAR COMPANY DRUG POLICY. More specific recommendations are listed below:

Workplace Changes

1. Provide a decaffeinated coffee and tea option where coffee and tea are already regularly provided. Employees are overcaffeinating themselves and undergoing the (pharmacological and psychological) effects of caffeine overuse.
2. Coca-Cola and candy machines are now in the workplace. Be certain that employees also have the option of buying sugar-free drinks, juices, and snacks other than candies and Coca-Cola.
3. Hang a bulletin board up in the workplace that posts current articles on health and information on drugs.

4. Make a no-smoking time-out room (one without fluorescent lights, which is comfortably decorated) where employees can go on their breaks to take some time for relaxation and quiet.
5. Regularly investigate working conditions. Check to see if smoking during spray painting and other chemical work is occurring, and if so, check to see whether or not this is dangerous to both the smokers and nonsmokers.

Programmatic Changes

1. Institute an employee assistance program.
2. Include an employee assistance counselor who can be seen off-site and anonymously (because any visit to an office in your particular type of workplace is highly visible). Provide an employee assistance counselor and/or referral service for employees who want help with smoking problems. Provide a counselor and/or referral service for employees who want help with their drug and alcohol problems. Be certain that employees understand that the contents of their counseling sessions are confidential.
3. Institute regular ventilation sessions. These encourage employees to speak up about tensions and pressures. A one-hour group meeting or a lunch group once a week—voluntary—will be of great help. Bring in an outside group leader or facilitator, one who is bound by the laws of confidentiality. Be certain that employees understand that their jobs are not at stake in these sessions.
4. Provide regular seminars on drugs, mental health, and stress. Be prepared for some discontent if these are made mandatory. Try to open these programs to family members of employees as well as to employees.
5. Be prepared to send an average of 10% of your employees per year through an addiction treatment program and its aftercare component, either via amending

the existing employee benefits plan or setting up an equal-access employer-subsidized benefit program.

Policy Changes

1. Make your drug and alcohol policy explicit.
2. Write this policy down and distribute it to all employees.
3. Be certain all employees understand the policy.
4. Review the policy regularly at company meetings.

2. Report to the "B" Corporation Regarding Employee Drug and Alcohol Abuse

Findings of Employee Survey. Forty-two employees of "B" Corporation were interviewed following initial meetings with Mr. K., Mr. D., and one employee who originally reported to Mr. K. the existence of a drug and alcohol problem at "B" Corporation. Mechanics, parts department employees, office staff, and sales personnel in both the used and new sales departments were interviewed.

The stated goal of the above-mentioned interview process was to "Get an idea as to the level of employee benefit utilization and employees' comments regarding their employee benefits utilization." The interview process served as an indicator of the extent of the employee drug and alcohol problem at "B" Corporation in two ways. First, an employee's benefit utilization increases with his or her drug and alcohol intake and with his or her drug and alcohol problems and possible addictive behaviors. Second, the interviewers who were employed to do this estimate were highly experienced in reading beyond the words to signs of drugs and alcohol use in the workplace.

Based upon the content of the interviews and the observations made during the interviews, it is clear that there is a marked drug and alcohol problem at "B" Corporation. This problem warrants extensive attention and immediate action. Recommendations are included later in this report.

Benefit Utilization Indicator of a Drug or Alcohol Problem

Note that 20.6% of those interviewed reported frequent use of medical benefits—by either the employee or the employee's family or both. Addicted families use medical facilities more than nonaddicted families by a factor of 8. High medical benefit utilization suggests but does not prove that there is a drug or alcohol problem among employees or their families.

Absenteeism Indicator of a Drug or Alcohol Problem

Estimated mechanics' absenteeism reveals that 13.8% (4 in 29 people) are responsible for 58% of the absenteeism and 10.3% (3 in 29 people) are responsible for 50% of the absenteeism. Estimated salespersons' absenteeism reveals that 19% (3 in 21 people) are responsible for 68% of the absenteeism. High absenteeism among a few individuals suggests but does not prove that there is a drug or alcohol problem among those individuals.

Symptoms Indicator of a Drug or Alcohol Problem

Remember that the symptoms discussed below are perceived based upon the observations and trained intuitive judgments of the interviewers. Of those interviewed, 20.6% presented symptoms of some kind of drug or alcohol use: 5.8% appeared to be "toxic" or in some state of withdrawal at work. It appears that the drugs being used by this 5.8% of those interviewed were marijuana, cocaine, amphetamines, and alcohol, not necessarily in this order of amount or extent of use.

Note that it is highly probable that the 20.6% group showing symptoms at the time of the interviews (while not appearing to be using on the job) was probably working under the remaining influence of some nonworkplace drug or alcohol intake or was in the withdrawal phase of such an intake. This group and the 5.8% who appeared to be using on the job present serious threats to the morale, health, and safety of all employees and waste and liability threats to your company. Judgment, coordination, attitude, and other capabilities are impaired in drug- or alcohol·using employees. An additional concern: Among the 20.6% not appearing to use drugs on the job but presenting symptoms of use off the job, there may be those employees who will use drugs or alcohol on the job on other days.

Attitudinal Indicator of a Drug or Alcohol Problem

Some of the interviewing was met with poorly disguised hostility. For example, one service mechanic was very hostile and kept his head under the hood of the car that he was working on and answered interviewers only in monosyllables. One young woman in the office was directly suspicious and hostile. It is unusual for one of our interviewers to be met with this form of behavior unless there is some type of problem in the workplace.

Interviewer's Outside Research as an Indicator of a Drug or Alcohol Problem in Your Industry

My research indicates that sales and repair shops such as yours range from 30% to 75% in drug or alcohol use among employees. Most companies similar to yours will benefit by implementing the following recommendations.

Recommendations. Based upon the findings of the on-site search and interviews and the general information we have collected about employee drug and alcohol abuse in auto dealerships, we recommended the following actions be taken at "B" Corporation:

1. The rewriting and subsequent posting of a new, more elaborate, and stronger company drug and alcohol policy.
2. The providing of a yearly drug and alcohol education

program for all employees. Group size should be between fifteen and thirty for employee nonmanagement seminars. Managers may need a smaller group size for more directed training in the handling of on-site employee drug problems.

3. The development of a list of treatment options available to employees who have drug and alcohol problems. This should be posted and distributed by mail within two weeks after the new drug policy is posted.

4. The instituting of behavioral and performance documentation techniques in all departments at "B" Corporation. These allow monitoring of employee performance.

5. The development and utilization of a computerized absenteeism and performance-tracking system with cumulative totals and other special capabilities such as absenteeism analyses by specific days of the week.

6. Other measures, including the instituting of "progressive disciplinary measures" suggested by "B" Corporation's attorney and the possible termination of certain employees, should be determined only after the implementation and review of the above steps.

ELEMENTS OF AN ESTIMATE REPORT

Despite their differences in estimate methods, estimate reports on employee drug and alcohol use usually contain the following elements:

1. An explanation of how the data were obtained.
2. The data.
3. Comments about the limitations of the estimates.
4. When requested by the employer, recommendations.
5. A verbal explanation and discussion of the contents of the report, which should accompany the written report.

Occasionally, employers who contract to have an employee drug and alcohol use estimate request that the reporter provide the names of specific employees who may be or are using drugs or alcohol at work. The reporter must clarify with the employer whether or not these names will be provided before beginning the research for such a report. I have consistently declined to provide the names of employees, stating that this is not the type of work that I or my colleagues do. This point is further elaborated below.

FACTORS IN EMPLOYEE DRUG AND ALCOHOL USE

Employee drug and alcohol use is influenced and even generated by several psychological, organizational, and sociological factors. Employers and managers need to be informed about these factors when they attempt to measure and then alleviate drug and alcohol use in their workplace. I have reviewed some of these factors from a different perspective in Chapter 2, but I include them here in order to indicate their relevance to the estimation of the extent of the drug problem.

Lack of Information

Most employees who end up in trouble with drugs suffer from a lack of information about how people become addicted and about how dangerous particular drugs are. Most employees who use drugs and alcohol even recreationally are generally unaware of the health risks involved. Most employees are also generally unaware of how to eat right "to keep fit" and to stay away from drugs. Every month, there is new information available on drug and health issues. It is difficult to keep up with this information growth. As a result, most employees settle for a lack of information. Unfortunately, this state of affairs can be dangerous and even fatal. For example, many persons become addicted to cocaine because they did not know or did not believe that it is a dangerous and sometimes fatal drug. New designer or lab drugs are often used by people who share these same misconceptions.

Worklife Stress

Worklife stressors include deadline pressure, pressure to be punctual, dealing with authority, protection of self-image, and competition for promotion, recognition, or the achievement of some other goal. These stressors combine with the general stress of economic survival (the employee has to work to make a living) to result in an ongoing tension. Drugs and alcohol have served as outlets and escapes for employees who have not learned other compensations for worklife stress.

Societal Pressures

We live in a society that advertises cigarettes and alcohol and glorifies legal and illegal drug use. It is difficult to be a member of this society and not feel the pressure to join the "Pepsi generation," "the happy hour," the drug-using crowd, and so on.

Peer Pressure

During a break at a seminar that I conducted, an employee came up and, almost in tears, commented that he had no friends at work because he would not drink or drug with any of them. Many employees feel pressure from fellow employees to drink or drug socially. It is viewed as being part of fellowship. It can be lonely to say "no." This is a frequently verbalized complaint among employees between the ages of eighteen and thirty-five.

Fear and Denial

Once someone is in trouble with a drug, fear and denial set in. Employees are afraid of losing the respect of their peers (by admitting that they are having trouble with a drug instead of "just using it"), and they are even more fearful of losing their jobs or being arrested when they step forward and state that they need help. Also, most employees are extremely uncomfortable with the idea of reporting someone else's drug problem. Fear and denial are barriers that employees confront when they attempt to alleviate employee drug and alcohol abuse. Sometimes, employers, denying their own or their companies' drug problems, contribute to the building of this barrier.

Each of these factors influences workplace behavior and drug and alcohol use by employees and, consequently, the estimating of the extent of the problem.

ISSUES IN REPORTING ESTIMATES OF EMPLOYEE DRUG AND ALCOHOL ABUSE

Recall that estimate reporting of employee drug and alcohol abuse is becoming a common practice. Those who participate in this practice are confronted by a combination of practical, professional, personal, and ethical issues. While these make such work professionally exciting, they also render it professionally and personally demanding. Among these issues are the following:

Practical Issues

Selecting an Estimate Method. The selection of an estimate method involves a consideration of the amount of time to be allotted to the research, the skills of the researcher, and the ease with which surveys, interviews, or other methods can be used in the work setting being studied. An understanding of what methods the employer and the employees will be most receptive to is important.

Determining the Accuracy of the Method Selected. Once an estimate method is selected, its accuracy must be considered. Most methods will provide underestimates of the amount of use because of employees' understandable reluctance to report illicit or wrongful activities. Employers must be informed about the questions of accuracy typical in this form of research, prior to the beginning of this research.

Collecting the Data. Data collection is often slow and tedious. A knowledge of the time involved in conducting interviews and tabulating the data from surveys or other research processes is essential. Contracting employers must be informed of the time involved in this process.

The Costs of the Research. Understanding the time and personnel practicalities in estimating employee drug and alcohol use will enable a researcher to estimate the cost of the project in advance.

Professional Issues

Responding to Requests to Do Undercover Work or Pose as Something One Is Not. Most researchers doing this type of work are psychotherapists, counselors, employee assistance or benefits personnel, or social scientists. These people are not professional actors or undercover agents and do best to deny this request.

Understanding One's Professional Background. Researchers must not commit themselves to forms of investigatory activity that run counter to their profession. If the researcher is a licensed psychotherapist, confidentiality issues are in the forefront. Employees may be confused about the role of the researcher. This confusion should be countered with a clear definition of the researcher's professional limitations and roles.

Understanding One's Professional Role during Research. Whether or not she or he is a psychotherapist, the researcher must address particular professional issues. The research must be accurate or state its accuracy level. It must be objective. The anonymity of the subjects—employees in this case—must be protected. Employers who ask for the names of employees are asking researchers to step beyond professional limits and should be told so.

Personal Issues

Coping with Scared, Unhappy, Angry, or Resistant Employees. When conducting research aimed at generating an estimate of employee drug and alcohol use, a researcher may have to interview or present questionnaires to employees who are uncomfortable with the research being conducted. Some of these employees will be coming from the perspective of chemical dependence, denying or angry about their drug problems. Others may be generally unhappy with their job descriptions, their pay, or their employers. In some workplaces, employees are intimidated by drug-using or drug-dealing employees, and their fears will be acted out during the research work. A researcher must be prepared to deal with the difficult personal interactions that may arise during the research.

Remaining Objective When the Research Brings Out a Subjective Response. As a result of the personal experience of the researcher while generating an estimate, the researcher may find his or her objectivity difficult to maintain. A constant alertness to this possibility will help to control the interference of subjectivity in generating an estimate.

Ethical Issues

Reporting More Than Was Requested. There will be times during the conducting of employee drug and alcohol use research when more information than the researcher would like becomes available. This should be reported if it falls within the original agreement with the employer and if it is professionally ethical.

Reporting Employee's Names or Specific Information Leading to the Detection of Their Names. Names of specific employees using or selling drugs at work may be mentioned to the researcher. Unless one has agreed in advance to provide such names, this information, as well as the names of those who reveal it, must remain confidential if the researcher is operating under the professional label of *psychotherapist*. Also, any details which can lead to the identification of employees should be carefully considered before being written into a final report. These should not be included in the report when their inclusion is equivalent to providing actual names.

Conducting Research That May Be Used as a Justification for Cutbacks in Employee Assistance. This is one of the most profound ethical questions in the fields of both employee assistance and social science research. Sometimes research produces information that leads employers to cut back programs and benefits that are helping employees. When a series of estimates of employee drug and alcohol use show no improvement over time, workplace decision makers may decide that their counseling or referral services are not working and may terminate them or cut back on them. Sometimes the funds are literally transferred to the security arm of the company, and an investigatory and enforcement emphasis may supersede the treatment and service emphasis which preceded it.

CONCLUDING REMARKS

In this chapter, I have shared an inside look at the measurement of employee drug and alcohol use and abuse. While the specific drugs used by employees are changing, we are a long way off from drug-free workplaces. Keep in mind that even OTC (over-the-counter) and prescription drugs can affect employee performance, productivity, well-being, and safety. Moreover, the quantification of employee behavior (turning behavioral events into statistics) will continue as employers increase their emphasis upon the measurement of indicators including employee performance as a predictor of productivity. As long as we want to generate statistics about employees, we risk losing real, humane, and treatment-oriented information about these employees. Their needs, their wants, and their problems with worklife become secondary to data about their behavior. In our work, we must refrain from losing sight of the human element—the cry of the heart that employee drug and alcohol use and abuse ultimately represent.

APPENDIX: EMPLOYEE SURVEY REGARDING DRUGS AND ALCOHOL

Please answer each of the questions on this survey and return it at the end of today's seminar.

Do not put your name on this survey. All of your answers are confidential and will remain that way. Thank you.

1. Your age

2. Your sex

3. Your present job (if employed)

4. The name of the company where you now work (if employed)

5. Number of years on this job (if employed)

6. Number of years with this company (if employed)

7. Do you live alone?

8. Do you have any preschool-age children?

9. Do you have any children ages six through twelve?

10. Do you have any high-school-age children?

11. Do you have any adult children (over eighteen)?

Please circle all of your answers to Questions 12 through 21. Each question asks you about more than one drug, so please be sure to answer every question in every column. Answers to Questions 22 through 25 will provide valuable supplementary information. Thank you.

	Alcohol	Mari-juana	Cocaine	Amphet-amine or speed	Any other drug (e.g., nicotine) Name it here: ____
12. Have you ever tried this drug?					
	yes	yes	yes	yes	yes
	no	no	no	no	no
13. Have you used this drug at least once within the past month?					
	yes	yes	yes	yes	yes
	no	no	no	no	no

	Alcohol	Mari-juana	Cocaine	Amphet-amine or speed	Any other drug (e.g., nicotine) Name it here:

14. How often do you currently use this drug?

	Alcohol	Mari-juana	Cocaine	Amphet-amine or speed	Any other
1 = never	1	1	1	1	1
2 = less than once a month	2	2	2	2	2
3 = once a month	3	3	3	3	3
4 = once a week	4	4	4	4	4
5 = 2 to 3 times a week	5	5	5	5	5
6 = daily	6	6	6	6	6

15. Do you feel you are having trouble with this drug at this time?

yes	yes	yes	yes	yes
no	no	no	no	no

16. Does anyone in your family (not including yourself) use this drug?

yes	yes	yes	yes	yes
no	no	no	no	no

17. Is anyone in your family (not including yourself) currently having trouble with this drug?

yes	yes	yes	yes	yes
no	no	no	no	no

18. Have you ever used this drug at work?

yes	yes	yes	yes	yes
no	no	no	no	no

	Alcohol	Mari-juana	Cocaine	Amphet-amine or speed	Any other drug (e.g., nicotine) Name it here:

19. Do you regularly use this drug at work? (Answer this only if you are employed.)

	Alcohol	Mari-juana	Cocaine	Amphet-amine or speed	Any other drug
	yes	yes	yes	yes	yes
	no	no	no	no	no

20. Do any of your fellow employees use this drug at work? If so, about how many of them do? (Answer this only if you are employed.)

	Alcohol	Mari-juana	Cocaine	Amphet-amine or speed	Any other drug
1 = yes, but very few of them	1	1	1	1	1
2 = yes, but less than one-third of them	2	2	2	2	2
3 = yes, about one-third of them	3	3	3	3	3
4 = yes, about half of them	4	4	4	4	4
5 = yes, about two-thirds of them	5	5	5	5	5
6 = yes, more than two-thirds of them	6	6	6	6	6

	Alcohol	Mari-juana	Cocaine	Amphet-amine or speed	Any other drug (e.g., nicotine) Name it here:
7 = yes, almost all or all of them	7	7	7	7	7

21. Do any of your fellow employees currently use this drug outside of work? (Answer this only if you are employed.)

	yes	yes	yes	yes	yes
	no	no	no	no	no

22. Would you benefit from more educational programs at work?

yes   no

23. What type of programs would you like to participate in?

24. Do you or any of your family members need counseling about alcohol, drug, smoking, or related problems?

yes   no

25. Please rate this seminar on drug abuse prevention here:

1	2	3	4	5
Poor	Less than average	Average	Good	Excellent

6

Drug Testing
A Test of Will and Right

On March 24, 1989, 267,000 barrels of crude oil were unleashed upon one of the world's most pristine environments, a portion of the Alaskan coast, causing what the editors of *Marine Log* described as "cataclysmic ecological damage." [1] A junior officer had been commanded to take control of the ship despite the fact that he was not legally certified to do so. The command had come from the senior officer or master of the ship, who may have been intoxicated on alcohol at the time. Six hours after the disaster, this senior officer's blood alcohol level was recorded at 0.06%, which suggests that, if he did not drink after the accident, it was close to 0.19% at the time of the accident. [2] This is almost double the 0.1% level at which motorists are determined to be legally "drunk" in many states, and more than double the 0.08% level at which people are legally drunk in California. (See the Blood Alcohol Level Chart in Appendix A of this chapter.)

When I heard about this disaster, I was immediately reminded of the 1978 Amoco *Cadiz* catastrophe, in which an oil tanker crashed into reefs off the coast of France and spewed its 230,000 tons of crude oil over the sea and shore. I happened to be visiting the area and stumbled into an unforgettably horrible visual experience. The sand was coated with oil. The waves were brown and too heavy to curl. It seemed to be raining oil, each drop coated with the dark slickness. I found it difficult to breath. But what was most unsettling were the accusing looks in the oil-filled eyes of the dying shorebirds who covered the shoreline for what seemed to be endless miles.

Industrial accidents will occur whether or not we use drugs. The Amoco *Cadiz* disaster was never blamed on drugs. Instead the cause was determined to be a malfunction in the hydraulic steering system, bad weather, and a time lag in the orders from the company's headquarters regarding the appropriate steps to take. [3] Perhaps, given the world's increasing awareness of the role of drugs in industrial accidents, other questions would have been asked of the same accident had it occurred in the 1990s. Unfortunately drug use increases the probability of accidents, accidents which, all too often, injure or kill innocent bystanders—wildlife and human life. Our understanding of this problem is more often than not an insulated understanding: It happens to someone else somewhere else. The accidents quickly enter the safe realm of statistics. Even dead people can be conveniently reduced to numbers. We are, therefore, distanced from the human face of drug-related accidents. Perhaps we need to be this distant in order to remain objective about the problem. Consider the effect that the following report has upon you. I have selected this report because, as it was explained to me, "only a few people died in this crash":

AIRCRAFT ACCIDENT REPORT
Trans-Colorado Airlines, Inc., Flight 2286

EXECUTIVE SUMMARY (EXCERPT)

About 1920 mountain standard time on January 19, 1988, N68TC, a Trans-Colorado Airlines Inc., Fairchild Metro III, operating as Continental Express flight 2286, on flight from Stapleton International Airport, Denver, Colorado, with 2 flightcrew members and 15 passengers on board, crashed on approach to Durango, Colorado. The two flightcrew members and seven passengers were killed as a result of the accident.

The National Transportation Safety Board determines that the probable cause of this accident was the first officer's flying and the captain's ineffective monitoring of an unstabilized approach which resulted in a descent below published descent profile. Contributing to the accident was the degradation of the captain's performance resulting from his use of cocaine before the accident.

FACTUAL INFORMATION (EXCERPTS)

Injuries to Persons

Injuries	Crew	Passengers	Total
Fatal	2	7	9
Serious	0	1	1
Minor	0	6	6
None	0	1	1
Total	2	15	17

Damage to Aircraft

The airplane was destroyed in the accident. Its value was estimated at $3 million.

Medical and Pathological Information

Autopsies indicated that both crewmembers of Trans-Colorado 2286 died from multiple impact trauma consistent with an airplane accident.

Blood, urine, vitreous, and bile samples from each of the crewmembers were submitted for toxicological examination to the Center for Human Toxicology of the University of Utah. The samples from the body of the first officer were negative for alcohol and drugs. The blood sample of the captain showed 22 nanograms/milliliter (ng/ml) of benzoylecgonine; the urine sample showed 22 ng/ml of cocaine and 1,800 ng/ml of benzoylecgonine. Benzoylecgonine is the principal metabolite of cocaine. Additional samples from the body of the captain were then submitted to a private laboratory in Sacramento, California, for a second toxicological analysis which was performed over a month later. The results showed the presence of 26 ng/ml of benzoylecgonine in the blood and 11 ng/ml of cocaine and 1,596 ng/ml of benzoylecgonine in the urine. The analyses were able to detect amount of cocaine in the blood as low as 10 ng/ml. The difference in the blood measurements between the two samples was attributed to measurement variation. The difference in the amounts of cocaine and benzoylecgonine in the urine of the two samples was attributed to measurement variation and/or the continued breakdown in the urine of the two substances.

The autopsy of the first officer's body included an examination of the liver. It showed no tissue pathology characteristic of alcohol abuse.

Survival Aspects

The airplane was crushed from the nose to the first row of passenger seats. Survivors' injuries ranged in severity from fractured vertebrae to muscle strains. One survivor also sustained first-degree frostbite of both feet.

At 2034, a local resident contacted Central Dispatch and informed it that a man had just reported surviving a plane crash. Central Dispatch sent a rescue vehicle to the survivor and it arrived at 2045. The survivor had walked until he arrived at the residence. Five other passengers, including a 23-month-old who was carried by another survivor, walked together about $1\frac{1}{2}$ miles over $1\frac{1}{2}$ hours to a highway. They then met a motorist who transported them about a mile until he met a responding rescue vehicle. The group of survivors was transported to a local hospital.

About 2226, the crash site was located. Rescue units from various local agencies, using snowmobiles, ambulances, ski patrol sleds, and a bulldozer arrived at the site 48 minutes later. Ten passengers and crew were at the site. The crewmembers and 4 passengers had been killed. Rescue of the survivors was hampered by snow, darkness, extreme cold and the remote location of the site. Two additional passengers died during extrication and one died a day later. Rescue efforts continued for over 1 hour after the first rescue personnel arrived at the site. The last survivor was transported from the scene at 0030.

Human Performance

THE CAPTAIN—After the accident, a corporate pilot contacted the Safety Board. He said that on February 24, while staying at a hotel in the Phoenix, Arizona area, he met a woman who said that she had been the fiancee of the captain of the Trans-Colorado airplane involved in the accident near Durango. The woman had the same name as that of the woman who had accompanied the captain, as his wife, on the trip to DEN [Denver, Colorado] in which the captain's bags were lost. The corporate pilot stated that the woman told him that she and the captain had been living together and that he had flown for a commuter airline based in DEN. Further, he stated that she said "I'm sure glad that we were able to bury him right after the accident, because the night before we had done a bag of cocaine . . . and I was worried that the autopsy would say there were traces of this in his system before he died."

The Safety Board attempted to contact the woman at the address that she had given to the corporate pilot. However, an attorney representing her informed the Safety Board that the woman had no information that could help the investigation, that she had not been with the captain during the 24-hour period before the accident, and that, in the woman's opinion, the captain was ". . . not a habitual user of cocaine, alcohol or other similar drugs."

The captain's parents told Safety Board investigators that they were unaware that their son had ever used cocaine. A close acquaintance of the captain, who had seen him almost daily from early 1984 through mid-1986, saw him again in the summer of 1987. In the interim between 1986 and 1987, she talked to him over the telephone but did not see him. She described him in the 1984 through 1986 period as "a very stable person . . . a nice guy . . . fun to be with." She described his demeanor, over a year later, as quite different than what it had been earlier:

He wasn't himself any more. I knew right then that there was some kind of drug problem. He acted, oh, very nervous like he was scared of something. He'd look over his shoulder a lot as if there was someone behind him when there wasn't. When I was over at his house, every time a car came through he'd jump up and look out that window. I thought he gained more weight than I had ever seen him gain before. And he was just real jittery.

The AME who had performed the captain's recent FAA [Federal Aviation Administration] medical examinations told Safety Board investigators that he had been surprised to learn of the results of the toxicological analyses. He described himself as unaware of the captain's drug use. He said that the captain's speech was coherent and that his behavior was unremarkable during the examinations.

THE FIRST OFFICER—Friends and acquaintances described the first officer as being in good spirits before the accident. He had successfully completed a pre-employment examination the day before the accident and was looking forward to employment with Rocky Mountain Airlines.

The first officer was reported to have regularly attended Alcoholics Anonymous meetings. In the late 1970s, the FAA received several anonymous reports that the first officer had violated the prohibition against consuming alcohol at least 8 hours before operating an aircraft. FAA inspectors investigated the reports but could not obtain evidence to support allegations.

* * * * *

The Safety Board believes that the research into the effects of cocaine use on performance suggest possible avenues of cocaine-related impairment of the captain's perceptual skills and abilities at the time of the accident. These include withdrawal effects, such as significant mood alteration and degradation, craving for the drug, and post-cocaine induced fatigue. Each of these effects, either alone or in combination, could have degraded the captain's abilities to fly as well as monitor the first officer's flying of Trans-Colorado 2286.

Without information about the amount of cocaine the captain ingested, when he ingested it, and his recent and long term history of cocaine use, the Safety Board is unable to conclude the extent of the cocaine-related impairment of his piloting and perceptual abilities.

Nevertheless, the evidence suggests that he had used the drug the night before the accident. If, as the corporate pilot related to the Safety Board, the captain and his friend had done a "bag" of cocaine the night before the accident, then according to a representative of the Drug Enforcement Administration, the couple had sufficient cocaine to stay up a good part of the night ingesting the drug. Given the known stimulant effects of the drug, the fact that he was not at rest while using the drug, and the likelihood of insomnia following cocaine use, with the fatiguing effects of flying for several hours before the accident, the Safety Board believes the captain's use of cocaine the night before the accident impaired his abilities to both fly and monitor the first officer's flying of the Trans-Colorado 2286, most likely due to fatigue. Therefore, the Safety Board concludes that the captain contributed to the accident by his use of cocaine.

Despite the inability to conclude the precise effects of the captain's cocaine use on his abilities at the time of the accident and despite the difficulty in making such conclusions following evidence of cocaine use, the Safety Board condemns the use of cocaine by an airman or by any individual involved in public transportation. The use of any illicit drug has no place in the transportation system. [4]

Can you control the mental soundness of your pilot when you fly on a commercial airline? I am against drug testing. I do not believe that anyone or any organization has a right to intrude upon my privacy. Yet, at the same time, I expect my taxes and some of the dollars I spend on goods and services to protect me from crime, injury, accident, and loss. My airline ticket is expensive enough that it should guarantee me that everything is

being done that can be done to ensure a safe flight. But what can
be done? What is going to be the surest, safest, most solid
guarantee?

We are caught in a moral crisis. How can the right to privacy
be fairly weighed against public safety? Drug testing raises this
moral dilemma to a visible and divisive peak. We must make
choices which are difficult and very uncomfortable.

I am reminded of the time when I was giving birth to my
daughter. I was in a hospital. I had been in labor twelve hours.
My husband had gone downstairs to handle some paperwork. I
was told that something was wrong. Suddenly, I was being
prepared for emergency Cesarean section surgery. Tubes were
jabbed into my arms, I was rushed to a special room, someone
ran in and broke my water. My own doctor was not there. I felt
that I had to speak up, to take control of this situation:

"How do you know this is necessary?"

"The baby's heartbeat had dropped precipitously."

I ran through a series of questions in my mind. Even in my
labor pain, I could tell that the decision to perform a Cesarean
on me was subjective. Suddenly I said it—the question that was
burning in my mind. I spoke calmly: "How many, if any of you,
have used alcohol or any other drug in the last forty-eight hours?
If you have, when, which drug, and how much of it?"

Four of the people in the room looked at me aghast. The
fifth laughed awkwardly. No one ever answered me. The Cesarean was never performed. My baby was born, whole and
healthy.

Didn't I have a right to know? Didn't I have a right to ask?
As someone who had worked in the addiction field for years, I
knew that it was quite possible that one or more of those attending me had used something. I have considered and reconsidered
this matter and still feel that I had to ask. I had a right to know.
But I could not get an answer. Where does this leave me? I say
that I am against drug testing. But the reality is that it may be my
only option in some cases. I would like to suggest that everyone

who buys an airline ticket interview the pilot before getting onto the plane and that everyone who has surgery interrogate the surgeon, nurses, anesthesiologist, and others in attendance before being cut open. But this ludicrous suggestion is difficult, if not impossible, to follow even for those who are willing. So what do we do? We consumers of goods and services have a right to know about their quality and safety. Testing may be the way to know this.

This pro-testing sentiment is growing. According to the 1988 survey of managers conducted by the American Productivity and Quality Center, 53% of all managers surveyed think random drug testing should be legal for all workers, 81% of all managers think drug testing should be legal as a preemployment requirement, and 94% think it should be legal as a preemployment requirement for sensitive jobs. [5] Another survey, taken in the late 1980s of *Industry Week* readers, found that an overwhelming 88% of the respondents would submit to a drug test if asked to; 70% did not view drug testing as a invasion of privacy; and 87% thought employers should be legally able to test. [6] This sentiment is fostered in an environment in which testing of many sorts is enjoying new status. Employment tests of cognitive ability have been available to employers for years, but many companies have avoided them because of their potential for lawsuits. After the Equal Employment Opportunity Commission's protective guidelines were instituted in 1978 to protect citizens from employment discrimination, most employers who were using employment testing as a means of hiring and promotion dropped their testing programs. Many employers reported consequent declines in the quality and productivity of their workforce. [7] This result may or may not have been caused by the reduction in employment testing.

Regardless of the relationship between employment testing and productivity, the issue has become highly controversial. Instead of fading away, testing has become increasingly prevalent in and around the workplace. Everything from job performance testing to cholesterol testing to psychological testing to AIDS testing to drug testing is now conducted. Although the legality of these and other tests has been and will continue to be tried in the courts, we are entering a sociopolitical state which has been described as a *testocracy*. [8] Admission into and opportunity in the workplace are increasingly determined by tests. A worker's reliability, competence, ability, and fitness for duty are being tested and measured in myriad ways. This may sound futuristic—all of one's relevant characteristics can be tested and reduced to numbers. But this is not surprising. Productivity is the goal. Efficiency is essential. Workers are only cogs in the massive economic machine. No wonder they are dazed.

Testing is here, most likely, to stay. Already federal agencies such as the Department of Defense, the Federal Railroad Administration, and the Department of Transportation are implementing mandatory urine screening. The Department of Defense began its large-scale drug-testing program in 1982. [9] The private sector was not far behind. By 1986, about 25% of the Fortune 500 companies were testing both applicants and employees for illegal drug use. [10] By the end of the 1980s, the majority of the largest employers in the United States had adopted a drug-testing policy, and some 20% of all employed in the United States work in businesses with a drug-testing policy. [11] About 3.5% of all employees tested in the United States test positive, the positive test rate in California estimated to be over 12%. [12] A growing number of job applicants are being drug-tested, and a surprising number of applicants are "flunking" these preemployment tests. Estimates are that the national "failure rate" may be as high as it is in California, 12%. [13] In many states the failure rate is several times higher than the national average. [14] In 1989, about 18% of the job applicants tested for illicit drug use tested positive. [15] About 40% of all employers in California conduct some form of drug testing, which is less than the national average of 53%. [16] It appears that drug testing is becoming an acceptable part of worklife. If you are under forty-five and are not self-employed, it is highly likely that you will be asked to take a drug test at some time during your work years. If you are over forty-five, you may also encounter a request that you be drug-tested during your work years. This may not surprise you when it happens. Drug testing may be just one of the many tests you will be asked, and maybe even compelled, to take. Entering the workforce, which almost everyone does, may be entering an exposure zone. What goes on inside your mind, body, and family may become information—data to be reviewed, tracked, analyzed, filed. What will the file with your name on it say?

TESTING BASICS

At this critical juncture in the evolution of worklife, we must examine drug testing for its broader implications. We must also know exactly what it is that drug testing can and cannot do. As employees and citizens, we must protect ourselves by keeping informed about the processes which measure our behavior. Let us briefly consider some basics of drug testing here.

Bodily Processes Which Affect Test Results

When a drug is taken, several processes in the body receiving it are activated. The drug is metabolized: It takes effect via the process of metabolism. When a drug enters the body, it usually attacks the nervous system. It also makes its way into the blood stream. The psychoactive effects of a drug come via the passage of the drug or its so-called metabolite through the circulatory system into the brain and nervous system. The drug then causes changes in behavior and perception.

While the drug is exerting its nothing-short-of-amazing effect upon the brain and nervous system, a second process, that of excretion, is also taking place. The blood passes through the liver, again and again. It is there that the drug is converted by enzymes into metabolites. These metabolites are electrically charged in such a way that they are more readily excreted through the urinary tract. By converting more and more of the drug to metabolites, the body is working to render the drug nontoxic, or as nontoxic as possible. Drug testing must take into account several aspects of the metabolization and excretion of a drug by the body.

Drug testing seeks to identify the presence (or absence) of a drug in the body being tested, and to determine which drug or drugs are present (or absent). However simple this may sound, there are many ambiguities in the testing process. For example:

1. Some drugs may have a metabolite in common. This means that a single test method may detect the presence of some drug but not reveal which drug is actually present. More than one analytic method must be applied in such cases. The "specificity" of a test method refers to its ability to specify accurately or identify the presence of a particular drug. [17]

2. The identification of the presence of a drug or its metabolite by means of testing says little, if anything, about the frequency with which that drug is used by the person being tested. A test does not provide any information about whether or not the user was using the drug for the first time, experimentally, or uses the drug regularly and/or addictively.

3. The amount of a drug used is not necessarily indicated by a test. The "sensitivity" of a test method refers to its ability to detect the presence of a drug. A test is "highly sensitive" if its "detection level" is high-powered enough to detect reliably the presence of a very small amount of a drug. [18] Even highly sensitive drug tests are rarely able to answer accurately questions regarding dosage or method of use.

4. Metabolism and excretion rates vary widely among individuals and among the drugs used by individuals. Detection periods—the amount of time after a drug has been used during which it can be detected by a test—are, therefore, only estimates. I have listed estimated detection periods in Appendix B of this chapter.

Testing Body Products

The human body produces various materials which can be tested for the presence of drugs. Another way to say this is that many materials produced by the body reveal the presence of drugs. Breath, blood, urine, skin, hair, and saliva have been tested for drugs. Because all drugs are distributed throughout the body by the blood, a blood sample provides the best yardstick of the potential effect of a drug on an employee's behavior and performance. However, blood testing is inconvenient, expensive, and not refined enough to clearly indicate the relationship between the amount of a drug present in the blood plasma and the degree of impairment. This means that job-performance-related actions taken as a result of a blood test are subject to legal scrutiny.

People are somewhat more willing to provide a urine sample than a blood sample. This willingness may reflect the sense that "I am going to be eliminating my urine anyway, but my blood—I need that." Or it may indicate that the use of the needle to take the blood test feels more intrusive than the demand for a sample of one's urine.

Urine is easily available and easily collected, and it is transported and analyzed cheaply. Urine-drug-testing technology is more advanced than blood-drug-testing technology, although laboratories must be highly competent in order to perform accurate tests. Some employees have actually demanded that, if they must take urine tests, they be allowed tests of their own performed at the company of their choice but paid for by their employer. This procedure will allow them to double-check the findings of the employer's testing service. Some unions have negotiated in favor of this option and have managed to attain it for their members. [19] This employee double-check of testing poses a critical set of issues. If the findings of the employer's test and of the employee's test conflict, ·the employer may face a legal battle. The employer who chooses to deny employees their own test threatens the credibility of the testing program and appears to be abusing her or his power.

General Testing Errors

Confirmation testing is testing which is done to confirm a positive finding in the first test. Although it consists of a second independent analysis, one which is usually more specific than the initial screening test, it is just as subject to error as the first test. Random error can occur when samples are mislabeled, instruments are not measuring accurately, or practical circumstances affect the testing process. Systematic error is an error which affects all of a certain type of sample. [20] For example, a false positive may occur when an employee has been in the presence of marijuana smoking but has not been smoking it himself or herself. (He or she has been *passively inhaling* the drug.) Or a metabolite of one drug may act so similarly to that of another drug that the two are confused. Therefore, even confirmation tests produce false positives.

Test accuracy rates range from 30% to 95%, depending on the drug or mix of drugs in the system, the test performed, and the laboratory doing the analysis. [21] Tests vary greatly in sensitivity and specificity. The more specific the test, the fewer the false positives for the presence of a particular drug. However, specificity usually comes at the expense of overall sensitivity. The more sensitive a test, the better it is at actually detecting the presence of any compound. A test may be highly sensitive, detecting even minute amounts of foreign material in the blood or body fluid, and at the same time unspecific, unable to determine precisely what individual compound rather than class of compounds is being detected.

Specific Methods of Urine Testing

It is incredible to witness the explosion of new methods of testing one's urine in order to determine what one has been up to. Entire laboratories are now devoted to the searching of urine for drugs. As we march into the futuristic testocracy that has invaded the present, we may sense that we are living out a fictional counterutopia, one in which there are infinite ways to monitor people. But we are not. These developments are as real as they can be. We and our bodily materials can become laboratory specimens at any time. We must arm ourselves with knowledge of the tests to which we or our urine may be subjected.

Thin-Layer Chromatography. TLC is not a form of tender loving care. It is a form of test called *chromatography* which is conducted on a thin plate (usually of glass) coated with silica gel. A urine sample is processed into a pure, concentrated form. Then, the concentrate is spread across a treated plate. The plate is placed upright in a tank containing a special organic mixture. Upon contact with the urine sample on the plate, this mixture will migrate upward in the tank, distributing and separating any drugs or drug metabolites present in the urine in their own respective spots. The plates are then sprayed with a series of chemicals that react differently to different drugs and drug metabolites. The drugs which are present in the urine sample can be determined by the color and position of the spots. This process, chromatography, is used in many tests.

High-Performance TLC. The HPTLC tests for drugs that appear in low concentrations in urine are an application of the same process used in TLC. The difference between the tests is that in HPTLC, the coating on the thin-layer plate contains smaller particles of silica. This method detects the metabolite of marijuana, which appears in urine at low concentrations.

Gas Chromatography. The GC process involves injecting a urine extract into a column in a chromatograph instrument which contains gas. This stream of gas is heated as it flows through the column. As the drugs in the urine are swept through the column, the high temperature of the gas volatilizes the drugs. The rate of movement or migration of each drug along the column depends on the molecular weight of the drug molecule. This length of time is measured and is used to indicate the specific drug or drugs which are in the urine.

Gas-Chromatography–Mass-Spectrometry. The GC-MS combination is usually used in confirmation testing when a specimen has screened positive for a drug. [22] Mass spectrometry performs two functions: It detects the presence of an unknown drug by its molecular weight, and then it shatters the drug into pieces to form what is called a *fragmentation spectrum.* Gas chromatography is included in this method in order to retain the length-of-time measurement described in the previous paragraph. Together, the results of gas chromatography and mass spectrometry provide reliable drug detection at a higher cost.

Enzyme Immunoassay. The enzyme-multiplied immunoassay technique (EMIT) is actually a mix of tests for commonly abused drugs. The EMIT uses antibodies to detect the presence of drugs in urine. Particular antibodies bind to particular drugs in the urine sample. The binding activity is then measured. The EMIT is used for a screening test or for a confirmation test when a different method was utilized in the initial analysis.

POLYGRAPH TESTING

Test methods have and will continue to rise and fall in popularity, as in the case of polygraph or lie-detector testing. Prior to its drug-related application, polygraphy was used by employers to establish the trustworthiness of job applicants and the truthfulness of employees in cases such as theft. In the mid-1980s, there was a wave of polygraphy to detect drug use among job applicants and employees. This wave was, for the most part, stilled as employers grew increasingly wary of the legality of polygraphy. The American Civil Liberties Union and others who question the constitutionality of such testing argue that the validity of polygraphy has yet to be proved. [23]

We have not seen the end of polygraph testing. Undoubtedly, new theoretical approaches, improved technology, and a shift in political climate may work together to bring a resurgence of demand for the polygraph test. In order to better prepare you for what may be your first encounter with the polygraph, let me share some sample preemployment screening polygraph tests. These were given to me, without the names removed, by a testing-company executive who was hired against my advice by an employer who hired me to do drug awareness training for the employees in his company. I have removed the names and numbered the reports to represent each subject.

Note that Applicant 1 declined to take the test when he heard what the questions would be. Applicant 2 had to reveal that he had had malignant cancer; however, he had no drug history. The remaining six applicants clearly had drug histories. (I have included a copy of the consent form that each applicant signed, before testing, in Appendix C of this chapter.)

APPLICANT 1

Age: 38

PERTINENT PRETEST ADMISSIONS: During the pretest interview, subject asked what questions would be asked during the polygraph examination. The questions were reviewed with the subject, and at that time, subject stated that he did not feel that to continue the interview would be in his best interests. Interview was terminated at that time.

RESULTS: NOT APPLICABLE

APPLICANT 2

Age: 47

PERTINENT PRETEST ADMISSIONS: HEALTH: Subject is in excellent health with last medical examination in 1984. In 1956, subject had surgery for malignant cancer in his left leg; he has since fully recovered. Had a minor shoulder injury while on job and had worker's compensation benefits. NO OTHER JOB APPLICATION PENDING. PERMANENCY INTENTIONS IF HIRED: Full-time permanent. NO MILITARY SERVICE. SCHOLASTIC BACKGROUND: B.S. in business. NO DEBTS. DRINKING: Moderate, 3–4 times weekly, never intoxicated. NO DRUG USE. NO DRUG SALES. NO GAMBLING. NO CONVICTIONS. NO JOB TERMINATIONS. THEFTS FROM EMPLOYERS: Most valuable theft was that of a stapler, valued at $3. All thefts from employers total under $3. This is the only theft from an employer.

RESULTS: NO DECEPTION INDICATED

"No deception indicated" (above) means that the polygraph did not find evidence that the applicant was lying. Applicants 3 and

4 also had no deception indicated, but after they had revealed a great deal about their drug use, convictions, and past.

APPLICANT 3

Age: 55

PERTINENT PRETEST ADMISSIONS: HEALTH: Excellent health with last checkup November of this year. No surgery, job injuries, or workers' compensation claims. Subject is currently applying for a workers' compensation claim. No other job applications pending; plans for permanent full-time employment if hired. SCHOLASTIC BACKGROUND: College graduate, special training in math and sales. TOTAL DEBTS: Total $2,000, broken down into several charge accounts. All payments current. DRINKING: Moderate daily usage; last intoxication was 2 weeks ago. Previously was alcoholic; joined AA in 1989. DRUG USE: Marijuana—currently uses 1 time per week; previously used (2 years ago) frequently on the job; last used 3 weeks ago. Cocaine—used once 3 years ago. DRUG SALES: Sold 1 lb. marijuana in 1985. NO GAMBLING. CONVICTIONS: Assault in 1985; 2 years' probation. JOB FIRINGS: One for "lack of production"; another for "commission conflict"; other terminations unclear. MOST VALUABLE THEFT FROM AN EMPLOYER: $100; last time stealing was two years ago.

PRETEST REMARKS: Alcohol, drugs, sale of drugs, conviction, firings, thefts, and falsified employment history on application.

RESULTS: NO DECEPTION INDICATED

APPLICANT 4

Age: 30

PERTINENT PRETEST ADMISSIONS: HEALTH: Subject is in good physical condition; last checkup was in 1983. No surgery. No on-the-job injuries. No claims pending. No other job applications pending at this time. Wants a permanent position with upward mobility into management in 1–2 years. SCHOLASTIC BACKGROUND: 2 years of college. TOTAL DEBTS: $1,300 for a car. Not behind in any payments. ALCOHOL: Subject has been a bartender for a long time and has drunk at work, consequently developing an alcohol problem. Subject realized in 1985 that he had a problem and joined AA but was not treated as an in- or outpatient in any medical facility. In 1989, subject drank on 3 occasions; once on a camping trip, brother's bachelor party, and the third was at his brother's wedding last weekend. Subject stated that when he does drink it scares him because he could very easily fall back into alcoholism. DRUGS: Cocaine 1 time per month, last time was 1 month ago; has used on the job 7 times, last time 1 month ago. Marijuana 2–3 times a week, last time yesterday; used very rarely on the job, last time 3–4 months ago. Mushrooms 4–5 times, last time 2 months ago. Purchased 1 gram of cocaine 1 month ago; sold small amounts to friends 1 month ago. NO GAMBLING. CONVICTIONS: 2 DUI's in 1 week, was fined about $2,000 and given 1 year probation, went through alcohol rehab program. FIRINGS: One for failure to show up for work. THEFTS: At another company, subject stole up to $20 at a time for a total of about $150. Stole a pair of hub caps from another employer.

RESULTS: NO DECEPTION INDICATED

Applicants 5, 6, 7, and 8 below had deception indicated. This implies that, if the polygraph is accurate, these applicants' involvement with drugs was even greater than they had stated.

APPLICANT 5

Age: 24

PERTINENT PRETEST ADMISSIONS: HEALTH: Subject is in fair health, having no recent medical exam. No on-the-job injuries, workers' compensation claims, or surgery. One other application pending. Full-time permanent position intended. SCHOLASTIC BACKGROUND: 3 years' college. Special training in biology. TOTAL DEBTS:

$700 in Visa. All payments current. DRINKING: Moderate, twice weekly; last intoxication was at Christmas. Does drink on the job. DRUG USE: Marijuana—used 20 times during past six months. Uses on the job. Cocaine—used twice in past year. Used on the job 2 months ago. In summary, subject stated that he had tried all known drugs, except heroin, at sometime in his life, particularly during his employment as member of a rock band. DRUG SALES: LSD, cocaine, marijuana, and speed. Last time was 1½ months ago. GAMBLING: Seldom; usually plays poker; most lost on one occasion was $300. NO CONVICTIONS. JOB FIRINGS: One, in September, for failing to show up for work. THEFTS FROM EMPLOYERS: Most valuable theft was a pair of shoes valued at $150 from a different company 5 years ago. Total of all thefts from employers is $200. Last time stole was in September of this year. Most cash taken was $20–$30.

PRETEST REMARKS: Drinking and drugs on the job, drug sales, job firings, and thefts.

RESULTS: DECEPTION INDICATED RE: Use and sale of drugs.

APPLICANT 6

Age: 42

PERTINENT PRETEST ADMISSIONS: HEALTH: Good health with check-up last year. Underwent stomach surgery in 1980. No job injuries or workers' compensation claims. One other job application pending. Plans for long-term employment if hired. No military service. SCHOLASTIC BACKGROUND: One year college, no special training. TOTAL DEBTS: Total $700 to a furniture store; all payments current. DRINKING: moderate, 2 times per day, last intoxication last night. DRUG USE: Marijuana—1–3 times per week, last used 2 weeks ago. Cocaine—3–4 times per year, last used 2 months ago. Heroin—2–3 times, last used 15 years ago. LSD—once, last used 10 years ago. Red devils—used 2–3 times, last used 15 years ago. NO DRUG SALES. NO GAMBLING. CONVICTIONS: Assault/battery, felony, 1980, 1 year in jail and 2 years probation; 1975, shoplifting from department store, 30 days in jail. JOB FIRINGS: One, when did not get along with sales crew; one from when sales crew was afraid of him and this was a problem; one for fighting over auto sales; one for arguing with salesman. All in the past two years. MOST VALUABLE THEFT FROM AN EMPLOYER: General office supplies. NO CASH STOLEN.

RESULTS: DECEPTION INDICATED RE: Job application/being fired from jobs/use of drugs/undetected theft. Subject was confronted with the results, but no further admissions were obtained.

APPLICANT 7

Age: 22

PERTINENT PRETEST ADMISSIONS: HEALTH: Subject is in good condition, injured his knee playing basketball and jumping from a ramp last week, has a workers' compensation claim pending; also had a claim pending on an injured finger with previous employer. Last checkup was 2 weeks ago. Surgery on injured finger. No other job applications pending at this time. Permanent job intentions. SCHOLASTIC BACKGROUND: High school graduate TOTAL DEBTS: $120,000: $33,000 for a Porsche, $12,000 to a bank, $75,000 for a home. Not behind in any payments; $3,000 in credit cards. NO DRINKING. DRUGS: Cocaine—2 times a month, last time 2 weeks ago, uses socially. Marijuana—1 time per month, last time 2 weeks ago, uses socially. DRUG SALES: At one company, sold 1 gram of cocaine to other salesmen; at another, 1 gram of cocaine; last time selling drugs was 3 months ago. Has quit selling since then. CONVICTIONS: 1987, nonpayment of tickets, paid fine. A DUI 6 years ago, 3 weekends in jail. FIRINGS: One in 1989 for concealing knowledge of another employee who had wrecked a car. THEFTS: Gasoline from both employers. TOTAL FROM ALL EMPLOYERS: Under $200. Last time was 5 months ago.

RESULTS: DECEPTION INDICATED RE: Use and sale of drugs, other than what was admitted to, and also the theft of money and merchandise other than what was admitted to.

APPLICANT 8

Age: 26

PERTINENT PRETEST ADMISSIONS: HEALTH: Subject is in good health with last medical examination unknown. Had a hernia at age 2 but it is no longer a problem. Has had no on-the-job injuries or workers' compensation claims. No other job applications pending. Intentions if hired: full-time permanent. MILITARY SERVICE: U.S. Navy discharge status and rank: E-2, general discharge. SCHOLASTIC BACKGROUND: 12 years, special training as a generalist. DEBTS: $5,000 (car loan and credit cards). Subject is month behind on all payments due, because of being out of work. DRINKING: Light, twice monthly, last intoxication was last Saturday night. DRUG USE: Marijuana—uses 1–2 times weekly, last used last night. Used one time on the job. Cocaine—uses once monthly, last used on Monday night. Used once on the job. Prior to 1987, subject admits that he used almost all drugs except for heroin. DRUG SALES: Sold 1 gram of cocaine last Monday night. NO GAMBLING. CONVICTIONS: 5 years ago, subject was convicted of a hit-and-run. Also, a court-martial for AWOL. JOB TERMINATIONS: One for being late to work. THEFTS FROM EMPLOYERS: Most valuable theft was that of an end mill, valued at $30. All thefts from employers total under $100. Last time stolen was 1 year ago.

RESULTS: DECEPTION INDICATED RE: Use of drugs.

POSTTEST REMARKS: Subject was confronted with deception indicated and further admitted that he uses marijuana daily and uses cocaine more heavily than was indicated in pretest remarks.

The employer who contracted with the polygraph test company to have these tests done was seeking applicants for sales and repair shop positions. He had been experiencing a high turnover rate, with theft, damage, morale, and absenteeism problems in his workplaces. He suspected that drugs were the explanation. There were 175 tests performed on applicants in a two-month period, but there were more than 200 applicants. About one-eighth of the applicants (including Applicant 1) declined to take the test, which was a voluntary one. The employer did not plan to take seriously the applications of those who declined polygraph tests; however, when he saw the results of these tests, he was uncertain as to how to proceed. On their polygraph tests, 95% of all his applicants were current users of marijuana and cocaine. This test result troubled him greatly. He had to hire 100 people to work at five different plants. The 25 who declined to take the tests may have had similar drug use patterns, but he had no way of being certain. In the end, he hired over 75 people who had admitted to relatively recent and/or regular use of cocaine and marijuana, many on the job.

"This is the industry today," he said. "We employers just keep passing these people back and forth. There's no way of getting around it."

Polygraph testing reveals just how far screening can go: One's personal life, one's behavior, one's *mind* can be screened. *Testing is intrusive*. It also reveals the moral dilemma in testing. On the one hand, would you like to be asked these questions in order to get a job? Is your right to privacy more important to you? *On the other hand, testing offers increased information about the possibility of drug-related workplace problems.* Would you like your surgeon or pilot to tell you when, how often, and how much he or she used of which, if any, drug? I would.

The problem with the use of polygraph or any other form of testing is it may not solve the problem it is intended to solve.

CRITICAL ISSUES

Is drug testing a rational effort to control a tractable social problem, or is it an invasive, inaccurate, expensive, and theoretically unsound reaction to a seemingly intractable social problem? *Does drug testing actually stop employee drug abuse and, if it does, at what expense to civil rights and freedom?* The availability of the highly intrusive technology to screen individuals for drugs is not an imperative to use it. We must monitor the advance of testing to be certain it is applied appropriately and fairly.

Is Testing Accurate?

The cost of urine screening ranges from a few dollars to $20. Whenever a test is positive, a second test to validate the findings should be conducted; the second, more expensive and precise analysis costs between $25 and $100 (these are 1989 price tags). [24] Employers, as purchasers of testing services, feel pressure to make their testing programs fit their budget. A significant number of employers choose analytical laboratories on the basis of cost. The quality of the findings of drug tests will continue to be a problem under these conditions. In the late 1980s, the U.S. Centers for Disease Control found that fewer than one-quarter of the laboratories they studied were performing acceptably in their tests for the presence of the five most commonly used drugs. [25] Without a guarantee of accuracy, employers are legally exposed to the risks of acting on false positives and of wrongfully discharging or wrongfully compelling employees into treatment.

Is Testing Effective in Achieving Its Intended Purposes?

No matter how accurate drug tests are or become, we must inquire as to whether they actually achieve what they are expected to achieve. The answer entails clarifying the goals of testing. Some view drug tests as measurement instruments rather than actual interventions in a company drug problem. Others view the possibility or "threat" of a drug test as a deterrent to drug use rather than merely a measurement of drug use. In order to clarify our societal motives for drug testing, we must ask if deterrence is a by-product or an actual strategy of drug tests.

We must also refine our knowledge of the efficiency of testing by asking if drug tests:

- Accurately determine whether or not an individual has used a drug.
- Accurately determine the prevalence of the problem among employees.
- Accurately document the abuse of particular drugs.
- Actually deter employee misuse of drugs.
- Actually deter legal (including alcohol) as well as illegal drug use.

Because we cannot answer any of the above questions with an unqualified yes, we must admit to at least some uncertainty about whether drug testing will solve or help to solve the problem of employee drug abuse.

When Should Testing Be Used?

Drug testing can be mandatory or voluntary. It can be required regularly, according to schedule, of all or some employees. It can be administered randomly, with or without a schedule, to randomly selected employees from a group of all or some employees.

Most employers find that they must choose between testing which is random, periodic, or for cause. This choice places the emphasis where it probably should be—on the purpose of the testing rather than on the design of the testing program. With few exceptions, the courts have found that a public employee can be required to submit to testing only if there is a "reasonable suspicion" of drug use or a "showing of cause." Impaired performance which seems to be related to drug use and actual observations of drug use have been found to provide reasonable suspicion. However, a mere suspicion that an employee uses drugs does not. [26] The courts have been reluctant to back truly random unscheduled testing of all public employees and have also resisted backing random unscheduled tests of private employees except where public safety is at stake. [27]

Can Testing Be Misused?

Some misuse of testing occurs as a result of human and technical error, including the mislabeling of samples, the misreading of test instruments, and the misrecording of data. Other misuse is due to unresolved ethical questions regarding the appropriateness of reporting test results to various members of the company or clients outside the company, and the extent to which an employer can ask an employee to provide body fluids to be tested. Still other misuse may be intentional. Intentional misuse of test results is, we hope, rare. It can occur when the wrong results are reported or the right results are reported in such a way that they cause unfair termination of an employee that the company would like to get rid of, whether or not she or he has a drug problem. Another misuse of test results occurs when they are put into the employee's permanent file and follow her or him from job to job and, worse, job application to job application.

Is Drug Testing Fair?

When CEOs, top managers, and political leaders can require testing of all but themselves, we have a systematic protection of the privacy of those "in power." Some employers have made an effort to make testing fairly distributed. In 1990, the Los Angeles Police Department was the first to require mandatory testing of *all* of its captains and commanders, its police chief, and its deputy chief. Under this testing program, anyone who tests positive is fired. Says the police chief of those who test positive, "They have no place in our department." [28] This 1990 testing policy was instituted as an add-on to the cadet testing program started in 1988, which covers some 8,000 supervisors and officers and which has fired about 10 police officers a year for drug abuse. [29]

While universal testing may sound more fair, we must ask ourselves if the intrusiveness of testing is diminished by subjecting all rather than only some employees to it.

Is Drug Testing Constitutional?

Although indications are that popular sentiment is pro-testing, the matter is by no way resolved in the courts and legislatures. Since President Reagan called for the federal government to become a drug-free workplace in his 1986 Executive Order 12564, testing of federal employees has been authorized when there is reasonable suspicion of employee drug use, unsafe practice, or counseling follow-up after treatment for illegal drug use. [30] But the constitutionality of both public and private employer testing has been vigorously questioned in the courts since that order.

In May 1990, the California Supreme Court dealt what was considered by some to be "a severe blow to companies with drug testing programs." [31] The court determined that when Southern Pacific Railroad fired an employee for refusing to take a random urinalysis drug test, it was acting illegally. This was the leading case in California's judicial testing of employers' rights to require employees to submit to drug tests. The court awarded the employee who had been fired, Barbara Luck, $485,042 in damages, ruling that her company's random drug-testing program impinged on her right to privacy under the state constitution. The court concluded that as a computer programmer, Luck was not in a "safety-sensitive" position, and that employers cannot test employees in nonsafety jobs on a random basis. An attorney for Southern Pacific Railroad predicted that other companies would end their random testing programs and test only under three conditions: (1) when there is probable cause; (2) when there is employee consent; and (3) when a truly safety-sensitive position is involved, which would give the employer a "compelling interest" in and justification for random testing. [32]

Shortly after employee Luck refused to take her drug test in 1985, the city of San Francisco passed a law restricting drug testing to cases in which the employee is using drugs or there is a clear and present danger of injury to others. At that time Southern Pacific terminated its random testing program. But for several years after that, the company was involved in appealing the findings against it and in favor of employee Luck. Its primary grounds for appeal were that (1) all railroad employees work in safety-sensitive positions and (2) the constitutional right to privacy does not govern the relationship between private employers and their employees. [33] Although the court ruled against Southern Pacific, these contentions of Southern Pacific warrant further discussion. Let's begin with the first argument. How can we be certain as to whether or not a job is safety-sensitive? The definition of safety is subjective. Who has the right to determine where public safety ends and begins? The second argument plunges even deeper into a moral quagmire. Is the relationship between the private employer and the employee a territory of its own? Can working people depend upon having their constitutional rights extend to their workplaces? When an employer pays an employee for work, what exactly is the employer buying: time, energy, service, or product, or a piece of the employee's life—flesh, blood, body, and soul?

We, and our courts, have not answered these questions. The U.S. Justice Department wrote, in support of a Boston Police Department plan to test its employees:

> Simply stated, in the context of the workplace, employees have no recognized absolute expectation of privacy that precludes an

employer from conducting reasonable inquiries into an employee's fitness for duty. [34]

Where Will Testing Lead Us?

I have repeatedly suggested that, if we are not watching its evolution carefully, worklife may evolve in an increasingly undesirable direction. Workers, no matter how well they are treated (some will be treated well while others will not be), may be increasingly viewed as cogs in a large machine, instruments or robots designed to march toward the mirage of progress. As we march, drug testing may appear to be a necessary form of protection and it may be exactly that. Job performance testing may replace drug testing if the courts find drug testing to be too invasive, or if employers become more wary of lawsuits. Performance testing, including random typing, coordination, and ability tests, may become the preferred means of ensuring quality on-the-job performance. However, commitment to the ongoing scrutiny of all forms of testing for any infringement upon human rights is essential. Testing may protect you as a consumer and as an employer, but what are the risks to you as a worker? What tradeoffs are you willing to make?

APPENDIX A: CALCULATING BLOOD ALCOHOL LEVELS

There is no safe way to drive after drinking. Even one drink can make you an unsafe driver. Drinking affects your Blood Alcohol Concentration (BAC).

Starting in 1990, in California, it has been illegal to drive with a BAC of .08% or more. Even a BAC below .08% does not mean that it is safe or legal to drive. The chart below shows a person's BAC level by weight, calculated by the number of drinks he or she has had. To calculate your BAC, use the chart below and subtract one drink from your drink total for every hour you drink.

For example, a 180-pound person consuming six drinks over three hours would have a BAC of .06%, which is still under the legal limit. (This is calculated by subtracting one drink from his drink total of six drinks for every hour he was drinking; therefore, his BAC is a three-drink BAC.) One drink is defined as 12 ounces of beer, 5 ounces of wine, or 1¼ ounces of 80-proof alcohol.

Weight (in lbs.)	Number of drinks								
	1	2	3	4	5	6	7	8	9
100	.04	.08	.11	.15	.19	.23	.26	.30	.34
120	.03	.06	.09	.13	.16	.19	.22	.25	.28
140	.03	.05	.08	.11	.13	.16	.19	.21	.24
160	.02	.05	.07	.09	.12	.14	.16	.19	.21
180	.02	.04	.06	.08	.10	.13	.15	.17	.19
200	.02	.04	.06	.07	.09	.11	.13	.15	.17
220	.02	.03	.05	.07	.09	.10	.12	.14	.15
240	.02	.03	.05	.06	.08	.09	.11	.13	.14

Source: California Department of Motor Vehicles. Cited in State of California Department of Alcohol and Drug Programs, *ADP Research Activity Memorandum*, Vol. 8, No. 5, December 1989, p. 5.

APPENDIX B: DRUG PRESENCE IN THE BODY: DETECTION PERIODS

Drug	Detection period
Amphetamines	
Amphetamine	2–4 days
Methamphetamine	2–4 days
Barbiturates	
Amobarbital	2–4 days
Butalbital	2–4 days
Pentobarbital	2–4 days
Phenobarbital	2–4 days
Secobarbital	Up to 30 days

(continued)

APPENDIX B (*Continued*)

Drug	Detection period
Benzodiazepines	
Valium (diazepam)	Up to 30 days
Librium (chlordiazepoxide)	Up to 30 days
Cocaine	
Benzoylecgonine	12–72 hours
Cannabinoids (marijuana)	
Casual use	2–7 days
Chronic use	Up to 30 days
Ethanol (alcohol)	12–24 hours
Opiates	
Codeine	2–4 days
Hydromorphone (Dilaudid)	2–4 days
Morphine (for heroin)	2–4 days
Methaqualone (Quaalude)	2–4 days
Phencyclidine (PCP)	
Casual use	2–7 days
Chronic use	Up to 30 days

Source: Cited in State of California Department of Alcohol and Drug Programs, *ADP Research Activity Memorandum,* Vol. 8, No. 5, December 1989, p. 5.

APPENDIX C: CONSENT FORM

Applicant Please Read Carefully

This is to inform you that as part of our procedure for processing your employment application and to confirm its contents, an investigative report may be made whereby information is obtained through personal interviews with third parties, such as family members, business associates, financial sources, friends, neighbors, or others with whom you are acquainted. This inquiry includes information as to your character, general reputation, personal characteristics, and mode of living, whichever may be applicable. You have the right to make a written request within a reasonable period of time for a complete and accurate disclosure of additional information concerning the nature and scope of the investigation.

The facts set forth above in my application for employment are true and complete. I understand that if I am employed, false statements on this application shall be considered sufficient cause for dismissal.

Date:_____ Signature of applicant:_____

As indicated above, we must confirm the information set forth in this employment application. Investigation of references, correspondence with your past employers, and interviews with your other associates may take days to accomplish. However, the information could be confirmed through the use of a polygraph examination, with the results usually obtainable within a matter of hours after the test. A polygraph examination is generally limited to confirmation of information contained in the employment application and is not concerned with irrelevant matters in your personal life. As set forth below, under the law we cannot require that you take a polygraph test, and we will give you your choice of the method by which we will confirm the information. In order to speed the employment process, we do request that you voluntarily consent to the examination.

California Labor Code, Section 432.2
Polygraph or Lie Detector Test as a Condition of Employment

No employer shall demand or require any applicant for employment or prospective employment or any employee to submit to or take a polygraph, lie detector or similar test or examination as a condition of employment or continued employment. The prohibition of this section does not apply to the federal government or any agency thereof or the state government or any agency or local subdivision thereof, including, but not limited to counties, cities and counties, cities, districts, authorities and agencies.

I will consent to a polygraph examination to verify the information contained herein.

Date:_____ Signature of applicant:_____

Tuning In on a Managers' Meeting
Growing Pains at Company L

An employer comes to an awareness of a company drug problem. This awareness grows in his or her mind. Finally he or she takes action: Communication is deemed important. Meetings are held. Policies are developed.

However straightforward the process may sound, the issues attending the development of a company drug policy are complex and, frequently, confusing. Right and wrong become territories with vague boundaries. The development of company drug policies brings to the forefront otherwise obscure dilemmas regarding levels of drug use, the legality of the drugs used, the rights of those who use them, and the biases of those who form the policies governing their use.

The following is an excerpt from the transcript of a company managers' meeting. Participants have been invited by the company's owner and chief executive officer to discuss the issues relevant to the development of the company's first drug and alcohol policy. Adding to this interesting team of managers is an unusual mix of invited panelists, including one representative from law enforcement, one from a drug- and polygraph-testing company, and one from the treatment community. Each of these invited panelists has worked with this company—

"Company L"—prior to this meeting. In Chapter 8 I analyze several critical issues presented in this chapter. I suggest that readers first read and react to this chapter, drawing conclusions independently of my discussion in Chapter 8. As a guide to readers I have made notes regarding key issues throughout the text. These are in italics and enclosed in rules.

CHIEF EXECUTIVE OFFICER (CEO): The purpose of this meeting is to set our own standards, to develop our own policy regarding drug usage in the workplace. We're struggling with this process. We're not really sure how we can put something down in writing. But I think that it's terribly necessary. A decade or so ago, the motion picture industry was depicting marijuana use and cocaine use as something that was fun, as a recreational activity. So a lot of the younger people were led down the wrong path; they were led to believe that it's okay to use drugs. And now we're seeing the results—we're seeing just how damaging misleading information can be. These once younger people have aged a bit and work for us now.

I'm not sure that every one of us has the same perspective on drugs. I think that one's age makes a difference. My age, for example, will give me a different outlook than perhaps—I'll pick you out—Walt, you're older than I am? (Laughter.) Because we come from different age groups, I expect that we're going to have different perspectives on drugs. I'm sure some of us (like me) feel that there should be zero drug use, and others may even feel that some drug use is okay. Is there a level of drug use which is acceptable? That's one of the problems. We don't all agree on this stuff.

And then, we will probably have difficulty confining the subject matter to drug usage within the workplace. Is that what we really should be addressing? Is there not also drug use in people's nonworkday lives? Doesn't this off-the-job use affect on-the-job performance? Can we, the corporation, interfere with employees' free time? Is it our right, as the employer, to dictate to people we're going to hire what they can do? And what about people we've already hired? Can we tell them what to do when they aren't at work?

Can we control employee drug use off the job?

The reason that each of you is here today is because you are responsible for hiring and managing people within your own departments. Just about everyone in this room has the authority to hire and fire in this company.

Another purpose of this meeting is to let our employees, customers, and competitors know that we not only are concerned about alcohol and drug abuse but are doing something about it. Our ultimate objective, at least from my perspective, is to have a truly drug-free workplace.

Is a drug-free workplace the ultimate objective?

The third reason for this meeting is that drug use certainly has a great financial cost to us. We know that drug use results in increased health care costs. We know that it results in absenteeism, lowered productivity, and increased comeback work in the shop.[1] Workers' compensation claims have also increased dramatically. And of course there's the problem of theft to support employees' drug usage. Well, I'm not going to go on and on with this list. Most of you are probably hoping I'll get off the stage right now.

Let's have each member of the panel say a little about his or her views regarding drug use in and around the workplace. I assume that each of our guests will see this problem from a different perspective.

Our representative from law enforcement might say, "Lis-

---

[1] "Comeback work," as its name implies, is work that is returned because it was not done well or completely the first time.

ten, we gotta stop this stuff. It's deadly, and we're out to arrest everybody we can and punish them for it." Our representative from the testing and preemployment screening company might want to field the issue from a different perspective.

TESTING REPRESENTATIVE: Right on. I'm really very concerned about safety in the workplace. That's what testing and screening are really about.

Safety in the workplace is of paramount importance.

CEO: And our representative from the psychotherapy and treatment community might say, "These are human beings, they are individuals, they're real, they're alive. They are much different from anyone else. We've got to do everything we can to bring them back to reality, to leading productive and full lives as well as to being productive employees." I've heard her say something like this before.

MANAGER A: Is there a specific goal for this meeting, like actually developing a drug and alcohol policy?

CEO: Yes. Developing a policy is the ultimate goal, but we may not get to it today. And there is more to this meeting. One of our objectives is to develop a uniform interpretation of the results of the preemployment tests we've been using. This is because our managers are calling the testing company about the results. They're asking things like "Well, what do you think about this guy?" when the person is borderline. And one of the reasons they're asking the testing company is that our central office hasn't told our managers, "Okay, hire this guy. Don't hire this one," and "This guy is out, this guy's in." In one department, an applicant might be out based on her or his test results, and in another she or he might be hired.

TESTING REP: So one of the objectives of this meeting is to help define what the levels of acceptability are in your company.

MANAGER B: What do you mean by "level of acceptability"?

The issue of level of acceptable use arises.

TESTING REP: What amount or level, past and present, of alcohol and drug use are you willing to tolerate among your employees? I say "past" because our preemployment tests ask people applying for jobs at your company what their past and present alcohol and drug use has been and is. It also asks about alcohol- and drug-related convictions. I say "present" because whatever level of use you are willing to hire people at may be the level of use you have to tolerate in your company.

We also need to discuss the issue of hiring amnesty today. This is especially important to your company because you need to expand your workforce, and whether you like it or not, most of your applicants have drug-using histories. Hiring amnesty is a way to hire somebody who has a borderline alcohol- and drug-using record. This is a way to get people into the company who you really think are going to be good employees even though they have an alcohol and or drug problem in their history. You can reserve the right to drug-test them later on, on an agreement basis. They also have to agree not to use alcohol or drugs henceforth.

MANAGER C: Henceforth? Are you talking about using on the job only, or anywhere?

TESTING REP: Well, that's one of the things we need to talk about today.

MANAGER D: That's really going to be a messy issue.

TESTING REP: That's the hard part. Yes, I know it is.

CEO: Because we can't really go past the bounds of working hours. Our policy manual is written in such a way that we can really only regulate on-the-job behavior.

TESTING REP: That's where preemployment polygraph testing has the advantage over urinalysis testing.[2] The urinalysis test can't tell where a person uses drugs. Polygraph can. With polygraph we can direct our questions specifically at on-the-job usage, or we can find out about general usage both on and off the job.

CEO: The problem is, if we confine ourselves to on-the-job use, we can't get at the problem of weekend use.

TESTING REP: But if people are using drugs three or four times a week, what are they going to be like when they get to work? How will they perform?

As managers, you hire and manage a group of people. And one of the things we want to be able to do is have you be aware of the drug problem, of the seriousness of the problem, and to have you be able to recognize people who work under you who have problems. This way you can do a good job of managing in this era of drug problems. The other important activity to be looked at is hiring, which is critical. That's one of the reasons our testing company is represented here.

Note the problem of trying to hire drug-free employees.

Sometimes the decision not to hire is easy. People are abso-

[2]At the time of this meeting, polygraph testing was still considered acceptable and useful by many members of the testing, corporate, and legal communities. Although this is no longer the case, issues of employees' preemployment and off-the-job use remain very relevant.

lutely out in left field, they've stolen, they're heavy drug users, they've had traffic problems and problems with the law, and you say, "No, we don't want them." Or you get them at the other end of the spectrum, and they're lily white, so you say "Great." But what about the people in the middle? And this is the hard part for you general managers. You are asking us, "Well, what do you think, should I hire this person?" And we're trying to throw the question back to you, saying, "This is hard for us to decide. Based on what you know about the demands of the job, should you be concerned about a person who admits to smoking dope at parties a couple times a month?" And maybe some of you will say, "No, that's OK." Others of you won't.

But what about the person who snorts cocaine or smokes crack two or three times a month? Maybe some of you would feel comfortable with that and others of you wouldn't. There are so many degrees.

Are some levels of use acceptable for some drugs and not for others?

So what we need to do is explore where, at what point, we've got to set your corporate hiring and firing policy in the alcohol and drug use area and then try to live within the range we set. If we say that we're not going to accept anyone having ever used any drugs, what happens? None of us hire anybody, right? We simply can't do this. Almost everyone has used or still uses at least some alcohol. We all know that most people under thirty years old have experimented with drugs; some are still using. Some use very occasionally. So, to say it again, we've got to determine what level of use is acceptable to the organization. Most of you have dealt with this problem in hiring and firing. You are going to be great resources in the development of a policy.

This company needs a unified view regarding acceptability, and a plan for what to do with borderline cases. You all need to feel more comfortable hiring or not hiring people and firing or not firing people.

Wait a minute. You have a question.

MANAGER E: Yes. I'm sitting here wondering how serious this problem really is in our company. I just can't tell.

Is our drug problem really a serious one?

ENFORCEMENT REPRESENTATIVE: Let me give you an idea of what we're facing in this city. Very close to 20% of our city population is using drugs. When you start thinking about that, and you take a room like this, 20% or ten of you are using drugs. That's a very, very hard figure and it's a good figure. Look around the room. Try and figure out who it is.

Here are some bigger numbers. Thirty-nine percent of all our high school kids coming out of school are using drugs. We have gone into companies in this area, where as many as 40% in the company are actively using drugs. So I feel that there is a very sizable problem.

I also see, however, that there is an honest change taking place in the local business structures that deal with drug abuse. Four years ago, when people from companies came to me, what they really wanted me to do was have enforcement go into the workplace and make everybody that was using drugs disappear. We're quite good at making people that use drugs disappear. Today, that's not what happens. Today, we see a really healthy change. Companies come in to us, asking for some advice because they're concerned about their alcohol- and drug-using employees. Now their questions are more like "How do we help our employee? We see him as a valuable asset." This change is honestly gratifying.

I'll tell you why it's gratifying. We've lost the drug war. There are more and more people entering this drug business; buying drugs; confiscating drugs; arresting people who use, make, transport, or sell drugs; and so on. And there are far more drugs out there today than there were a few years ago. The price of drugs is dropping rapidly. The price of heroin, which is the king of drugs, has gone from, last year, $300 a gram to, today, $80 a gram. A phenomenal decrease. Cocaine has gone from $120 a gram to $85 a gram, and often even less.

If someone comes to me from a company and says, "I think we have a drug problem," I don't put someone from the police force inside the company to do a little number there anymore. What we do now is try to evaluate the problem, because we do not have the staff to deal with people who use drugs; we honestly don't have the personnel. There are too many. The only thing our enforcement division is after is the dealers—most important, the dealers who are using force and violence to maintain their anonymity within companies.

Some employees experience the threat of force and violence by drug dealers seeking to maintain anonymity within their company.

There is always force and violence, or at least the threat of it in the drug business. If someone buys some drugs and then says, "I'll pay you tomorrow," and then doesn't have the money to pay tomorrow, the intimidation and often the threat of or actual violence begin. In many cases this leads right to employee theft: "Well, I can't get it today, but I will get the money." The desperation leads to theft when it would never have occurred otherwise. That's the cycle of things we see in the business.

Desperation can lead to theft in the workplace.

Now what can I say about the devastation we see? People like you in this group here, who have never been around the jail system, cannot know. There is nothing more demoralizing in a person's life than the first time in jail or the prison system.

Everything your mind can conceive of goes on behind the walls of jail. You ought to think about what I'm saying. Everything your mind can conceive of is going on. It's not a pretty business. But the bottom line for you and me is this: There are still far more people not using drugs than there are using drugs. I should say that we haven't lost the drug war entirely. But it is a great problem. The only real chance for change is through groups just like this one today. People are beginning to show honest concern for the employee, and that's what I hope you are doing here today.

CEO: Thank you, Lieutenant. And now, let's hear from our treatment community representative. I think you probably recognize a lot of the faces here.

TREATMENT REPRESENTATIVE: Just about all of them, yes. I have had the pleasure of conducting the employee seminars on drugs and health awareness for this company. Almost every employee has attended. The attendance was made mandatory, and family members' attendance was optional. I learned a tremendous amount about this organization as I usually do when I conduct these seminars, and a lot of wonderful people sat in the audiences and told me that there were no drug or alcohol problems here in this company.

How much do we know about our own company?

A lot of other wonderful people sat in the same audiences and told me things like "Prove to me that crack is dangerous," and "Tell me why my friend should quit," and "Tell me how to talk to my friend who's using." No one spoke in the first person. No one ever said, "Tell me why I should quit." Yet, in many cases, I recognized the spoken language, the body language, the denial, the emotional and physical symptoms around cocaine, crack, marijuana, alcohol, and other types of drug abuse and addiction. One of your employees came to me during a break in one of my seminars and said, "I don't have any friends here because I won't drink with that group, and I won't use drugs with the other group of people I work with. I don't use drugs at work or anywhere else, and so I'm very lonely at work." This is a painful reality. Nonusers are lonely in this company.

Peer pressure to drink and drug is great among employees.

This isn't the only company in which I've seen this kind of thing. Many people enter a workplace or begin a job, never having had a problem with a particular drug, or any drug at all, and then develop that problem while on the job. Sometimes they've used drugs in the past and sometimes they haven't. There is a great deal of social pressure to drink and drug in and around the workplace. This pressure arises not just as a result of television watching and not just because of the neighbors, spouses, drinking buddies, and others who drink and drug, but because of fellow employees who use drugs, abuse drugs, and abuse alcohol.

The majority of employees in trouble with alcohol and drugs are in a state of denial. But individuals are not the only ones in the state of denial. Entire organizations can be, and I find this level of denial over and over in workplaces, where employers, managers, and co-workers say, "There's no drug problem here. I don't have a problem, and so there can't be one next to me, or else I'd know about it," or, "Maybe there is a drug problem here, but it's not my problem." We cannot afford to talk this way. Chemical dependence is a painful problem, one of the most painful problems I've seen and I've been preoccupied with social problems for most of my adult—all of my adult life. I think chemical dependence is really killing us. It is undermining the very soul of our society and the élan of our businesses. So we've got to take this time to communicate with each other. I appreciate the fact that your CEO has made this meeting possible. He has brought the different viewpoints of the panel together, in the same place, to talk to you and to hear what you have to say and want to do about chemical dependence among your employees.

Many companies are in a state of denial about their drug and alcohol problems.

TESTING REP: As far as I can see, the drug scene has changed somewhat since the 1960s, simply because in the 1960s drugs were condoned, many people thought they were OK, many thought drugs were hip. But today this is not so much the case. Drugs aren't really that acceptable in the workplace anymore. Drugs are accepted a lot more socially, at home: "What I do at home is nobody's business; my friends come over," this type of thing. But in the workplace, drugs are not so OK, and people are really frowning on them. Drug use is becoming a moral problem.

Yet, people still see drugs being used these days; however, because of peer pressure, they don't "rat" on their co-workers. So drug use in the workplace is implicitly condoned until the user eventually surfaces and is treated or got rid of in some way.

Drug use in the workplace is implicitly condoned.

But you wonder what damage drugs can do in a workplace? What about a surgeon? I know of prominent surgeons in San Francisco right now who are on cocaine. They're using cocaine, I know they're using cocaine. Any one of you people could be operated on by these people. What would you think of that, if you knew that these people were using cocaine? How about an airline pilot out there, for crying out loud, that's flying this bird from here to LA and you're commuting on it and you know that he just had a few lines of cocaine or he has just smoked some crack—are you going to get on that airplane? And then you say,

"Well, what's this got to do with our company?" Well, you know what it has to do with you. You've got $800,000 worth of machines right out that door there and more elsewhere. You've got a woman who's taking that company car I see just out there so she can go smoke some crack in the park—which you've already had happen here. And you've got the mechanic that's going to test out some of this large packing equipment while he's on pot or pills. You don't know what kind of condition the equipment is in or how it will look when it comes back. Or who he'll hurt. And then something happens to that company car or that equipment—and this has already happened here—and all of a sudden your company is liable for what's happened out there.

There's a problem for you. You do have a problem here. I'm sure that if any one of you people in here knew that you had a person working under you who was going out in one of your company cars and was snorting coke or smoking crack in it, or burning up weed in it, or drinking in it, you wouldn't have that person around very much longer. We lose $100 billion a year throughout the United States in retail because of drugs. Drugs alone. And that's through people being unreliable, not showing up for work, workers' comp, and on-the-job accidents. That's a heck of a figure. You're dealing with this type of loss right here, but maybe not as much as you were a few years back because now you're doing drug education and some preemployment screening.

CEO: I have a few comments here. Once we know that some of those people on our staff, in our employ, do have drug problems, where does our liability end? I don't know. I'm not really clear on this.

Where does the employer's liability begin and end?

Say we've got a guy in the service department who's working on brakes and he's just finished a line of cocaine (which he probably just has). My God, you know his head's not on right, he's not going to put the car back together right. I need to know what our liability is since we knowingly have an employee using drugs and we're letting him work on a car like that? And what about our sales people, the ones representing us to the public? Should they be allowed to represent us if they're not thinking straight? I don't think so. Should people in the office who work with more exact figures than anyone else in the company, millions of dollars worth of exact figures, and who are responsible for the final accounting be allowed to work for us if we know or even if we suspect they use drugs?

Should people who we know or suspect use drugs be allowed to work for us?

And what about if they drink a lot? I don't know really where the beginning or the end of the problem is. I don't know how far downhill we're going to go, or how much we're going to be able to put a dent in the problem. But we're sure as hell going to try, I'll tell you that. Chuck, are you still awake?

Where does the problem begin and end?

MANAGER G: Yes, of course. (Chuckle.) I woke up when you mixed drinking in with drugging. They are different, you know.

Is drinking the same problem as drugging?

CEO: Well, we have to decide how different very soon. I wonder about this myself.

I'd like to get into some questions now. I'm hoping that you will all put on your thinking caps and throw our panel some good questions here.

C'mon, Chuck. Would you stand? You don't have to stand, I'm only kidding.

MANAGER G: Sure. Let's keep this really loose, okay?

MANAGER H: I think the biggest problem the company has is we managers. We don't know how to proceed and some of us don't want to. We don't think it's our job to fight the war on drugs. We weren't hired for that.

It may not be the job of a manager to deal with the drug problem.

If indeed a manager has an employee who is taking drugs, how does that manager prove he or she is actually taking drugs anyway? If the employee has an alcohol problem and goes out to lunch and has five or six beers and comes in half loaded, you can tell because you can smell it. But with drugs you can't.

Managers can detect alcohol use more easily than drug use.

You can sometimes see a behavior pattern change, but you don't know whether that behavior change is because the employee had a fight with his wife or if he's been drugging. And if indeed we think we know, what do we do? What are the legalities involved in trying to find out if indeed he is or has been taking drugs? Can we just outright ask? I feel as if we're behind the eight ball.

Can managers outright ask if an employee is on alcohol or another drug?

TESTING REP: Well, I had hoped for some easier questions to start off with!

MANAGERS: (Laughter and coughing.)

TESTING REP: I can tell you what I see. A lot of the companies are now seriously looking into using preemployment waivers that allow several things upon being hired, one of which is drug testing, and another of which is search of person and personal possessions on company property. And there have been several court cases that have been very supportive of searches. It is, in fact, an arrestable crime to be under the influence of any illegal drug.

One of the dangers of going into a company and teaching people how to do drug searches is that we turn some of the people we train into "supernarcs." Then they're out nabbing everybody—at least trying to get everybody taken into custody—and that's not good.

Managers should not be detectives.

What I see is three things that companies have been very successful with. One is having the knowledge of what to look for, having a few conscientious people trained to look. A second is confrontation: bringing the employee in and putting it right up front and saying, "We think you're under the influence." The third is professional help. Working with people in trouble with drugs and alcohol takes professional help. I can't do it. I'm a tester. It takes a trained treatment professional to be able to deal with those people.

CEO: This is a good time to talk about the symptoms of drug and alcohol problems. The folks on today's panel were good enough to give a listing of symptoms, which I'll pass out so each department has one, one for each of the managers. Let me start by saying that there is something that you can do to help: Watch for these warning signs. I'll read the list aloud. First of all, look for frequent mood changes; overcomplying in order to cover up; secrecy or isolation from other employees; frequent trips to the bathroom; spaciness; redness of eyes; excessive defensiveness or a short temper; loss of initiative; and a radical change in work habits. These are just some of the signs; there may be others.

Remember that alcoholism and drug dependency can affect not only the health and welfare of the employee with the problem but also the safety and well-being of your other employees. So that's kind of a good starting point.

TREATMENT REP: One of the other things that I have noticed is abrupt changes—not just in work habits. Radical changes are on your list, but let's include changes in grooming, speech patterns, posture, facial grimaces, facial coloring, interests, and friends. So, look for unusual changes. Now, I don't know what your turnover rate is; I don't know if you have a chance to know your employees long enough to know when somebody is going through a radical change in more than just work patterns. But that's something I watch for.

One of the drug-related things we see is changes in the user's perception of time. At first these changes are subtle: "Oh, did it really take me ten extra minutes to do that this time?" "Oh, am I really one-half hour late?" Eventually the shift in perception is less subtle. This is not surprising. Think of your own lives. You have a schedule. You get up in the morning, you clean yourself up, you eat three times a day, and you sleep at about a certain time in the evening. People who are using drugs lose organization of time and the perception of time as something that can indeed be organized. Their cycle breaks. They get up at strange and unusual hours, they don't sleep when they should, they stay up late hours, they do not eat as they should, their meals are irregular, and they are consistently late for appointments and for work.

Something else that you may see as a symptom of drug use is that users' perception of themselves changes over time. You, as the manager, are aware when employees' productivity drops, when they become generally irritable, when they show a lack of concern about their job performance. This can be indicative of some kind of problem. It may be drugs. Many employees in trouble with drugs go on believing that they're top-notch, that everything's going fine. It is almost impossible to convince them that they've got a problem, that there's anything wrong.

And if you try to confront an employee who you think is in trouble with drugs, you need to be backed up by a very clear policy for this confrontation. I think you (Manager H) asked, "How do you confront an employee on this issue?" I have some concerns about this procedure. One must be very careful, because many other problems in life besides drugs and alcohol can cause some of the symptoms we've listed. So while we—to use the verb *policing*—are policing our employees, we must remember that these symptoms are just indicators; they are not necessarily indications of the fact that drug or alcohol use is going on.

Employers who confront employees must be backed up by a written company drug policy.

CEO: We certainly don't want any of you out there to think that each time you get up to go to the bathroom or rub your nose, someone is watching! We don't want to cause paranoia.

MANAGER J: Let me ask you a question. Same question, I guess. How do you approach an individual if you suspect that he or she is using a substance? And how do you approach that certain individual if you honestly feel that he or she does have a drug or alcohol problem. Can you call him or her into your office and just have a little chitchat? We have a situation here where you have the unions, which are very touchy about approaching their members individually. We've even had the union's business agent come up to talk to its members who work for us about this problem.

ENFORCEMENT REP: This company, like most companies, needs a drug policy with procedural rules: Who will do the approaching? What are the steps in approaching? Where do you overstep

your legal bounds? When are the rights of the employee in-
fringed upon if she or he is or is not a union member?

Company policies must have procedural rules.

MANAGER D: I also wonder how I will make the other employees
feel when I approach someone. Do they say, "Well, so-and-so's
been called in. Will it be me next? And even if I'm not using,
gosh, my eyes are so red today. I'm a person who has red eyes
often. And my eyes are so red today. Will they call me in next? Is
my job being threatened?" And what does this kind of anxiety
do to productivity? Morale? Turnover rates?

So I agree it should be very clear, especially to the managers, what the steps are, and the employees should know the
steps of approach as well.

CEO: Well, it looks as though we'll be able to get drug testing into
the current rounds of the new union agreements. I don't know
what to do about your nonunion employees though. We're
going to find this out, soon.

The other day I must have sent eight people down for a
preemployment test. You gave them polygraphs. And one individual really 'fessed up and said, "On my bachelor party I really
went up to space, but that was the last time I used and that was
a year ago." So we had this individual, and I don't know what
the legalities are, so I said, "Well, would you be willing to give
me a note in your own handwriting that I, so-and-so, if hired
will submit to a drug test at random?" He says, "I'll be more
than happy to do that." But the following morning he says, "I
don't think I want to do that." I really wanted to hire him and I
didn't. So you see, we are caught between a rock and a hard
spot.

TESTING REP: Well, I can tell you this, that the only positive way
for anyone, even with the best of training, to tell that someone is

under the influence of a drug is by means of a drug test. You need a drug-testing policy of some sort to be effective.

CEO: Only one of our branches is in San Francisco, but just recently, the Board of Supervisors in San Francisco passed an ordinance stating that a company cannot, in any way, shape, or form, have an employee submit to a drug test. So I guess we need a different policy for the departments in the San Francisco branch.

TESTING REP: That's true, they did pass that ordinance. We're not doing as much work in that city currently.

MANAGERS: (Weak laughter.)

TESTING REP: In my view the anti-drug-testing law is really invalid. It's a crime to be under the influence of illegal drugs. Users can go to jail.

MANAGER M: I wish I'd been through the employee drug awareness program and other company meetings last fall, because I've heard a great deal about it in the two-and-a-half months I've been with the company. My perception as a new person is that the attitude of our employees toward what this company is trying to do about drugs and alcohol is very hostile.

Employees may be hostile to company efforts.

I listened very carefully to what you were saying earlier, about confronting an entire company about a drug problem and basically being told by a lot of people, "We don't have a problem." We do have a drug problem here. I can tell.

I think we're talking about two separate issues: how to handle the people we currently work with and how to handle people we're thinking of hiring. And I think it's a lot more complicated to discuss how to handle the people that we have already hired. New people will follow new rules and procedures. It's the others I worry about.

I also wonder about follow-through. We had the drug awareness program last fall, and we all know we have a problem. But what do we do next? There's a great deal of hostility toward even discussing it here. A lot of people are afraid of what the boss will decide to do. And when I try to discuss it one-on-one or at a meeting in my department, I am also told that we have no problem. Then, later, one person will come forward and secretly say, "We have a very serious problem." There's a conspiracy of silence that's just incredible.

MANAGER B: People are scared.

MANAGER M: Even the people who have no problem whatsoever are afraid or just don't want to talk about it.

Even employees who have no drug problem are scared.

TREATMENT REP: Of the groups that I worked with here at the company, there was one that stood out as being the most hostile. I asked them at the end of one of the seminars what the hostility was about. They openly explained that they objected to the seminars' being mandatory. I asked them if they would have been there if the seminars hadn't been mandatory, and most of them said, "No, of course not." And I said, "But did you learn anything while you were here?" and I'd say three-fourths of them said, "Yes, definitely." That was the same group that walked off with a coroner's report on a cocaine-related death which I'd passed around and a few other things, and that was the same group that later had at least one member tell me one of his co-workers was using a lot of cocaine and didn't think he had a problem. A lot of the behavior that I dealt with in that seminar was much like what I find when I'm working in treatment settings, working in treatment with people addicted to drugs. By the way, the coroner's report was that of a healthy young man who died of what could be called a cocaine overdose with less than the known lethal dose in his body.

The seminar groups I worked with weren't all of the same opinion, though. But some of them didn't like the idea of employee drug awareness programs being mandatory for all and done on paid time for some employees but not for others. Your salespeople complained, "I'm losing time when I could be earning money while the union people are being paid for being here."

Should employee drug awareness programs be mandatory?

And your union people said, "This man (the boss) has no right to require my presence here, because I'm union." Yet, the union rep came to a seminar and told me that he thought it was great.

Other employees were grateful for the program and brought their spouses and children. So there was a lot of mixed response. I would do it again. I think that a lot of people learned something from the program. And the most hostile ones are the ones who are still voicing negative opinions, while the others who appreciated the program are not speaking up. I did receive a letter from one of the people in the most hostile group which said, "You have to understand, we've all been drug users, but most of us are taking care of this problem ourselves. And we just want you to know it's nothing personal." It was a very sweet letter. But after meeting them, I wasn't convinced that they were all taking care of the problem themselves.

Are employees handling their addiction problems on their own?

ENFORCEMENT REP: Let's address another issue, the problem of whether or not to lump alcohol and drug problems together.

There's one very real difference: Illegal drug use is against the law. And maybe that's the subterfuge. I personally can't get upset about a guy that takes a drink when he gets home at night, but I have zero tolerance for someone who goes home and uses coke or crack or smokes a joint. I probably speak for at least half the people here.

MANAGERS: (Half of their hands are raised for a moment.)

CEO: At least all of these people! (He points at the hands.)

Are legal and illegal drug use the same?

TREATMENT REP: What we are talking about here is a sign of the double standard with which the entire society is struggling.

ENFORCEMENT REP: And even when it comes to drugs, there are double standards. Look at H.M. Corporation. The only thing they screen for are the hard drugs. They don't screen for marijuana. For some reason they don't look at marijuana as a problem.

Is marijuana use as serious as hard drug use?

CEO: So do you have a policy in your police department as to what constitutes an acceptable level of drug use and which drugs are acceptable?

What constitutes an acceptable level of which drugs?

ENFORCEMENT REP: In our department, years ago, no drugs were allowed—if applicants for a job with us had any prior use, we couldn't use them, we wouldn't take them. And then suddenly we couldn't get anybody to apply for a job with us, ever, because it was right during the Vietnam war. So we switched our policy down to no drug use within a year of starting work with us, and still we couldn't get anybody. So now we're down to six months prior to starting work with us and a promise never to use drugs again.

Employers must hire some people with a history of drug use.

MANAGERS: (Everybody is talking at once.)

CEO: So the other questions that I have for you three on the panel is: If someone uses drugs casually, what is the likelihood of that person's escalating into a serious drug or alcohol problem? That's question number one.

How likely is casual use to lead to a serious drug problem?

Question number two: How successful are drug addiction rehab programs? What I'm trying to find out is: If people have a history of a drug problem in the past and have been in treatment, is the drug problem likely to remain in the past? Or will it come back after we hire them? If they have been in treatment and now have what they consider only a "recreational" or "light" amount of drug or alcohol use, how likely is it that they will escalate, and what are they likely to escalate into?

How successful is treatment? Is it safe to hire people who've been in treatment? What if these people are using a little?

TREATMENT REP: I take it that you are asking these questions because you require this information in order to design your company drug and alcohol policy?

CEO: Yes. I'm struggling to determine what, if any, is a level of acceptable past and/or present use of each drug and how to decide who to hire.

Is there an acceptable level of use?

TREATMENT REP: Last fall, in the seminars, I talked about moving from "experimental use" to "regular use" to "being in trouble with the drug" to "being addicted to that drug" and how so many people slip from experimental use through these stages right on into addiction. And the boundaries of these stages are all very hazy—they overlap. I'm finding that, in working with people from about age ten to sixty—this is a broader age range than that of your employees—of the people who say they are experimental users, at least half are now really regular users of drugs. By the way, I'm including alcohol as a drug here. We've been taking polls. We've been taking anonymous surveys. We've also been interviewing people who come into treatment to get these data. Of the people who are regular users of things like cocaine, I just haven't seen any who have no problem with that drug. In fact, with cocaine, the recreational use I've seen is in most cases actually the "having-trouble-with-that-drug" stage. And regular use is already verging on addiction, if it isn't addiction. So depending on the drug, people who report being regular users may already be addicted to their drugs. They can even be honest on lie detector tests and still not reveal the truth. That's a pretty thorough form of denial.

Consider cigarettes—nicotine is also a drug. It's true that a lot of regular cigarette smokers are already hooked on nicotine. A lot of regular drinkers are already dependent on a certain amount of alcohol to calm down or to get through a work week. I suggest that a policy which tries to have several different provisions for several different drugs will become very complicated to implement. If we go this route, the policy must be carefully worded.

A policy that attempts to make different provisions for different drugs will be very complicated to implement.

CEO: Well, as some of you managers are already aware, what I've been doing lately is having new employees sign something. I have been giving them amnesty at the preemployment level. Whatever they've done in the past is their business. But they must stop all drug and alcohol use on the job and all working under the influence upon beginning work in this company, and they must agree to drug testing. I have them write it down in their own words, making a promise to play by the rules.

If you don't lay down the rules, you're just not going to get a response. It's been my experience that you can't appeal to people. If you don't lay down the rules and be open with them about what the rules are, then you've got a serious problem. I do want some feedback regarding how this hiring amnesty program is doing. I would definitely appreciate some feedback.

MANAGER N: I'm confused. What are we actually asking people to do, especially new hires? To give up the use of drugs, period, or are we asking them to restrict their use of drugs and alcohol to their own off-the-job time and their weekends? And I also wonder, if we have a so-called recreational, experimental drug user, are we going to basically say, "I accept your cocaine use; just keep it separate from the workplace." How?

What is it that we are asking employees to do: never to use or never to use on the job?

CEO: This issue is central to the whole meeting. It's important that we work toward an agreement on this. We may want to change our simple rule, "No use of drugs or alcohol on the job." We also need to express to employees the fact that we enforce this rule very rigorously within the organization, and that a potential employee's ongoing or recent prior drug use causes us concern. We want to say that we would like to employ them, but we would like as a condition of their employment for them to allow us to test them for drug use in the future at our discretion. Now, what we will do if we go this route is to have a form all worked out, something they might even copy in their own handwriting—it has a much stronger impact that way. Then we hire people on that condition. Then they're allowing us to retest them as we see fit, if we suspect something, or in using the "at our discretion," it doesn't even mean that we have to see them showing evidence of drug use; it means we could send them down for a test virtually anytime at will.

What's your question?

MANAGER D: Well, now you might have it in the manual that employees are prohibited from using drugs during their attendance at the workplace, and in the preemployment agreement they sign this rule. Then you send them down for a urine or some kind of drug test on some Monday. What if they smoked pot on the Sunday just before that? It would most likely show up. Is this fair?

Is it fair to test for off-the-job use?

TESTING REP: Now, on a polygraph, you can differentiate. On a urine test, you cannot.

MANAGER D: That's what I'm saying, you send them down for a urine test.

TESTING REP: Testing could be polygraph testing.

MANAGER D: Okay, whatever, but if you wanted to send them down for a urine test . . .

TESTING REP: That's a decision your company must make, but if it's urine test, obviously you're going to have to draw a line somewhere. If you have the rule "Don't do drugs in the workplace," then you're going to be very limited in the testing procedures you can apply. Your company policy may have to change with the technology.

MANAGER A: Excuse me. May I ask exactly who is going to define acceptable limits for our organization and who's going to determine the drug policy for our organization?

CEO: I think we're now attempting to receive input from all of you on these matters. Then, probably Pat, Jim, myself, Dan, maybe with the help of the panel here, will come up with something. And we'll certainly have further conversations with all of you before we actually put it down in writing.

MANAGER A: What are we talking about concerning the time frame for this policy?

CEO: I hope to have something maybe within six weeks.

MANAGER G: I have a question regarding polygraphs. I'll be the first one who's an advocate from the start that it does work and certainly makes our job of hiring a little bit easier. But there have been a lot of television shows on the bad side of polygraphs, and I'm wondering what the future of polygraph testing is?

TESTING REP: Right now it's unsure. To say the least. What's happened, to give you the gist, the unions have come up with $15 million to fight polygraph testing on a national level. We know that for a fact. The polygraph people in the United States are a very small minority. We don't have $15 million. At least the American Polygraph Association doesn't have that much money. Consequently, we don't have the lobbyists and things like that. I'm glad you brought that up, actually. What's helping us the most are people that we run polygraphs for. Employers can help us keep polygraph testing an approved, legal method.

CEO: But since the future of polygraph testing is uncertain, we have to have a policy that does not rely on it. Let's end this meeting here for now and reconvene next month. I personally would like to thank our panel for coming today and making their time available, and thank you all very much for being a part of our ongoing process.

*　*　*　*　*

Polygraph testing has become increasingly difficult to defend in a court of law. As a result, this company went on to design a drug policy which did not include this means of controlling "the problem." After struggling with a number of methods aimed at stopping employee drug use, this company found itself focusing on the surprising issue of acceptable use. Instead of asking what it could do to halt all employee drug use and abuse, the company asked what level of use of which drugs would be acceptable or most acceptable given the fact that the majority of its applicants had drug-using histories. I will say more about this ironic development in the following chapter.

8

Is There an Acceptable Level of Use?
The Question of the Hour

Every one of us, whether we are employers or employees, must do some soul searching about the issues raised in the managers' meeting transcribed in Chapter 7. The managers' questions are quite common in company discussions regarding employee drug use, and the answers to these questions affect us all. For example, *is our drug problem really a serious one?*[1] is asked with great frequency, and with a certain prejudgment that there can indeed be such a thing as a drug problem which is not serious. When I ask employers and managers what a drug problem which is not serious would look like, they say, "A few employees smoke a few marijuana sticks a day," or "One employee has to go in for treatment once a year."

"Do you have one of these problems which is not serious in your company?" I sometimes reply. Typically, managers are divided as to whether the problem is serious or not serious, and whether it exists at all. However, their superiors or the owners of their company tend to reply, "I don't know whether the problem is serious or not. Maybe you can tell us," or, "Yes, the problem is serious. It's costing us a lot of money."

[1]In this chapter, I highlight the questions and statements that I have pulled from the dialogue in Chapter 7 in italics for ready identification.

Two things are evidenced in these conversations. One is that people in companies do not always agree about the existence and the extent of the problem. The other, and perhaps more critical, is that many people in the business world believe that there is, or can be, a drug problem which is not serious. We can extract this pivotal message from the discussion in the previous chapter. In this chapter, I intend to pull questions and comments out of that discussion and talk about them in a way that helps us arrive at what is, or should be, the question of the hour: Is there a level of acceptable use? Let's consider some of the questions I highlighted in Chapter 7.

EXAMINING TYPICAL QUESTIONS ABOUT EMPLOYEE DRUG USE

Is drinking the same problem as drugging? Time and again, our double standard, which favors alcohol, a legal drug, over illegal drugs, rears its ugly and deceitful head. Of course drinking is the same as drugging: Drinking *is* drugging. One of the key messages in this book is that we must expand our notions and definitions of drugging in order to understand how pervasive drugging actually is.

Are legal and illegal drug use the same? Again, the basic difference between illegal and legal drug use is that one is against the law while the other is not. The use of cocaine or amphetamines or heroin in the workplace or outside the workplace can have obvious legal consequences for the user. It is a crime to use these drugs. Most use of alcohol in or out of the workplace is not against the law. This is why many official company parties serve alcohol and many official company happy hours are held in bars.

Is marijuana use as serious as hard drug use? Notice that each of these first few questions reveals that the managers are attempting to differentiate between types of drug use. Again, we can read between the lines and see that a general notion exists which says that some levels or types of drug use may be less serious than others. In this case, the questioner is focusing on marijuana, a drug which is viewed as being pharmacologically different and legally less serious than harder drugs such as crack or heroin. Marijuana has found itself a strange social niche in the gray continuum of legality and acceptability, between alcohol, which is legal and socially acceptable, and "hard" drugs, which are not. But how many readers would want their children's bus drivers, their bankers, their surgeons, or their airline pilots to work under the influence of marijuana? A minority, if any, of my readers would make a deliberate choice to do business with these people.

How likely is casual use to lead to a serious drug problem? Again, an effort is made to differentiate between acceptable and nonacceptable drug use. There is another question hidden within this question: Is casual drug use all right if it does not lead to serious drug problems? We are, again, confronted with uncertainty regarding the demarcations (1) between a drug use problem which is not really a problem and one which is, and also (2) between a drug use problem which is not a serious problem and one which is serious. If my airline pilot casually uses cocaine just before flying, or my auto mechanic casually (if this is possible) takes a hit of crack before putting my car back together, or my doctor casually smokes marijuana just before doing surgery, or my child's bus driver casually drinks wine at lunch before driving the kids home, there is a drug problem. Somebody is working under the influence of a drug and it is affecting my well-being. Do we wait until there is an accident to call it a serious drug problem? This, of course, was not the overt focus of the question at the head of this paragraph. The questioner was more than likely attempting to find out if all casual use leads to the problem of addictive use. No, not all casual use leads to a full-blown drug addiction. Some casual use is experimental or social and stays that way. A great deal of casual use becomes regular. However, regular users may or may not be able or willing to distinguish between regular and addictive use. Whether or not they can distinguish, they may continue to call themselves regular users while becoming addicted users. Definitions can fool us. And we are quite readily and willingly fooled about the complex issue of drug use in and around the workplace. Let's delve further into the tangle of complexities presented by employee drug use.

EXAMINING THE COMPLEXITIES

The participants in the meeting transcribed in Chapter 7 revealed some significant details about their workplace culture. For example, they indicated that, in a company where there are severe problems with illicit drug use, *some employees experience the threat of force and violence by drug dealers seeking to maintain anonymity within their company.*

In this disturbing situation, some employees work in fear of other employees. The workplace does not feel safe or predictable. There is an atmosphere of forced protection and denial. Lies, even among those who would not necessarily choose to lie about or cover up co-worker drug use, are fostered by impending violence.

Whether it occurs on or off the job, the use of illicit drugs such as cocaine, crack, speed, and ice by employees feeds into an atmosphere of dishonesty and uneasiness in the workplace. Cocaine and speed—their smoked versions, crack and ice—have taught us how quickly addictive a drug can be. Addiction to an illegal drug fosters its own special mix of desperation. This desperation includes fear of discovery, fear of arrest, fear of being fired, and, above all, fear of not being able to get enough of the drug. As the participants in the managers' meeting noted, *financial desperation can lead to theft in the workplace.* The erosion of order in the workplace is one of the consequences of the entry of illegal drugs into the workplace.

The erosion of order in the workplace is a social process:

Peer pressure to drink and drug is great among employees. Working can be tedious, or boring; and it can be lonely. Humans want to feel connected to other humans. In the workplace, loneliness, disconnection, and alienation are common, especially in settings where employees do not find fulfillment in their work. Working people naturally seek to counteract their feelings of being part of a production machine—their robotlike sensations, their losses of identity—by trying to find social outlets for their individuality. Social interaction allows individuals to express themselves, to express their feelings. Social interaction *feels* personal; it *feels* as if connection is being made. All too often, in order to fit into a company culture or subculture, employees attend social get-togethers with their co-workers where alcohol and other drugs are the medium of interpersonal exchange.

The depersonalization of the worker occurs as the personality, the will, is subsumed by the corporate personality, the company will. While it may appear beneficial for the company organization, the repression of the self is tension-producing for the organization of the soul of the individual worker. The pain of self-repression is often obscured by the rewards of company involvement. But the vigilant self seeks an outlet, even if it be via drugs. The self also seeks to drug the pain of suffocation. Drugs are thus welcomed into the workplace by workers who feel that they need drugs in order to cope.

One of the most unsettling comments made during the managers' meeting was that *drug use in the workplace is implicitly condoned.* The speaker who made this comment was referring to the way co-workers respond to peer pressure not to "rat" on or report drug-using employees. This is but one part of the conspiracy to condone drug use. On an unspoken level, some degree of drug use, especially alcohol use, is accepted by employers. Why? One reason for the acceptance is that alcohol is legal. Another reason is that bosses often use alcohol and are known to do so. Thus, it would be difficult to deny employees what management so clearly does not deny itself.

However, there is more to the story. So much about work-

life is compulsory: Be at work at a certain time. Do a certain
thing. Function at a certain level. Behave a certain way. Those
who seek to harness human energy intuitively understand its
limitations. Some degree of drug use is implicitly condoned because employers intuitively understand that employees need a
breakout mechanism. They need some way to relieve the pain of
suffocation and the pressure of disindividualization and dehumanization. Controlled use of alcohol and other drugs is a
controlled breakout. Employers find controlled use preferable to
outright rebellion and riot. Employees can be controlled in a
controlled-use organization. The hypocrisy, or denial, of a controlled-use organization is that it *is* a drug-using organization.
Many employers choose to deny this because (they claim) they
have no official policy stating that controlled use is acceptable.
However, they are wrong. As is revealed in the typical policy
included in Chapter 9, controlled use of alcohol is often explicitly described as being acceptable in company policies. In the
case of illegal drugs, policies usually describe these as being
unacceptable, and yet, when these policies are implemented
there is often a tolerance of a limited use of some illegal drugs by
some employees. The hypocrisy extends further when we consider the uses of caffeine and nicotine by employees. These
drugs are rarely referred to in company drug policies because
they are not considered drugs by the authors of these policies.

A controlled-use organization is an employee-controlling
organization. An organization that explicitly prohibits some
drug use while it explicitly and implicitly condones other drug
use seeks to control employees by allowing them to do what
they are going to do anyway. The basic premise, albeit unspoken, is that when employees break rules, they undermine
control much more than they do if they undermine control within the rules.

Most employers deny that they condone drug use among
their employees, even implicitly. This denial is, of course,
grounded in the overarching condition with which we are faced,

which is that *many companies are in a state of denial about their drug and alcohol problems.*

EXAMINING TYPICAL POLICY QUESTIONS AND ISSUES

When employers confront the matter of employee drug use, numerous policy issues arise. For example, whatever questions employers and their managers may raise regarding the seriousness of employee drug use, there seems to be a basic agreement that *safety in the workplace is of paramount importance.* That the safety of the consumer is of equal importance is also generally agreed upon, although I continue to be surprised when I hear it emphasized less frequently than workplace safety.

Liability

One of the most basic policy questions that employers either ask or attempt to ask without being certain of what it is that they are asking is: Is the drug problem the employer's problem or does it belong to the society? If the problem, at least in part, is the employer's problem, does that employer's involvement end as employees leave the workplace parking lot at the end of the workday? Most of the time, when employers ask the above question, they are actually asking, *where does the problem begin and end?* and *where does the employer's liability begin and end?* In some instances, the employer can be held legally responsible when he or she sends an intoxicated employee home and that employee gets into an accident on the way home. The employer's liability therefore can extend far past the workplace. It also can extend far past the workplace when a consumer is injured as a result of an intoxicated employee's poor judgment at work. An intoxicated auto mechanic who does not fix the brakes on a customer's car, although thinking he or she has fixed these brakes, can extend the employer's liability out to the highway.

Managers' Roles

Employers delegate responsibility for the day-to-day management of employees to their managers. This means that managers come face to face with the actual difficulties of *managing employee drug use*. The participants in the managers' meeting reported in Chapter 7 raised a number of issues regarding the management of employee drug use. For example, they pointed out that *managers can detect alcohol use more easily than drug use*. However, they also claimed that regardless of their ability to detect employee drug use of various types, *it may not be the job of a manager to deal with the drug problem*. The drug problem brings with it a number of emotional reactions, including fear (*even employees who have no drug problems are scared*) and hostility (*employees may be hostile to company efforts*). Managers may not be prepared to handle these issues. This is not what most managers have been trained to do. The managers also indicated that *managers should not be detectives*. They should not be expected to spy upon or investigate employees. They do not view undercover investigation as being their line of work.

Managers sometimes feel that they are expected to engage in direct confrontation of employees who are suspected of having drug problems. In the meeting reported in Chapter 7, managers inquired, *can managers outright ask if an employee is on alcohol or another drug?* Even if managers have the right to ask employees such questions, they may not have the skills to deal with the reactions to such a confrontation. And even if they have received some training in this area, every action that employers expect their managers to take in this area should be specified in writing.

Need for Written Policy

Employers who confront employees must be backed up by a written company drug policy. All steps and actions that employers and their managers take to counter employee drug use must be taken according to policy. Moreover, *company policies must have procedural rules* to back them. These procedural rules must be clearly stated and checked by legal counsel for their legality. I will address policy and procedure in more detail in Chapter 9. Company drug policies must answer a number of questions asked by the managers in Chapter 7, including *is drinking the same problem as drugging?* and questions as to whether or not drug testing offers more certainty regarding the actual level of employee drug use than do other methods.

At first, workplace drug policy seems to be quite simple: Don't use drugs at work. However, as we have seen in the discussion in Chapter 7 and the review of the issues in this chapter, the matter is much more complex. The most complicating factors are that a wide range of drugs that have a wide range of effects are being used at widely varying frequencies in widely varying amounts. However, *a policy that attempts to make different provisions for different drugs will be very complicated to implement.* Because most drug users are polydrug users, a company that attempts to maintain a separate policy for each drug will be applying different rules to the same individuals when they are using more than one drug.

Whatever the content of a policy, its goals must be clear. The managers asked several questions which revealed their confusion regarding the goals of workplace drug policy, especially when it concerns employees' use of drugs off the job: *What is it that we are asking employees to do: never to use or never to use on the job? And can we control employee drug use off the job?* If we can find a way to effectively control employee drug use off the job, do we have a right to? These concerns point at a larger question: How far can public or private employers reach into the private lives of employees? Employees who use alcohol or any other drug off the job may come to work under the influence of that drug. Even if they don't come to work high on that drug, they may come to work with a hangover or withdrawal, a letdown or nervousness, or a craving for more of the same or another drug. How? Their bodies may not have completed metabolizing, excreting, and recovering from the dose of that drug. In other words, even employees who use drugs only off the job can come to work under the influence. Again we are confronted with the issue of acceptability: How much of a particular drug at what time of the work week is acceptable?

THE QUESTION OF THE HOUR

We are ultimately going to have to ask ourselves: *Is a drug-free workplace the ultimate objective?* And if it is, what do we mean by a "drug-free" workplace? Is a truly drug-free workplace achievable? What about *the problem of trying to hire drug-free employees* which the managers alerted us to? As they pointed out, *employers must hire some people with a history of drug use.* Given that they must do so, employers and managers wonder, *are employees handling their addiction problems on their own?* And, if they are doing so, *how successful is treatment? Is it safe to hire people who've been in treatment? What if these people are using a little?* But what is "a little"? Where should employers draw the line?

We return to the question of the hour: *What constitutes an acceptable level of which drugs?* Or stated from another angle, *are some levels of use acceptable for some drugs and not for others?* We know that they are. Nicotine, alcohol, and caffeine are legal drugs which affect the mind and body during and following their use, and which, therefore, can affect job performance in some way. An addiction can be formed to each of these drugs, and therefore, many casual, social, and regular users of these drugs may be unaware of their dependence upon them.

Any way we choose to approach the problem, there will always be a certain percentage of working people who work under the influence of some drug or drugs. The drugs will change over time. So may their legality. But their deteriorating effects, whether blatant or subtle, upon overall workplace performance will continue to be with us. It is time to shake ourselves out of our communal denial, our shared daze, and learn to function with this problem instead of proceeding as if we can entirely alleviate it.

9

Drug-Free Workplace Policy
The State of the Art

You begin a new job. You are handed a piece of paper which says, "Company X: Drug and Alcohol Policy." You are asked to read it and then you are asked if you have any questions about it. You ask your questions if you feel comfortable doing so. You get the basic message: *Don't*. But don't do what? Is the message clear? Do your co-workers understand it?

The creating of an effective workplace drug policy is an art, an art which we are still developing. Setting the pace for this development is the Drug Free Workplace (DFWP) Act of 1988 (U.S. Congress, Section 701 et seq., 1988), which became effective on March 18, 1989. This act applies to employers who are awarded property or service contracts of $25,000 or more by any federal agency; to individuals who enter into any other contract with a federal agency (in any amount); and to all recipients of federal agency grants (in any amount). If they are individuals, these contractors and grantees must certify that they will not engage in the unlawful manufacture, distribution, dispensation, possession, or use of a controlled substance in the performance of the contract activity. If they are organizations, they must certify that they will provide a drug-free workplace by the following five means:

1. *An employee notification statement* (a drug-free-workplace policy issued to employees).

2. *A drug-free awareness program in the workplace that states* the workplace policy; the options for counseling, treatment, and assistance; and the penalties for violation of the policy.
3. *Notice to the government agency of convictions,* which requires that the employer notify the contracting or granting agency within ten days of an employee drug-statute conviction for a workplace violation.
4. *Employee sanctions and rehabilitation,* which requires that employers impose sanctions or require satisfactory participation in a drug abuse rehabilitation program by any employee who is convicted, within thirty days of receiving notice of the conviction.
5. *Good faith effort,* that is, an effort by the employer to continue to maintain a drug-free workplace by implementing these requirements. In order to implement the requirements of this law, employers begin by writing the required employee notification statement or, as it is often called, the drug-free workplace policy. Next, they must find a way to provide their employees with drug awareness training. [1]

In this chapter, I will focus primarily upon the first of the five requirements of the Drug Free Workplace Act: the statement of notification (which is the policy itself). I also touch upon drug awareness training, conviction reporting, and sanctions as they pertain to policy. I discuss rehabilitation (treatment and recovery) issues in Chapters 10 and 11; I have discussed the related matter of drug testing in Chapter 6.

The federal Drug Free Workplace Act of 1988 suggests an ideal toward which employers who contract with the federal government are enjoined to strive. As the states moved to enact similar legislations and to extend the drug-free workplace mandate to other employers, the phrase "drug-free workplace" became a catch-all for a new upgraded vision of the workplace.

The drug-free workplace thus joined the hallowed ranks of all-American apple pie, flag, and Mom symbology. But that may be all it is—symbology.

WHAT IS THE PURPOSE OF A DRUG-FREE WORKPLACE POLICY?

There is nothing wrong with national symbols. They serve as reminders of ideal conditions which we can strive to achieve, once we envision them. Most of us would agree that to have every workplace become a drug-free workplace is a laudable goal. And the workplace can be the hub of social change. After all, Otis Bowen, the U.S. Secretary of Health and Human Services, claimed in 1986, "The health and safety of our workforce, and indeed the future of America, may well depend on the extent to which business, labor and industry can develop an appropriate response to the epidemic use of drugs that plagues this Nation." [2] Perhaps, having had no clearly measurable success in the war on drugs, waged via other routes, the government was shifting the focus to the workplace. And why not? The workplace is the hub of the American economy, of productivity. It is a place where almost every adult American goes almost every day. The workplace is an excellent catchment area for serious public health problems, such as drug abuse.

The purpose of drug-free workplace policy is to bring about a change in the behavior of adult Americans. It seeks to remedy the public health problem. Specifically, drug-free workplace policy seeks to keep drugs and the influence of drugs away from the workplace. More generally, as Otis Bowen suggested, the purpose of drug-free workplace policy may be to protect the future of the nation.

There is a lot riding on drug-free workplace policy. Yet, just how free of drugs can a drug-free workplace be? Can policy make a difference? The starting point for anyone writing a drug-free workplace policy is to understand the goals and objectives of that policy. I have outlined these in the section below. Although few workplace policies have thus far followed such a detailed and clearly structured outline, employers would do well to consider doing so.

PRIMARY OBJECTIVES OF A DRUG-FREE WORKPLACE POLICY

Workplace drug policy is evolving. Eventually we may see alcohol treated more as other drugs are in policies, and smoking policies incorporated in drug policies. If you have a drug policy where you work, be certain that it makes the following items clear. If it does not, consider suggesting that it be rewritten.

OBJECTIVE 1: To control the possession, use, and sale of drugs at or around the worksite.
1.1. Definition of drugs: This typically is spelled out to include illicit and otherwise controlled drugs. Ideally, alcohol and nicotine will also be included. However, alcohol is usually separated (as in Objective 2 below), and nicotine is usually covered in a separate smoking policy.
1.2. Definition of possession: This typically is spelled out to mean in, on, or around one's person. The definition details the handling of prescription drugs, the keeping of drugs in "closed containers" in private vehicles, and related issues.
1.3. Location of possession: The boundaries of the worksite must be clearly spelled out. These boundaries will vary in companies where traveling salespeople, ships' captains, off-site construction workers, and other employees make the worksite a mobile location.
1.4. Definition of use: This usually includes minimal use, so as

to discourage all use. The definition should address time of use as well.

1.5. Definition of sale: This should be clearly detailed.

OBJECTIVE 2: To control alcohol possession and sale at or around the worksite.

2.1. Definition of alcohol as a drug: Alcohol is typically discussed separately in a policy statement, primarily because its possession is legal and because it is a socially acceptable drug. A discussion of the definition of possession of alcohol is usually omitted but should be included. When it comes to alcohol, use, and not possession, is usually considered the only potential problem. This may not be a realistic approach.

2.2. Definition of use: Use of alcohol on the job, use of alcohol off the worksite during work hours, and use of alcohol at company-sponsored social functions are all limited, usually in different ways, by a policy statement. Typically, policies are inconsistent in their use rules. Consistency is important in this area.

OBJECTIVE 3: To define the meaning of presence of alcohol or other drugs in the body.

3.1. Definition of presence: This should go beyond the use of subjective phrases such as "impaired performance" or "under the influence" because the presence of a drug in the system is measurable, for example, via blood alcohol level or urine screening.

3.2. Conviction reporting: When and to whom convictions are to be reported should be spelled out, including the violations covered (such as DUIs) and reporting protocol.

3.3. Testing for presence: This should be spelled out especially well, including a specification of:

3.3.1. What type of test or tests will be used.

3.3.2. Under what conditions (preemployment, during employment, etc.).

3.3.3. Location of test and collection procedures to be used: sample collection, chain of custody, interpretation of results, and training of those responsible in the process.

3.3.4. Consequences of refusal to be tested.

3.3.5. Protections (confidentiality, privacy, preknowledge, and consent).

    3.3.5.1. Consultation, training, education, assessment, and referral.

    3.3.5.2. Who is covered, at whose discretion, and under what conditions (e.g., automatic referral on first violation, reasonable accommodation, management discretion on second violation. Based on company policy, collective bargaining agreement, and pertinent legislation).

    3.3.5.3. Consequences of refusal of referral.

    3.3.5.4. Guarantees of confidentiality.

OBJECTIVE 4: To specify the consequences of a violation.

4.1. Consequences of possession violation.

4.2. Consequences of use violation.

4.3. Consequences of presence violation.

4.4. Consequences of sale violation.

4.5. Specific consequences should be specified:

    4.5.1. No hire in the case of an unsatisfactory preemployment screening.

    4.5.2. Probation and monitoring in the case of employee drug use.

    4.5.3. Evaluation and treatment of addicted employees.

    4.5.4. Progressive discipline in cases of repeat episodes, in which the consequences evolve from treatment to discipline and the discipline becomes increasingly strong.

4.5.5. Discharge protocol when an employee must be terminated.

4.5.6. The role of employee assistance; the in-house or external counseling and referral service available to all employees.

OBJECTIVE 5: To specifically address smoking policy within the drug policy.

5.1. Definition of smoking: What is smoked, how it is smoked.

5.2. Definition of location (if any) where smoking is allowed.

5.3. Consequences of violation.

OBJECTIVE 6: To specify utilization of employee assistance services.

6.1. Who is covered, at whose referral.

6.2. What conditions warrant an automatic referral to employee assistance; consequences of refusal of referral.

6.3. Required participation by all employees in employee drug awareness training.

OBJECTIVE 7: To enhance company communication at all levels. Policies rarely, if ever, address this issue; however, it is the key to policy success. I return to this issue at the end of this chapter.

A TYPICAL POLICY

The following is a typical drug-free workplace policy, which is actually a composite of the policies in use at several different companies. Note that this policy does not take the form outlined above. This design is more common than the explicitly detailed design outlined above. A policy need not take the form of the above outline; however, the more organized and clearly subheaded a policy is, the better use employees and employers can make of it.

Sample Drug and Alcohol Policy

Employees involved in the use of mood-altering drugs and/or abuse of alcohol are likely to have more workplace accidents, incur greater amounts of lost time from work, and perform their job requirements in a substandard manner. Company X does not wish to intrude in the private lives of its employees; however, it has an interest in employee health and well-being as they affect workplace productivity and job safety. Company X is committed to the highest standards of service to the consumer and a safe work environment for its employees. Therefore, in accord with this commitment (and with the Drug Free Workplace Act and other federal directives, collective bargaining agreements, etc.), Company X establishes the following policy, to be adhered to by all employees of this company.

I. Possession, Sale, or Distribution of Illicit Drugs, Controlled Substances, or Alcohol at or around the Worksite. Possession, sale, or distribution of illicit drugs or unauthorized controlled substances at or around the worksite or on company property is prohibited. Unauthorized possession, sale, or distribution of *alcoholic beverages* at or around the worksite or on company property is also prohibited, except as part of a company-sponsored social event or in appropriately sealed and wrapped gift packages. This exception applies only to alcohol. Violations will result in disciplinary action up to and including discharge.

II. Off-Worksite Use of Alcohol. Unauthorized off-premise use of alcoholic beverages during the course of the workday is prohibited *except* as part of a company-sponsored social event. Violation will result in disciplinary action up to and including discharge.[1]

---

[1]Readers will note that although most policies specify such a violation, there is room for considerable debate regarding such practices as the two-martini business lunch.

III. Presence of Illicit Drugs, Controlled Substances, and Alcohol

A. The presence of illicit drugs or unauthorized controlled substances, as determined by appropriate body fluid testing, is prohibited.

B. Being under the influence of alcohol equivalent to .05% or higher of blood alcohol concentration (BAC), as determined by body fluid or other accepted testing mechanisms, is prohibited. Violations of Section A or B will result in disciplinary action up to and including discharge.

IV. Body Fluid Testing. Preemployment urinalysis will be conducted by a medical facility selected by the company to determine the presence of illicit drugs or unauthorized controlled substances. If the test is confirmed positive for such substances, the candidate will not be employed. Reapplication for employment may be considered after forty-five days.

COMMENTS ON THE TYPICAL POLICY

The above typical policy covers many of the basics. Note that the controlled use of a legal drug, alcohol, is explicitly allowed. The rules for alcohol differ from the rules for other drugs. Also note that smoking is not referred to at all. This is not an oversight but an indication of a relative acceptance of nicotine or a sense that nicotine is not a drug. Also consider the difficulties in defining the boundaries of the worksite. It is important to define the worksite carefully for employees so that it is clear that the worksite is any location during any normal working hours where an employee is engaged in performing company duties.

EMPLOYEE DRUG AWARENESS TRAINING

Employee drug awareness training for all employees is now required of employers who fall under the federal Drug Free

Workplace mandate. Many other employers are using this approach as a way of preventing drug problems in their workplaces. Education can be effective in prevention. The content of training should include:

- Definitions of drugs.
- How drugs work.
- Effects of varying levels of and frequencies of use.
- How a hangover, withdrawal, and/or craving can affect job performance.
- Specific effects of specific drugs (i.e., impaired coordination).
- Definitions of experimental, social, regular, and addictive use.
- Symptoms of addiction.
- How addiction comes about.
- Codependence in families and workplaces.
- The consequences of the use of particular drugs: public law and private law (company policy).
- Careful explanation of company drug policy.
- Testing (how it works and when it will be used).
- Mental health prevention of drug problems and addiction.
- Physical health prevention of drug problems and addiction.
- Stress reduction exercises.
- Communication training and activities.

I have learned that communication activities comprise one of the most important items on the above list. I have conducted many training seminars on employee drug awareness. The participants in these seminars have taught me a great deal about the need for communication. I recall one seminar which was presented to forty employees (all men) who worked in the "shop" at their company, servicing company vehicles.

About thirty minutes into my initial presentation on how drugs work, three participants stood up and demanded that they have a few minutes to address a different subject. They wanted to discuss whether or not their boss actually had a right to make the drug awareness seminar compulsory. They also wanted to express a great deal of anger about the way that management treated them. Their unified resistance to proceeding until they had had time to air their grievances convinced me that this was a necessary step. I asked the participants in the seminar to rearrange the chairs (which were set up in classroom-style rows) into a large circle. I explained that I was a licensed therapist as well as an instructor and that their boss and I had agreed that anything said in these meetings was to be confidential unless the person who said it requested otherwise. I then spent an hour listening to these employees express frustration and anger. At first, the anger was directed toward management. After about thirty minutes, I noted that the anger was directed toward worklife in general. By the end of the hour, several employees were talking about their personal anxieties and how using alcohol at the end of the workday was soothing to them. These employees were concerned that management was eventually going to try to control what they did off the job. They wanted to know (1) if this was a possibility and, if so, why off-the-job alcohol and drug use mattered, and (2) if alcohol and drug use were going to be "lumped together" and why.

This group conversation accomplished several things. First, it opened the door to the drug awareness seminars when employees finally *wanted* to know the answers to the above questions. Second, as participants reported, they felt better when "somebody finally took the time to listen," and they were able to express anger and talk about their feelings. Above all, when the anger evolved into a discussion of personal anxieties, I saw how important it is for employees to have an opportunity to be heard, to communicate. It was clear to me that there were legitimate concerns about the way management was behaving, and that there was a great deal of work-related stress in the lives of these employees. It was also obvious that personal problems, work-related stress, and disgruntlement with management were tangled together, seemingly inseparably. As a result of this meeting, the company's employees were given a regular opportunity to communicate with management. The company began a communications training program for all employees at all levels. Within months, the workplace atmosphere had changed for the better. Employees were also provided with an employee assistance program in which they could sort out their problems, whether personal or organizational.

Communications activities alone do not eliminate a company drug problem, but they do serve as an important vehicle for profound company change. Escape from the dimension of denial in which so many drug-using companies exist is fueled by ongoing efforts to communicate truth. Workplace drug policy must incorporate company communication activities in its content to achieve its goals.

10

Where the Buck Really Stops
Employee Use of Treatment Services

There is a large and expanding enterprise out there. It is called *drug treatment*. Drug treatment focuses on drug (including alcohol) addiction at the *individual* level. I emphasize individual level because, although entire families occasionally come in for treatment, entire neighborhoods and entire companies do not. Certainly chemical dependence affects individual people, but it also affects entire organizations. Still, drug treatment programs have not moved right into our workplaces to treat us all.

So, at this time, we have individualized drug treatment. If individualized drug treatment is going to be even part of the answer to the drug "problem," then it must be effective and affordable. Neither of these characteristics of treatment is an absolute given. If you or someone you know has ever enrolled in or referred an employee to drug treatment, you have become aware of this predicament firsthand.

THE UNWIELDY COST OF CARE

Treatment is costly and the bill appears to be increasing. Several trends are contributing to the escalation of addiction

The research for and writing of this chapter was supported in part by a postdoctoral fellowship from the National Institute of Mental Health.

treatment costs. Among these is the expansion of the addiction treatment industry. Many treatment purchasers are being encouraged to "overbuy" services despite the lack of evidence that the more dollars spent on treatment, the more effective it will be.

Employers who seek to determine the most cost-effective method of addiction treatment must recognize that not all employees require the same treatment pattern. Unless treatment is responsive to individual characteristics, it is not only costly but of poor quality. There are distinct gender and ethnic differences in the use of general mental health services. These differences suggest that addiction treatment utilization is also sensitive to specific patient characteristics such as gender and race. There are also numerous psychological and organizational barriers to the effective use of employer-sponsored treatment. Some of these barriers to treatment affect employees with different characteristics differently.

The evaluation of the cost-effectiveness of treatment must always be underscored by a deep understanding of its utilization: Which employees use which forms of treatment, and what factors affect their utilization patterns?

Trends Influencing Cost Escalation

Corporations face rising costs as employee benefit plans expand to include addiction treatment. [1] At least forty states now require employers to include coverage for alcohol and drug rehabilitation in their company health insurance plans. [2] Other pressures that contribute to the rising costs experienced by corporations include "cost-shifting," where inflated bills are submitted by hospitals to traditional corporate health plans to offset the effect of payment cutbacks being made by Medicare. [3]

Cost escalations faced by employers are also associated with several overarching social trends. First, there is a growing demand for, and an increasing utilization of, both inpatient and outpatient mental health services, whether or not they are aimed at addiction. [4] Because an estimated 50% to 80% of all complaints heard by physicians have a significant emotional component or have no organic base [5], new mental health services may be needed even where they are not yet demanded. Although outpatient mental health service utilization has increased more rapidly than has inpatient utilization, the number of hospital admissions and inpatient days for mental health care have also increased markedly. [6] Although addiction treatment has traditionally been viewed as a physical health service, it is increasingly treated within the context of mental health services within corporations. Second, there is a growing and specific demand for, and increasing utilization of, both inpatient and outpatient addiction treatment services. [7] Third, there is increasing disagreement and misjudgment regarding the appropriate duration and mix of inpatient and outpatient care in addiction treatment. [8] Addiction treatment is a less finite and more ambiguous process than many forms of physical health care. Quite often, the patient is unable to perceive clearly (or to admit) the onset of addiction, and quite frequently, both the patient and the provider are unable to discern the termination or continuation of an addiction problem. In the specific case of addiction treatment, the potential for relapse is always present; there are no absolute guarantees in the prevention of relapse. The more we know about addiction, the more we must admit to the ambiguity of treatment's effective limits.

Increasing demand and increasing ambiguity are accompanied by another, and perhaps the most critical, trend: The cost of addiction treatment is increasing. Consider the historical roots of this trend. Since the twelve-step self-help program of Alcoholics Anonymous was founded in 1936, it has provided cost-free access for all persons who choose to attend. The decades following the establishment of Alcoholics Anonymous have brought further developments in addiction treatment. In the 1940s, the first detoxification programs and halfway houses appeared. In the 1950s, therapeutic communities for the treatment of alcoholism were developed. Other forms of treatment were inspired in the 1960s, when federal funds were made available for various forms of experimental treatment and for occupational alcoholism programs. [9]

The Expanding Treatment Industry

The private sector eventually realized that there was a market for addiction treatment. In the early 1970s, the first for-profit hospital alcoholism unit opened its doors. In the almost two decades that followed, hospital addiction programs began to compete for patients and for income. Although in 1978 the American Hospital Association reported that there were a few investor-owned for-profit alcoholism–chemical-dependency inpatient units (a total of 17 with 277 beds among them), in 1987 there were 84 of them with 1,730 beds among them. [10] During these same years the number of alcoholism–chemical-dependency inpatient units in nongovernment not-for-profit hospitals increased from 262 (with 5,404 beds altogether) in 1978 to 564 (containing 14,105 beds altogether) in 1987. [11]

It has been suggested that financial gain was one, if not the primary, incentive for this growth and for the expansion of program lengths. By 1976, many 14-day hospital programs were extended to 21 days, and many 21-day programs were extended to 28 days. There was, however, little, if any, clinical evidence to support this extension of the standard hospital stay. Research surveys indicate that financial incentives motivated this structural change in treatment. In the 1970s, hospitals were suffering from cash flow problems. The average overall occupancy rate of hospitals appeared to be dropping (from 80% occupancy in 1970 to 76% in 1978). [12] Hospitals responded by increasing the number of beds assigned to treating addiction. It has been argued that by increasing the length of stay for addiction treatment, hospitals have not only filled beds, but they have created waiting lists and increased hospital income. Today, some programs charge as much as $25,000 for twenty-eight days.

From 1980 to 1983, total inpatient chemical-dependency programs increased 42%. [13] Advertising and marketing on the part of chemical-dependency treatment programs proliferated. Corporations and their employee assistance, human resources, and health benefits programs were increasingly solicited by addiction treatment programs. The Office of Technology Assessment of the U.S. Congress has concluded that treatment providers have convinced treatment purchasers to "overbuy," encouraging the "use of the most expensive services available, namely inpatient medically based treatment," whether necessary or not. [14] Employers and their employees have been, and continue to be, confronted with a broad range of options for the treatment of chemical dependency. Corporations continue to struggle to determine which are the most cost-effective methods of treating addiction and which of these methods their employees are most likely to use. These goals are potentially at odds because efforts to get employees into treatment and to help them remain in treatment run counter to efforts to reduce the money spent on treatment. Employers face the rising costs of untreated employee addiction, on the one hand, and the rising costs of addiction treatment and/or addiction treatment coverage, on the other.

The Issue of Varying Utilization Patterns

Yet the problem is not clear-cut. No one pattern or combination of inpatient and outpatient care best suits all persons in need of treatment. A utilization pattern that may be considered cost-effective for a married white male without children and with job security and a management position may not be effective for a single black mother of two pre-school-aged children with little job security, a low salary, and a nonmanagement position.

Extensive research regarding the utilization patterns of specific employee subpopulations would aid employers and policymakers in designing programs to encourage participation in treatment as well as to control costs. As employee assistance and managed-care services proliferate [15], they must recognize the special needs and tendencies of specific employee subgroups. Managed care has come to be known as the "fourth party" in and the "gatekeeper" of treatment, in that it controls the utilization (as a gatekeeper) of health care benefits and services for insurance and benefit providers (the "third-party payers"). Gatekeepers can help reduce health care costs if, and only if, they have a technical understanding of the treatment utilization behaviors and needs of specific gender, race, and other subpopulations.

GENDER DIFFERENCES IN MENTAL HEALTH AND ADDICTION TREATMENT UTILIZATION

The research literature contains studies which consider the different characteristics of the mental health service utilization of males and females. [16] The sociological and health services literature frequently reports that women use ambulatory mental health services to a greater extent than men. For example, a study of a representative sample of 2,000 adults found that of all those who sought mental health care, 66% were women and only 34% were men. [17] Studies suggest that women have a significantly greater probability of mental health service use. They also use a significantly greater level of outpatient, ambulatory, or "walk-in" mental health care services. [18]

Differences in Mental Health Utilization

There are sparse data regarding inpatient mental health service utilization among men and women. Studies show that men are more likely than women to be involuntarily committed. [19] However, general admission rates for men and women vary substantially between private and public sector hospitals. In state and county mental hospitals, the admission rate (per 100,000 civilian population) is greater for males (220, 92 of which are voluntary admissions) than for females (111, 45 of which are voluntary). On the other hand, in private general hospitals with psychiatric facilities, the admission rate is about the same for men and women: 62 for men (53 being voluntary) and 63 for women (56 being voluntary). [20] These statistics suggest that there may be socioeconomic factors which determine which mental health treatment people receive.

Differences in Addiction Treatment Utilization

Data indicate marked differences in alcohol and drug treatment utilization rates. The National Drug and Alcoholism Treatment Utilization Survey conducted in 1982 reported that of the almost 300,000 individuals in treatment for alcoholism, 78% were male, and 22% were female. Of those in treatment for drug abuse, 70% were male, and 30% were female. [21] In 1984, of the almost 600,000 alcohol-related discharges from short-stay hospitals in the United States, 836 (per 100,000) were male, and 339 (per 100,000) were female. [22] These figures inspire an important question: Is the proportion of females who utilize treatment representative of those who need treatment, or are females underrepresented in the treatment population?

The common perception that fewer women than men suffer from chemical dependence derives largely from the incentive that society provides for women to "go underground" with their drinking and drug problems. When labeled "alcoholic," women face not only the negative community attitudes toward alcoholism that are experienced by men, but also the moral stigma attached to their being alcoholic wives and mothers. [23] Time and again, I have found that women perceive themselves to experience greater personal and social costs when entering addiction treatment. They also perceive themselves to have greater concerns regarding job loss when undergoing addiction treatment. Employed women are more visible than women who run their households on a full-time basis. Their alcohol and drug problems become more apparent to the outside world at work. Women tend to drink alone and to be "closet drinkers" more than do men. [24] Yet the effects of their addiction follow them to their workplace. Although men experience more job-related problems and arrests as a result of their drinking, women tend to experience more "illness other than hangovers." [25] These illnesses affect job attendance and performance.

Because of processes of self-selection and entry into treatment, gender-related differences in the utilization of treatment are inextricably linked to treatment outcomes. Studies which focus on gender issues in addiction treatment have reached conflicting conclusions regarding the outcome of males' and females' participation in treatment. A large proportion of these studies show no significant differences or show that sex is completely unrelated to treatment outcome. [26] On the other hand, a National Center on Alcohol Abuse and Alcoholism Treatment Program Monitoring System study found that women actually showed greater improvement after 180 days of treatment than did men. [27]

VARIATION IN MENTAL-HEALTH-SERVICE UTILIZATION AMONG ETHNIC SUBPOPULATIONS

The existing literature addresses the characteristics of and notes the differences in mental health service utilization among subpopulations such as those determined by race. [28] Recent research has begun to look specifically at the utilization of mental health benefits by employed populations and their dependents, disaggregating the data across ethnic and other sub-groups. Among the conditions indicated by the research in this area is the marked variation in the level of service use and the type of service use among ethnic groups. [29] For example, a large study in which I was involved reported that blacks had a 24% and Hispanics a 14% higher probability of using inpatient mental health services than whites. The inverse was true for outpatient service utilization, with blacks registering a 40% lower use of outpatient services than whites, and Hispanics a 38% lower rate. [30] We must ask whether this variation reflects differences in patients' preferences or in providers' referrals. [31] If the latter is all or part of the explanation, do some health professionals refer blacks and Hispanics to inpatient treatment more frequently than they do whites for purely clinical reasons or for other, more social, reasons such as clinician bias or implicit racial prejudice? [32]

Whether biased or unbiased, clinical judgment plays an important role in referrals to treatment and in decisions regarding the pattern of treatment. A major review of the research on minority utilization of mental health services found that "Blacks are more likely to be involuntarily admitted; less likely to receive individual psychotherapy [33]; and more likely to be medicated, placed in seclusion, and denied privileges [34]." [35] There is a distinct need for further research on specific differences in white, black, Hispanic, and Asian utilization of services and on racial differences in the responsiveness to mental health intervention. [36] Without an extension of this type of analysis into the arena of addiction treatment service utilization by employees of different races, employers are limited in their efforts to ameliorate the drug "problem." Even if it seems as if every employee who has a drug problem has the same problem, it is certain that not every employee has the same treatment needs. No matter how much money we throw at the addiction problem, we will be wasting it if we do not address the special needs of special subpopulations.

THE COST OF UTILIZATION OF DIFFERING
FORMS OF TREATMENT

Variations in general mental-health-service-utilization be-havior have been documented. It is now becoming important to measure these differences in terms of the differing costs of vari-ous utilization patterns. There is an obvious lack of research regarding the costs of addiction treatment utilization by specific subpopulations.

Cost-Effectiveness Comparisons

By contrast, extensive research concerning the cost-effec-tiveness of various forms of treatment does exist. Studies com-pare short- and long-term hospital stays and inpatient and outpatient treatment options. New evidence suggests that inpa-tient hospital treatment may not be the best option for alcohol and drug addiction treatment. In 1984, Bechtel Corporation pro-duced a study comparing the costs and the effectivenesses of the inpatient and outpatient chemical-dependence treatments that a random sample of its employees had received in two different years, 1980 and 1983. The data showed that there had been a shift in the nature of corporate referrals from predominantly inpatient in 1980 to predominantly outpatient programs in 1983. With this shift, Bechtel Corporation's total treatment cost dropped dramatically, from $119,000 for the treatment of 27 em-ployees in 1980 to $13,000 for the treatment of 26 employees in 1983. This dramatic change in total costs and average cost per patient was not paralleled by any change in treatment outcome. In fact, the outcome measure (measure of treatment success) remained 71% for both the inpatient and the outpatient groups. Moreover, the drop in expenditures did not reflect a parallel change in the treatment utilization rates in the geographical area (the San Francisco Bay Area). In fact, these rates increased 45% from 1980 to 1983. Assuming that the measure of treatment success employed by Bechtel was reliable, Bechtel's shift to out-patient from lengthy hospital treatment was cost-effective. [37]

Questioning Traditional Modes of Treatment

The relatively nascent view that traditional modes of treatment for chemical dependence may not be clinically or economically justified has been expressed by a variety of players in the referral, treatment, and benefit process. Researchers William R. Miller and Reid K. Hester conducted an extensive review of twenty-six controlled studies comparing in- and outpatient treatment models. They concluded that "Third party reimbursement policy should discourage the use of cost intensive residential models." [38]

Miller and Hester also concluded that "American treatment of alcoholism follows a standard formula that appears to be impervious to emerging research evidence, and has not changed significantly for at least two decades." [39] Other research has also questioned the necessity and the efficacy of inpatient treatment of addiction. Although expenditures on inpatient treatment are significantly higher than those on outpatient treatment, a growing body of literature claims that the outcomes of these two different forms of treatment are similar. [40] And where they are dissimilar, the treatment outcome for patients who received all or most of their treatment on an outpatient basis may actually be more positive. This finding reflects the greater opportunity afforded by the outpatient status for integrating treatment into the daily family and worklives of patients. [41]

Short-Term versus Long-Term Treatment

Another area of empirical research has been the comparison of the costs and the outcomes of short-term (and thus less costly) and long-term (and more costly) inpatient stays for addiction treatment. While studies differ in the lengths of stay that they have evaluated, many of them conclude that there is no justification for prolonged and costly hospital treatment. [42]

All of this research pertains to the cost-effectivenesses of treatment. Short-term inpatient stays are less costly than long-term, and outpatient care is less costly than inpatient care. If the outcomes of these forms of treatment are similar, then long-term care is not cost-effective.

The cost of addiction treatment can range from no fee (when twelve-step programs such as Alcoholics Anonymous, Cocaine Anonymous, and Narcotics Anonymous are used without other programs) to many tens of thousands of dollars (when prolonged or repeated inpatient treatment is involved over a period of several months and years). Most insurers place a ceiling (either annual or lifetime) on their levels of expenditure per case of individual addiction treatment. Employers face skyrocketing bills for addiction treatment coverage [43] when they pressure insurers to raise their ceilings. Employers face skyrocketing losses in productivity when they do not provide effective addiction treatment.

Employers under Pressure Turn to Managed Care

Based upon the continuing belief that enough addiction treatment will alleviate the problem of employee alcohol and drug addiction, many employers felt mounting pressure to pay larger premiums to cover more generous employee benefits during the 1980s. As a result, employers began to question the belief that more (treatment) is better. They also began to call for improved treatment outcome measures on the new premise that better treatment is better. This premise calls into question longstanding beliefs such as those that claim that longer (28-, 35-, 45-, and 60-day) inpatient stays are always more effective in breaking addiction than either briefer (5- to 14-day) inpatient stays, outpatient treatment without inpatient stays, or brief inpatient treatment combined with long-term outpatient treatment.

The demand for better treatment has somehow translated into a demand for less expensive treatment or better managed utilization of treatment. This has been true all over the health care industry rather than being restricted to the addiction treatment field. By 1990, over 60% of all major employers offered health maintenance organization (HMO) benefits to their employees. [44] An HMO is a health care organization which provides health care in return for a preset amount of money on a per member per month basis. HMOs were one of several new patterns of health care cost, reimbursement, and utilization control that emerged in response to increases in the cost of general health care in recent decades. PPOs (preferred-provider organizations) are another. PPO plans contract with individual providers, selected by the PPO, to receive a discount for their services. Many PPOs have a utilization review (UR) component which monitors the level and type of use by individuals who are covered by the plan.

Whether in the form of an HMO, a PPO, or some other form of *managed care*, employers are increasingly turning to managed care as the answer to skyrocketing health benefit costs. By the mid-1990s, it is expected that at least 75% of all major employers will offer HMOs and 90% of all employers will provide HMO, PPO, self-insured (employer-insured), or other managed-care plans to their employees. [45] Consequently, by the mid-1990s, some 85% of all payments for hospital inpatient services and some 75% of all payments to physicians will be covered by some form of fixed-price managed-care payment system. [46] As addiction treatment coverage, services, and providers fall in the domain of managed care along with other health and mental health services, the characteristics of care change. If a national health care system is adopted in the United States, it may usurp or replace managed care. However, national health care is also going to involve use control in some way. We have entered the era of public- and private-sector health-care-utilization control. Future addiction treatment utilization will reflect this development.

The old notion that the more dollars spent on care (usually as a result of more inpatient days), the better the outcome is being challenged. [47] Concurrently, the consumers of addiction treatment services—the employees who need the help—are exhibiting variations in their utilization of the different forms of addiction treatment. It is time that treatment and referral become more sensitive and fine-tuned to individual differences. Whatever form they take, the gatekeepers of addiction treatment must recognize individual differences. It is becoming increasingly clear that, as the National Academy of Sciences Institute of Medicine states, "There is no one approach that is effective for all persons with alcohol problems. Consequently, matching the type of alcohol problem with the appropriate treatment is central to effective intervention." [48] The same holds true for the treatment of addictions to other drugs. As I contended at the beginning of this chapter, the evaluation of the cost-effectiveness of treatment must always be underscored by a deep understanding of its utilization: Which employees use which forms of treatment? What variables affect their utilization patterns? And which forms of treatment are most effective in treating which types of addictions? It is time for a concerted and humane effort to answer these questions. Treatment which does not seek these answers is not treatment. Managed care which does not seek these answers is not effectively managing care.

Recovery in the Workplace
An Obstacle Course?

"Recovery" is the central goal of addiction treatment. The notion of "recovery" says that recovering from addiction is possible, but that it is a continuous process, one that must last a lifetime. The general consensus is that it is dangerous to say that an addicted person "has recovered." It sets him or her up for the illusion of completion while all the forces drawing him or her back to using drugs continue to lurk in the wings.

One of the greatest challenges confronting companies that have addicted employees is to get these employees in for treatment. Another is to keep them in recovery. Because recovery is often related to the entrance (and, in many cases, the reentrance) into treatment, it is important that employers look for and try to overcome the obstacles to this entrance and reentrance. A third challenge is to realistically evaluate the effectiveness of the treatment used by employees. Yet another, and perhaps greater, challenge is to question the basic understanding of recovery upon which many recommendations, decisions, and actions are based.

OBSTACLES TO PARTICIPATION IN EMPLOYER-SPONSORED TREATMENT

There are two critical levels upon which obstacles to participation in employer-sponsored treatment are found. The first is the individual level and the second is the organizational or company level.

Individuals' Reluctance to Seek Help

The reluctance of an addicted individual to seek help from anyone in or outside the workplace is a typical part of addictive behavior. Several of the elements of reluctance are detailed in Chapters 2 and 5: lack of information, fear, denial, and family codependence. A brief review will be sufficient here: Employees who have problems with alcohol and drugs frequently suffer from a lack of information about the dangers they pose to their own physical and mental health and to that of their families and co-workers. Whether or not they lack full information, employees experience fear of job loss, social and workplace stigma, and other forms of reprisal such as police involvement. When experiencing this fear, these individuals develop intricate patterns of denial, in which they seek to avoid admitting the truth about their drug problems to others and to themselves. Many employees who are having trouble with drugs may have developed long-term family-life patterns which resist change—even if the change is that the employee in trouble with drugs gets help and gets out of trouble. The combination of lack of information, fear, denial, and family codependence serves as a powerful barrier to an individual employee's entry into treatment. However, the organization in which the individual is employed also contains numerous obstacles to entry into treatment.

Barriers in Company Referral Processes

The second level upon which barriers are erected is the organizational level. I have described the organizational counterparts to the individual level of lack of information, fear, denial, and codependence in Chapters 2 and 5. Whatever information the individual lacks is lacked by many of her or his co-workers and supervisors. Her or his individual fear and denial are couched in an environment of organizational fear and denial. Because the work environment shares elements of a typical family environment, workplace codependence and coinvolvement run rampant. Well-constructed barriers in the company referral process appear. Some of these organizational barriers are the following:

1. *Attitudes and beliefs of supervisors about the nature of alcohol and drug addiction.* These attitudes and beliefs may stem from a general lack of information [1]; from the application of common stereotypes which make it difficult to recognize the early stages of alcoholism [2]; or from views that persons in the later stages of alcoholism are "hard to reach." [3] Supervisors tend to more readily refer employees who are illegal drug users for treatment than they do problem drinkers, about whom they tend to remain more ambivalent. [4]

2. *Systemic denial among employees, co-workers, supervisors, and case managers.* The denial-based manipulative skills of the addicted individual as well as denial among his or her family, friends, co-workers, and workplace supervisors and managers serve as barriers to entry into treatment. [5] Employers may be reluctant to admit that "one of their own" (or so many of their own) has a highly stigmatized condition such as addiction. [6] Such an admission is viewed as a threat to the public image of the company.

3. *The drive for autonomy among supervisors.* Department supervisors, who are the most likely members of the work organization to encourage employees to get treatment, may be resistant to passing the problem on to employee assistance or other designated programs. This resistance is attributed to a sense among supervisors that they should handle problems that they have with the employees they supervise independently [7], without seeking help from other members of the company hierarchy. Supervisors also tend to believe that they should stay

away from the personal lives of their employees. [8] Involvement in the referral process is also viewed as a risk by many supervisors, as it can jeopardize their status within the company or with the union or may result in lawsuits for themselves or their employers. [9]

4. *Socioeconomic characteristics of the workforce.* Of all the obstacles to participation in treatment, the specific socioeconomic characteristics of the troubled employee are not viewed as being highly critical. However relevant demographic characteristics (such as gender, race, age, marital status, family size, and parenting status) and economic characteristics (such as occupational level and salary) may be, they are not recognized as major hindrances to participation in treatment. Consider gender and parenting issues. Married and single women with children are reluctant to enter and then remain in treatment when they have no reliable child care to cover for them during their absence. [10] Job security (which is usually related to occupational level), income (affecting the amount of and quality of child care that can be purchased), and marital status all play a role in forming this socioeconomic obstacle to treatment.

These are just some of the many obstacles to entry into addiction treatment. There are many employees with drug problems who do not seek employer-sponsored or any form of help as a result of these obstacles. For those who do seek help, there are other obstacles to recovery in the workplace.

KEEPING EMPLOYEES IN TREATMENT AND RECOVERY

When an employee enters treatment, the hard work has just begun. The rate of compliance with outpatient follow-up programs which "follow up" on compliance with inpatient hospital treatment is disturbingly low in most mental health and psychiatric care. [11]

The Tendency to Drop Out

One reason for dropping out is that hospital patients frequently are under the impression that outpatient aftercare is just that: "after" care. Accordingly, many treatment programs are changing the name of this program component to *ongoing* or *continuing care.*

There are several other explanations for treatment dropout. All too often, inpatient treatment providers place little emphasis on outpatient treatment and worse, inpatient treatment providers frequently discourage or devalue the role of outpatient psychotherapy in recovery. There are also practical explanations for treatment dropout. There is often too much time lapse between discharge from inpatient care and entry into outpatient care; and, there is frequently not enough social support to encourage involvement in ongoing care. [12] When employers or their employee assistance personnel are involved in referral for treatment, they can best ensure compliance with the inpatient and outpatient programs by providing as much positive moral and social support as they can and by supervising treatment participation.

As I suggested in Chapter 10, there is disagreement among professionals regarding the most effective length of stay in treatment and the relative effectiveness of in- and outpatient treatment. Some research demonstrates that outpatient treatment is just as effective as inpatient treatment.[13] Other research indicates that the chances that a recovering person will comply with an outpatient treatment plan increase as the length of that person's preceding inpatient hospital stay increases. [14] In other words, the effectiveness of outpatient treatment is dependent upon the use of inpatient treatment and the length of that inpatient treatment.

Whatever the most effective treatment may be, motivation is critical in promoting the involvement in and the success of the treatment process. Goal setting promotes motivation when the goals are to attain new benefits specific to a clean and sober lifestyle—benefits that outweigh the perceived benefits of using drugs. This has been demonstrated in studies of persons being treated for alcoholism. [15] Recovering employees often need as much coaching in general goal setting as they do in the more specific elements of recovery.

The Stigma Factor

There are other factors contributing to the tendency to drop out of treatment. One is the stigma factor. Returning to work after being in treatment for drug addiction can be awkward, embarrassing, and demoralizing. If co-workers or managers know about the treatment and have no understanding of the difficulty of reentry, they can appear unsympathetic even when they are not.

Reentry Crises

Reentry into the workplace can be an intense experience. Even if there is no stigma in the workplace (either because no one knows about the treatment or because everyone is support-ive of it), there is a crisis of adjustment: A new drug-free ap-proach to the challenges of life, including work, must be gener-ated. This can be a stressful process. Furthermore, being an addicted person in recovery—especially "early" recovery—is frequently experienced as being a person whom co-workers, bosses, and friends are cautious of, a person who may have no way of being certain that the havoc caused by the drug use is truly over.

The I-Can-Do-It-Alone Mode

Many a recovery is foiled by the I-can-do-it-alone-I-don't-need-anyone response to reentry. The intense stress of having to make a new life, even if it is a better life, can lead some persons to isolate themselves and to pull away from the world around them.

Substituting Work for Healing

One of the greatest misappropriations of personal energy is the substitution of working for healing. Even if recovering persons do not use their drugs while they are working, they are not doing everything that they can do for themselves by increasing their working hours. Past the point of reasonable involvement in it, work is used as a way of avoiding confrontation with the self.

When Am I Well? Relapse Prevention

Relapse prevention has become one of many addiction treatment buzz words. This is, of course, because prevention of relapse is the ultimate aim of all addiction treatment. A distinction is sometimes made between lapse and relapse. Lapse is a process (one or more slips or mistakes) that may or may not lead to relapse (return to the addictive behavior and pattern). Two definitions of relapse are commonly used. One is that it is "a recurrence of symptoms after a period of improvement," and the other is a "backsliding or worsening." [16]

The most effective approach to relapse prevention is to focus on preventing relapses and/or recovering from lapses when and if they occur. The risk of relapse is determined by the interaction of individual, situational, and psychological factors: Depression, inadequate motivation, stress, lack of social support, environmental reminders of the drug to which one is addicted, physical exhaustion, and illness can be factors which set off powerful cravings for one's drug or drugs of choice.

OBSTACLES TO EVALUATING THE EFFECTIVENESS OF TREATMENT

One of the greatest difficulties in chemical dependence treatment is evaluating or monitoring its success. Because the possibility of relapse is ever-present, success is never a finality. Monitoring must therefore be longitudinal, rather than a one-shot deal.

The measurement of outcome in the treatment of chemical dependence is not only controversial and difficult, it is also extremely complex. When employers or the agencies they hire do the referring for treatment or pay for treatment by insurance which covers treatment, program success rates are economically as well as psychologically critical. The difficulties of measuring success are many. They include more than the problems of tracking the behaviors of an employee over time and maintaining her or his willingness to report on the course of her or his recovery regularly for years.

The primary controversy encompassing the measurement of treatment outcome is found in the operationalization of the term *outcome*. When the ideal outcome is referred to, the phrase "100% clean and sober" usually comes to mind. But what does "100% clean and sober" actually mean? Clean and sober of what? Of all drugs or only of the drug to which the employee thought he or she was originally addicted? And if outcome is defined as being clean and sober of all drugs, how is the term *drugs* defined? Illegal drugs only? Alcohol as well? Prescription and over-the-counter drugs? Caffeine and nicotine? If the use of any or all of these drugs can trigger dangerous cravings for the original drug of choice, perhaps their use should be included in the outcome measurements.

And what about the progress that a twenty-year addict (who used his drug more than once a day every day for twenty years) makes from 0%—no days clean and sober—to a month or several months at a time clean and sober? This is definitely progress. This is a positive if interim outcome achieved along the way to the goal of becoming 100% clean and sober. But is this outcome going to make a difference in overall productivity at work?

Further questions about the measurement of outcome data arise when changes in the quality of treated persons' lives are considered. It may be that changes in sleep, eating, and emotional patterns are critical outcome measures whether they are achieved concurrently with 100% sobriety or along the way to the realization of that goal. Unfortunately, this notion is viewed as backward and somewhat heretical. The first goal of treatment is expected to be 100% clean and sober, even though the quality-of-life changes that may maintain sobriety should actually come first.

It helps to think of treatment evaluation as being fourfold. As dictated by what I call the *quadrad model*, outcome data can be organized into four categories. (I have included in this chapter's appendix data from a study in which I applied this model.) The first category is the *frequency-of-use outcome*, the most traditional evaluation of the effectiveness of drug treatment. Because the primary goal of treatment (and of employers who sponsor treatment for their employees) is to reduce and eliminate drug use, this measure is always a critical indicator of clients' progress in recovery and program effectiveness.

I added three other evaluative categories to the first in order to capture less obvious but equally important changes that individuals may experience in other dimensions of their recovery. The second of four evaluation measures in the evaluation quadrad is *longitudinal symptom reduction*. Employees arrive in treatment with a plethora of presenting symptoms. These symptoms represent their level of distress as well as suggest their degree of on-the-job impairment. (The data in the appendix show a dramatic reduction in the reported symptoms.) The third evaluation measure is *attitudinal change*. Chemically dependent employees' attitudes must change for their workplace behaviors to improve. Treatment can affect change in clients' attitudes toward drugs, as the program under study here has done. The fourth evaluation measure is *change in the quality of life*. Without an improvement in quality of life, the quality of workplace behavior does not really improve. (As in the other evaluation categories, the data presented in the appendix report positive change.) The treatment evaluation quadrad should thus include:

Quadrad I: Frequency-of-use outcome measures
Quadrad II: Longitudinal symptom reduction
Quadrad III: Attitudinal changes
Quadrad IV: Change in the quality of life

This evaluation quadrad provides a valuable perspective on client progress and program quality. No one arm of this quadrad would present a balanced picture of the course of recovery.

RETHINKING "RECOVERY" AS "DISCOVERY"

Recovery in the workplace is complicated not only by workplace factors, but by the larger social confusion regarding the ultimate meaning of recovery. The standard jargon of addiction treatment calls addiction a disease and calls the time spent getting well a recovery from disease. According to this line of thinking, anyone who has once been addicted will be a lifelong "recovering addict." This disease–recovery model has helped many thousands of people confront and work on their chemical dependence. The concept of lifelong recovery has also helped their friends and relatives appreciate the continuing seriousness of addiction long after the addict has stopped drinking or drugging.

It is important to recognize the philosophical limitations as well as the value of the disease–recovery model and how these limitations affect the addicted person's ability to stop being chemically dependent.

First, the disease–recovery model of addiction helps to remove the element of blame: If addiction is a disease, then it is not the addict's fault that she or he is addicted. This model relieves the addict of some social stigma and blame but allows the focus to remain on the individual rather than on the relatively "well" society. It avoids seeing the pervasive problem of societal chemical dependence. Second, the disease–recovery model also holds the general level of treatment to the individual level, although laudable current campaigns use public funds in "Call for help" and "Just say no" slogans. If society focused a substantial portion of attention, energy, and money on treating chemical dependence at a societal level, we could make quality treatment available to everyone. "Call for help" and "Just say no" campaigns would include messages that we are all part of "the problem" and must all participate in alleviating its symptoms.

Third, the disease–recovery model views lifelong "recovery" as the only positive change away from "disease." Other positive options are never suggested. Since recovery, by its very name, is convalescence, lifelong convalescence means the person is perpetually getting over a "bad thing that once happened." Recovery itself may or may not be growth, although many people grow psychologically and spiritually during recovery.

Fourth, the disease model uses the term *recovery*, and recovery justifies use of the disease model. Addiction is individual sickness, and its aftermath is getting well. We are snared in this conundrum. Our minds and hearts are trapped by the words we use.

Try for a moment considering chemical dependence as a challenge or struggle that some humans are going through for all of us. They are searching for a way out of individual, societal, and planetary stress, exploring frontiers as others have explored uncharted continents on Earth and as still others will explore the solar system and outer space. When they find an answer, no matter how large or small, they have made a discovery.

The postaddiction discovery process makes its actors into pioneers, even leaders, in spiritual development. Persons who enter lifelong discovery seek answers for themselves and for others. How can we as individuals and as a species transcend crisis?

To some onlookers, drug addiction, especially cocaine addiction, is a "luxury problem" for people "who have nothing more serious to be troubled by." Looking across socioeconomic lines and into other nations, large and small, poor and rich, we can see that chemical dependence is an insidious and global reality. No matter who encounters the anguish of addiction, the pain is the same. Addiction is the great equalizer.

Addiction is a strange kind of world war in that the best weapons against it are understanding, caring, and respect for human dignity and peace. Anyone who is addicted or works with or lives with addicted persons experiences the ravages of war and visits the battlefields between the mind, body, and soul where this war between life and soul death rages. The dark side looks overpowering; standard weapons will not work. Only a sustained stream of light can conquer the dark.

Many persons who have been addicted to drugs have discovered that the key to living drug-free is to develop a spirituality. Although their versions of spirituality differ, spirituality has great importance for them. Out of suffering, the addicted individuals have discovered the great gift of being and a reverence for life. Every crisis provides an opportunity to be "only human," to struggle and to overcome—to transcend. It is time we awarded these individuals our respect, rather than labeling them diseased and postdisease recoverers. It is time we discovered the message in their discovery of the fragility and sanctity of life. We must call recovering addicts *discoverers* and rename *recovery,* calling it *discovery.* Because that is what it really is.

APPENDIX: APPLICATION OF CHEMICAL-DEPENDENCE TREATMENT-EVALUATION QUADRAD*

The following data were obtained in an evaluation of a drug treatment program which consists of a repeatable one-week social-model residential component and eighteen months minimum of outpatient treatment. During its first four years, this program, the Cokenders Alcohol and Drug Program, saw an increasingly diverse group of clients. Most socioeconomic categories are represented by the client population. Over the four years, 75% of those who enrolled were men. Of all clients, 43% were single, 36% were married, and the others were separated or divorced; 68% had no children, and 17% had children aged twelve and under; 7% of the clients had not finished high school, 32% had attended school for enough years to earn a high school diploma, 31% had some college, 19% had a bachelor's degree, and the remainder had earned a master's or doctorate degree or another credential in addition to the bachelor's degree. 5% were unemployed, while the other 95% listed a broad range of occupations; 51% of all clients were employed in white-collar occupations, 5% were homemakers, and 30% were employed in what are traditionally referred to as blue-collar occupations; 42% reported that they earned annual incomes of from $10,000 up to $30,000, 36% reported from $30,000 up to $65,000, and 13% reported from $65,000 up to $150,000. Those who participated in this study (about 30% of the total population, which was 850 at that time) fell into these same demographic groups in approximately the same proportions.

Frequency-of-Use Outcome Measures

The frequencies of use at intake revealed a high chemical intake profile among the clients who participated in this study. These data are listed in Table 1.

Given the baseline data in Table 1, clients could be tracked and asked to report their frequency of use of cocaine, alcohol, and marijuana over time, following their entry into treatment. Data regarding these frequencies of use are listed by drug and level of use over time in Tables 2, 3, 4, 5, and 6.

As indicated in Table 2, the majority of clients were abstaining from all cocaine use from within one to two years of beginning treatment. At the time of intake, the majority of clients reported using cocaine two to six days a week (30.7%) or once a day (15.5%) or more than once a day (32.0%), for a total of 78.2% of all clients using from two days a week to more than once a day. Within from one to two years of intake into treatment, 89.8% of all clients reported that they were not using cocaine. These data show a marked improvement in clients' drug use profiles.

The majority of clients also significantly reduced their rates of alcohol consumption from within one to two years of beginning treatment. At the time of intake into treatment, 69.3% of all clients were using alcohol from two days a week to more than once a day. Within from one to two years of intake into treatment, 64.0% were using alcohol once a month or less, and over half of these clients (34.0%) reported that they were not using alcohol. See Table 3 for these data.

The majority of clients also stopped using marijuana from within one to two years of beginning treatment. As listed in Table 4, at the time of intake into treatment, 71.7% of all clients were using marijuana from once a month to more than once a day. Within from one to two years of intake into treatment, 82.0% of all clients reported that they were not using marijuana.

Based on the above longitudinal frequency-of-use data, at intake the typical client was using cocaine at least twice a week

(78.2%), alcohol at least twice a week (69.3%), and marijuana at least once a week (54.1%). The effect of treatment was markedly positive within one to two years after intake, with the majority of clients clean and sober from cocaine (89.8%) and marijuana (82.0%) and a notable percentage of clients using alcohol less than once a month or never using alcohol (48.0%).

The typical client was also drinking caffeinated coffee at least once a day (69.2%) and using nicotine at least once a day (64.0%). The data in Tables 5 and 6 also reveal that there was no parallel increase in caffeine and nicotine intake and that, in fact, the percentage of those who were not using caffeinated coffee or nicotine markedly increased.

The profile of the individuals in treatment for chemical dependence in the program under study here is one of positive change (reduction and cessation of drug intake) from within one to two years of admission into the program. However, frequency-of-use data alone tell little about the way the lives of recovering individuals change during recovery. While the goal of complete cessation of drug use seems to be approached by continuous reduction of use, some clinicians do not view reduction of use as success. However, when the measures presented by the evaluation quadrad described in the text are combined with frequency-of-use data, a more comprehensive and realistic picture of recovery is generated.

Symptom-Reduction Outcome Measures

Clients arrived at intake with a host of presenting problems. Every participating client listed many physical, psychological, and social symptoms. The ten most common physical symptoms that participants in this study reported upon intake were loss of energy, physical deterioration, sinus problems, insomnia, headaches, general health failure, heart palpitations, lost sex drive, sore throat, and shaking. The percentages reporting these symptoms are listed in Table 7.

The ten most common general psychological symptoms reported at intake were depression, irritability, anxiety, fears, paranoia, concentration problems, loss of interest in friends, loss of interest in nondrug activities, memory problems, and suspiciousness. (See Table 8 for percentages.)

The ten most common states of mind and the ten most common social symptoms reported at intake are detailed in Tables 9 and 10.

Clients reported that their symptoms reduced dramatically over time, as is demonstrated in Tables 11, 12, 13, and 14.

The reduction of physical, psychological, and social symptoms over time indicates that the participants were experiencing changes in their lives following their intake into this program. Together with overall changes in their frequency of drug use, the picture of the recovery process generated is one of significant change for the better. A continued fleshing out of the picture is provided by the remainder of the quadrad data.

Attitudinal-Change-Evaluation Outcome Measures

The majority of participants in this study entered the program with the goal of being 100% clean and maintained this goal over time. The changes in goals regarding future drug use (longitudinal) were reported as listed in Table 15.

While the goals regarding future drug use stayed about the same (as indicated in Table 15), the attitudes about drugs changed. Changes in attitudes toward drugs are listed in Table 16.

Note (at the bottom of Table 16) the large percentages of respondents who listed specific attitudinal changes within one and two years of intake. The majority of specific changes written in by respondents fell into three categories: increased awareness of the negative effects of drugs, lowered tolerance of other drug users, and increased awareness of one's own addiction. Overall, the participants' changes in attitude were significant and constructive. Yet attitude changes must be accompanied by measurable changes in behavior and experience such as those offered by the other quadrants. The remaining quadrant offers yet another dimension of measurement.

Quality-of-Life-Evaluation Outcome Measures

A series of questions were asked the participants regarding their subjective ratings of general changes in their lives. They were given the opportunity to report no change or some change. If change was reported, their answers were broken into categories of degree, such as worse, a little better, better, much better, or change without an evaluation of quality.

Changes in Emotions: Within one year 13.8% reported that their emotions were "a little better" and 63.3% reported that they were "much better." From one to two years, 23.1% reported "a little better" and 66.7% reported "much better."

Changes in Social Life: Within one year, 12.1% reported that their social lives were "better" and 53.3% reported "much better." From one to two years, 22.0% reported "better" and 46.3% reported "much better." A little over 20.0% continued to report a difference without a "better" or "worse" evaluation during the first and second years. Many of the respondents in the latter category noted that their responses were neutral because, although the overall changes were positive, they had had difficulty making the transition from having drug-using to having no drug-using friends.

Changes in Family Life: Within one year, 13.1% reported "better" and 56.1% reported "much better." From one to two years, 25.0% reported "better" and 60.0% reported "much better." The unspecified changes dropped from 17.8% the first year to 10.0% the second.

Changes in Energy Level: Profound changes in energy level were reported over time. Within one year, 17.1% reported have "more energy" and 57.7% reported having "much more energy." From one to two years, 7.1% reported having "more energy" and 88.1% reported "much more energy."

Changes in Eating Habits: Within one year, 15.1% reported "a little better" and 56.6% reported "much better." From one to two years, 28.2% reported "a little better" and 46.2% reported "much better." The level of unspecified changes stayed a little over 10.0% from the first to the second year.

Changes in Sleep Patterns: Within one year, 11.2% reported "more erratic," 7.5% reported "a little better," and 64.5% reported "much better." From one to two years, none reported "more erratic," 12.2% reported "a little better," and 70.7% reported "much better."

These data allow us to question the simple outcome indicator of cessation of use in evaluating the treatment of chemical dependence. Do frequency-of-use as well as quality-of-life measures reveal that lifestyle and patterns can be changed in a chemically dependent population without necessarily generating total sobriety first? Can total sobriety follow other changes in attitude and lifestyle rather than precede it? Perhaps lifestyle change is the foundation for a solid and lasting recovery.

Whatever the answers to these questions, it is clear that there is a case for the multidimensional approach to treatment evaluation modeled by this quadrad.

*   *   *   *   *

*This study was made possible through grants from a number of donors. Special thanks to donors Don Lucas of the Lucas Dealership Group in San Jose, California, and Dan Carlson of the Ark Foundation in Moraga, California. These data are drawn from an evaluation of the Cokenders Alcohol and Drug Program which was published in Angela Browne, "New Perspectives in Chemical Dependence Treatment Evaluation: A Case Study," *Employee Assistance Quarterly,* Vol. 4, No. 2, March 1989.

Table 1. Frequency of Use at Intake

	Cocaine	Alcohol	Marijuana
More than once a day	32.0%	17.2%	14.2%
Once a day	15.5	19.0	11.5
2–6 days a week	30.7	33.1	5.2
Once a week	10.6	13.8	13.2
2–3 times a month	3.7	4.6	6.8
Once a month	1.9	3.7	10.8
Less than once a month	1.9	2.5	8.1
Never (not using now)	3.7	6.1	20.3

Table 2. Cocaine: Frequency of Use over Time

	Within intake	1 year	1 to 2 years
More than once a day	32.0%	2.6%	0.0%
Once a day	15.5	0.0	0.0
2–6 days a week	30.7	4.3	4.1
Once a week	10.6	1.7	0.0
2–3 times a month	3.7	2.6	0.0
Once a month	1.9	3.4	0.0
Less than once a month	1.9	12.1	6.1
Never (not using now)	3.7	73.3	89.8

Table 3. Alcohol: Frequency of Use over Time

	Within intake	1 year	1 to 2 years
More than once a day	17.2%	2.5%	2.0%
Once a day	19.0	5.7	2.0
2–6 days a week	33.1	9.0	16.1
Once a week	13.8	8.2	10.0
2–3 times a month	4.6	17.2	6.0
Once a month	3.7	5.7	16.0
Less than once a month	2.5	7.4	14.0
Never (not using now)	6.1	44.3	34.0

Table 4. Marijuana: Frequency of Use over Time

	Within intake	1 year	1 to 2 years
More than once a day	14.2%	2.5%	2.0%
Once a day	11.5	3.3	0.0
2–6 days a week	15.2	4.9	2.0
Once a week	13.2	5.7	2.0
2–3 times a month	6.8	3.3	4.0
Once a month	10.8	2.5	2.0
Less than once a month	8.1	10.7	6.0
Never (not using now)	20.3	67.2	82.0

Table 5. Caffeinated Coffee: Frequency of Use over Time

	Within intake	1 year	1 to 2 years
More than once a day	34.4%	24.2%	27.7%
Once a day	24.8	10.0	19.1
2–6 days a week	13.6	7.5	8.5
Once a week	7.1	5.8	4.3
2–3 times a month	3.1	4.2	0.0
Once a month	2.4	0.8	0.0
Less than once a month	2.7	2.5	2.1
Never (not using now)	11.9	45.0	38.3

Table 6. Nicotine: Frequency of Use over Time

	Within intake	1 year	1 to 2 years
More than once a day	47.6%	53.4%	44.0%
Once a day	16.4	0.8	2.0
2–6 days a week	5.2	2.5	2.0
Once a week	1.7	0.8	0.0
2–3 times a month	0.7	1.7	4.0
Once a month	1.7	0.0	0.0
Less than once a month	1.0	0.8	0.0
Never (not using now)	25.5	39.8	48.0

Table 7. Ten Most Common Physical
Symptoms Reported at Intake

Symptom	Percentage reporting symptom
Loss of energy	39
Physical deterioration	31
Sinus problems	25
Insomnia	23
Headaches	20
General health failure	17
Heart palpitations	14
Lost sex drive	14
Sore throat	13
Shaking	13

Table 8. Ten Most Common General Psychological
Symptoms Reported at Intake

Symptom	Percentage reporting symptom
Depression	40
Irritability	38
Anxiety	37
Fears	28
Paranoia	27
Concentration problems	27
Loss of interest in friends	26
Loss of interest in nondrug activities	26
Memory problems	25
Suspiciousness	22

Table 9. Ten Most Common States of Mind Reported at Intake

Symptom	Percentage reporting symptom
Think I am addicted	44
Feel I cannot refuse drug(s) of choice	39
Feel loss of control over drug use	39
Feel like binge-using	34
Feel unable to stop using drugs	34
Prefer drugs to food	30
Feel a real need for drug(s)	29
Prefer drugs to family activities	29
Fear of being discovered as a user	28
Feel depressed when using	28

Table 10. Ten Most Common Social Symptoms Reported at Intake

Symptom	Percentage reporting symptom
I miss work because of my drug use	41
I make excuses because of my drug use	40
Other people object to my drug use	33
There is fighting or arguing because of my drug use	32
My spouse objects to my drug use	31
I borrow money because of my drug use	28
I have used 50% or more of my savings because of my drug use	26
I am in debt because of my drug use	25
Breakup of my family is threatened because of my drug use	24
I have no money left because of my drug use	20

Table 11. Percentage Reporting Physical Symptoms over Time

Specific symptom	At intake	During first year after intake	From 1 up to 2 years
Loss of energy	38.7	13.4	4.0
Physical deterioration	30.6	9.4	2.0
Sinus problems	24.6	13.4	12.0
Insomnia	22.5	10.2	2.0
Headaches	20.0	8.7	6.0
General health failure	16.7	6.3	2.0
Heart palpitations	13.9	6.3	2.0
Lost sex drive	13.9	6.3	4.0
Sore throat	13.2	7.1	4.0
Shaking	13.0	4.7	2.0

Table 12. Percentage Reporting Psychological Symptoms over Time

Specific symptom	At intake	During first year after intake	From 1 up to 2 years
Depression	40.4	25.2	14.0
Irritability	38.1	21.3	16.0
Anxiety	37.4	26.8	8.0
Fears	28.3	16.5	6.0
Paranoia	26.9	7.9	4.0
Concentration problems	27.1	11.8	6.0
Loss of interest in friends	25.5	5.5	6.0
Loss of interest in nondrug activities	25.5	3.1	4.0
Memory problems	24.8	4.2	0.0
Suspiciousness	22.0	7.1	4.0

Table 13. Percentage Reporting Symptoms over Time
("States of Mind")

Specific symptom	At intake	During first year after intake	From 1 up to 2 years
Think I am addicted	44.0	30.7	10.0
Feel I cannot refuse drug(s) of choice	40.1	9.4	8.0
Feel loss of control over drug use	38.7	7.9	6.0
Feel like binge-using	34.0	3.9	4.0
Feel unable to stop using drugs	34.3	7.1	8.0
Prefer drugs to food	29.5	7.9	4.0
Feel a real need for drug(s)	28.5	11.8	4.0
Prefer drugs to family activities	28.5	5.5	2.0
Fear of being discovered as a user	28.1	8.7	2.0
Feel depressed when using	28.1	8.7	2.0

Table 14. Percentage Reporting Social Symptoms over Time

Specific symptom	At intake	During first year after intake	From 1 up to 2 years
I miss work because of my drug use	41.0	9.4	0.0
I make excuses because of my drug use	40.0	7.1	2.0
Other people object to my drug use	33.0	9.4	4.0
There is fighting or arguing due to my drug use	32.0	9.4	4.0
My spouse objects to my drug use	31.0	9.4	4.0
I borrow money because of my drug use	28.0	3.9	0.0

(continued)

Table 14 (*Continued*)

Specific symptom	At intake	During first year after intake	From 1 up to 2 years
I have used 50% or more of my savings because of my drug use	26.0	7.1	2.0
I am in debt because of my drug use	25.0	12.6	6.0
Breakup of my family is threatened because of my drug use	24.0	8.7	4.0
I have no money left because of my drug use	20.0	4.7	4.0

Table 15. Goals Regarding Future Drug Use over Time

Goal	Intake	Following intake up to 1 year	From 1 up to 2 years
Don't know	1.0%	0.9%	2.2%
100% clean	68.2	76.7	71.7
Continue alcohol, cocaine, and/or marijuana	6.6	0.9	0.0

Table 16. Changes in Attitudes toward Drugs over Time

Attitude change	Within 1 year	1 to 2 years
No change	2.8%	0.0%
Change		
Want more drugs	0.0	0.0
Want less drugs	11.9	4.9
Don't want drugs	26.6	61.0
Listed other specific changes (an open-ended question)	58.7	34.1

Why Can't a Woman Be More Like a Man?

Gender and Chemical Dependence in the Workplace

The men and women that we find in our workplaces are the men and women who live in and create the society in which workplaces exist. Men and women are different, but they share the experience of being. They deal with many of the same pressures and respond to these pressures in many of the same ways. In a society and a world full of people using chemicals to change their moods and physical sensations, it is not surprising that many working men and women are chemically dependent. These people are part of the larger "chemical society" in which they live.

Many of them were already consuming large amounts of refined sugar and caffeine as children. The sugar was taken in the form of candy, ice cream, soda pop, cake and pastry, and other foods not considered "sweet," such as catsup, cereal, fast food, and convenience foods. (As do sugar, caffeine, and related compounds "sneak" into children's diets via cola drinks, candies, and chocolate. Children react to sugar and caffeine, and many even become dependent on these chemicals. Sugar and caffeine do what other drugs do: They affect moods and physiology via blood sugar, brain functioning, and artificial "swings" in body chemistry.)

Many of today's working people "started young" on the chemical roller-coaster rides of sugar and caffeine. In adolescence, peer and media pressures introduced them to the highly alluring effects of nicotine. In their late teens and early twenties, the drinking of alcohol was viewed by peers not only as socially acceptable but as *socially desirable*.

By the time they reached the age of twenty-one, they may have been brainwashed into believing that their regular consumption of cigarettes and alcoholic beverages was important in defining them as active, popular, attractive, and happy persons. Moreover, they were acculturated to the highs and lows of smoking and drinking by watching the adults around them drink and smoke and by their own intakes of sugar and caffeine. Their minds and bodies were programmed to accept chemically induced highs and lows by the time they were introduced to the nicotine, alcohol, and maybe even the Valium, codeine, marijuana, and cocaine so common in our adult world.

In addition to societal and environmental pressures to depend on chemicals such as sugar, caffeine, nicotine, alcohol, pain killers, diet pills, tranquilizers, marijuana, and cocaine to "feel right," working men and women experience special gender-related challenges that can cause them to turn to chemicals in order to cope. Let's take a look at women's and men's paths to drug use and addiction. As we do so, let us keep in mind that the use of any amount of a drug in order to "cope," whether it be regular or addictive use, *is* chemical dependence.

WOMEN AND DRUGS

Women who use drugs do so for many of the same reasons as men. Their addictions are just as severe and their withdrawals are just as painful. Just like men, women are flesh and blood and body and soul. They do, however, differ in significant ways. And because of these differences, particularly differences in socialization, women often follow different paths into addiction. They absorb the American Dream of material wealth, comfort, and success in different ways and at different stages of life than do men. And yet, they define themselves, all too often, in terms of their relationships to men. Consider these female roles:

The Chemically Dependent Female Adolescent

The chemically dependent female adolescent is a teenage girl who has been drinking "on the sly" for several years. Perhaps alcohol is readily available in her home. She's seen her mother drink socially, perhaps daily, and it seems sexy and sophisticated to her. Men seem to like women who drink. When her girlfriends begin to drink socially, she is "way ahead of the game." Naturally her friends look up to her and boys notice her, and this feeling is rewarding, even if she is already feeling the pain of addiction. She is driven by a modern American image of what it means to be a "cool" or "hip" girl, an image that includes drinking. She is also driven by the new female "machisma"—an "I-can-do-what-the-boys-do" image. The chemically dependent female adolescent can remain trapped in this adolescent perspective far past her teens.

The Coaddicted Wife of an Addict

A woman who feels dependent upon her addicted mate may become dependent on the fact that he is addicted. In this situation, the women's own self-image is dependent upon the fact that her husband needs her and that she is his *rescuer*. Some women in this situation follow their mates into actual chemical dependence so as "not to be on the outside." Often the woman becomes highly addicted to her mate's addiction—a chemical dependence one step removed. She may remain addicted to her mate's addiction even if she stops her own drug use.

The Chemically Dependent Wife of a Social User

Some women begin drinking or drugging socially with their mates but are unable to stop at this level of use. They eventually develop an addiction to a chemical substance. Women in this situation may have mates who do not become addicted and continue to use the problem substance socially. The men often defend their unhelpful social drugging and drinking behavior by saying, "I'm not going to change my lifestyle just because she couldn't handle it and got hooked."

The Chemically Dependent Single Woman

While the single or "unattached" life has gained greater respect and has become more alluring in recent years, there are single women who may have actually "married" a chemical— become addicted to drugs in place of having a close interpersonal relationship. In addition, many young single women feel pressure to use drugs in order to "fit in with the crowd." So either way they can be trapped into using drugs: using with the crowd as a result of social pressure, using without the crowd as a result of loneliness.

The Chemically Dependent Woman Married to a Nonuser

Some women bring the drug-using behaviors that they developed while single into their married lives. Others respond to social and workplace pressures or a lonely marriage by "making friends with chemicals." Either way, these women are among the least likely to seek help, because both their marriages and their parental rights may be threatened if their addictions were to become known.

The Chemically Dependent Woman Working in a Competitive Occupation

Women have moved in large numbers into occupations once totally dominated and occupied by men. Many career-oriented women have become drug users out of a feeling that if their male colleagues are drinking and using drugs as part of the realization of the American Dream, they should be, too. Some of these women report that their male colleagues are using alcohol or drugs with their clients and customers—and that the only way to stay competitive is to also use these chemicals. A portion of these women becomes increasingly chemically dependent. Women who take time off from work in order to receive addiction treatment feel that they are more heavily stigmatized than are their male counterparts. "You see, a women just can't handle this job" is a typical reaction. Many women compete for jobs and careers which once were or continue to be dominated by men. While working for lower pay, they struggle to demonstrate their competence, to equal if not to surpass the performance of their male counterparts, or simply to hold their own. Women are thus understandably reluctant to seek help for their addictions in their workplaces.

The Chemically Dependent Woman Experiencing Job–Family Role Strain

The tugs of motherhood and homemaking responsibilities compound with the standard pressures of working life (such as competition, deadlines, commuting, and avoiding tardiness and absences) to place working women under intense pressure. They get home from work exhausted. Yet, somehow, the household must be managed while these women bring home the bread. They end up spending a large portion of their paychecks or a large portion of their time off (and usually both) replacing the hours they have taken away from household management to go to a job outside the home. They go back to work drained. Moreover, many women are seeking "success" in the career and job market because they feel it is expected of them, because they expect it of themselves, and because *they simply cannot afford to fail*. They need the income. And, above all their basic needs, there emerges a craving for some kind of help—all too often help takes the form of a drug.

ADDICTION, DEPENDENCE, AND POWER

One thing that chemical dependence among women can teach us is more about the general nature of dependence. In a society where competitive individualism is applauded—among men and among women who attempt to make it in a "man's world" or to transform a man's world into a people's world—to be dependent in any mode, chemical or otherwise, is to be a lesser member of society. Of course, the dream, the myth of independence, is merely a myth. In reality, no one is completely independent. But we are talking about degrees—degrees of dependence. While the healthy forms of dependence are actually interdependence and are survival-oriented, many forms of dependence, such as chemical dependence, are unhealthy. In fact, they are self-destructive.

Women's chemical dependence problems provide us an uncanny insight into the nature of dependence. Today, women are confronted with a dual stress system. On one front, they face the pressures inherent in their traditional roles as wives, homemakers, and mothers. On the other front, they are accosted by the various demands of modern worklife and career activities. In the former system, women are economically dependent upon

male providers. The consequences of historically ordained economic dependence include legal and psychological dependence.
Women, as a class, have been encouraged to be, expected to be,
allowed to be, and willed to be explicitly dependent for most of
history. For those female persons, already conditioned by history to accept dependence, chemical dependence is merely one
more link—an easy link—in a long chain of subservience.

Let's oversimplify matters for a moment, inventing extreme
types to better understand the situation. These women have
given their power brokers—be they lawyers, mayors, fathers,
husbands, lovers, or sons—control. Both the controllers and the
controllees in these situations suffer and benefit in their roles.
Controllers, the men in dependent women's lives, bear the burdens of responsibility for economic support and at the same
time enjoy having power over the women they "protect." Controllees, the women in their dominating men's lives, bear the
burdens of subordination to their economic supporters along
with the freedom from economic responsibility that their role
yields. Although even the most traditional men's and women's
roles are in no way this simple, or this distinct, the dependence
conspiracy is most apparent in this type of male–female relationship: It takes two players to make at least one dependent.

Now, let's assume that one of the players is an inanimate but
powerful chemical. Being a nonliving item, this controller does
not experience the sensations of burden or of power. But the controllee, the woman using the powerful chemical, bears both the
burden of subordination and the freedom from responsibility associated with dependence upon this chemical. If the controllee is
a drug addict, the burden of subordination is the anguish of addiction. The freedom from responsibility is the escape from the
problems of coping with real feelings and the challenges of real
life as they are experienced while one is straight or sober.

But the dependence conspiracy is warped when one of the
players is merely a collection of inanimate molecules. How can a
drug be a power broker? It is the addict who surrenders her

power to the chemical, shackling herself to its control. In this sense, she imbues it with her own power. The drug is nothing until it enters her body. She, the addict, is the power broker now. She deposits her power in a thankless and unexpressive chemical bank. She chains herself to its chemical control. She gives the drug power over her self. She keeps giving away her power until she has no self. Then the chemical becomes, in effect, powerful. This relationship to drugs (including alcohol) is easy for a woman to slip into. She has been conditioned to dependence throughout history.

In this way, addiction is dependence and dependence is power. Dependence *is the power* to shrug the responsibility for self-control off onto someone or something else (in this case a chemical). Addiction is the power to keep shrugging until all self-control is lost, until the nature of the controller, the drug, overtakes the biochemistry and the soul of the user. Here the drug user becomes the drug abuser. Self-control is surrendered or transformed into self-abuse.

This pattern of addictive progression is common to men as well as women. Still, we can learn something special from women who abuse drugs (abuse themselves with drugs). Both the traditional male–female role model and the once male-oriented, now male and female job-and-career-person, model are paradigms for addictive dependence. Drug and alcohol addiction are not restricted simply to women who live out the extreme forms of subservience to men. In fact, few women today, even those in the more traditional roles of housewife and mother, would describe themselves as "dominated" or "subordinate." Furthermore, the burgeoning female labor-force participation rate has not reduced the female drug abuse rate. In fact, women's consumption of alcohol and other drugs appears to have increased as their participation in the workplace has increased. [1] This is a key piece of information. It poses at least two possibilities: (1) entry into the workforce makes a problem with drugs more visible, or (2) entry into the workforce encourages the development of problems with drugs. Whatever the meaning of this un-settling correlation between female labor-force participation and female drug consumption, it appears that women's escape from traditional forms of dependence upon men has not been accompanied by freedom from dependence upon chemicals. If any-thing, women are sharing what were once men's drug problems.

MEN AND DRUGS

Men are forgotten people. They are the unthanked brute shoulders upon which the modern world has been built. They have constructed a vast number of impressive ships, millions of roads, countless cities. They have carved out a place for women and children to live in a world full of natural threats to survival. Men have moved entire mountains in the name of ideas.

And still, there is tremendous social pressure placed upon men to achieve "more." This pressure can carve a driven, empty quality into a man's character. It can dig a hole in his soul. Men who use drugs are frequently seeking to fill this emptiness and, at the same time, to drug away—to deny—the unpleasant and stressful sensations caused by the endless pressure to achieve the elusive American Dream.

The American Dream and Drugs

What is it about the chemical dependence conspiracy that invites otherwise independent men into its web? What factors drive even economically comfortable men into chemical depen-dence? Once they come of age and enter the workforce, they become aware of all of the pressures of worklife that their fathers have been facing. Straightforward pressures, such as being on time, being dressed appropriately, and behaving properly, are compounded by the more complex demands for performance and achievement in the face of competition. Lurking behind these stresses is the awareness that failures may bring economic hardship and threaten masculinity.

The Chemically Dependent Superman

The desire to achieve like a superman is enough to drive some men to drink or to use relaxing or downer-type drugs— allowing them to decompress after or even during work. And the same desire is enough to drive other men to use uppers or stimulants, such as speed or cocaine, in order to feel that they can produce or achieve more. While riding high on a stimulant, an ambitious man may experience an illusory sensation of hypercompetence. During the hypercompetent high, he may work, uninterrupted, for long periods of time—all day, all night, all day *and* all night. He feels himself to be more creative, more productive, more brilliant, more of a high achiever. This state is a gratifying one for the competitive man who finds that he must "stay way ahead just to stay on top and stay on top just to avoid ending up at the bottom." This pressure or distortion of values existed in his mind prior to his beginning the use of a stimulating drug; however, any mind- or mood-altering chemical affects its user's perception of reality enough to exaggerate an already-existing distortion of values. High achievers who are addicted to cocaine or another stimulant find cocaine to be a drug which feeds their hunger for stimulation and for pressure. When an individual develops an addiction to this drug, *the illusion of hypercompetence it renders eventually leads to the degradation of actual competence.* Illusions of hypercompetence and actualities of hypo- or undercompetence are thus the paradoxical outcome of addiction to the neurostimulant. For these men, many of them otherwise "emancipated," addiction is dependence, and dependence renders the dangerous illusion of power.

The American Dream of wealth and success has been pursued by millions of men in search of the good life. They've taken *all the right steps* to achieve success. Men led the way. They suffered the earliest scars. They opened the first doors to the dream. (The women's movement made it possible for many women to follow.)

Tragically, some men, upon achieving something which approximates the American Dream, find it to be a waking nightmare. They find that a lifetime spent striving to achieve the American Dream, whether or not they achieve it, can be a very hollow, mechanizing experience. Values become distorted or dissolve altogether. Disillusionment sets in. The dream made a lot of promises. It told men that they could demonstrate their manhood by throwing themselves into some all-American dollar-oriented effort. (It told women that they could gain the economic and social power of men by pursuing the American Dream that was once virtually restricted to males.) The dream has fostered materialistic goals and materialistic rewards. Unfortunately, the dream has been betraying men (and now women, too). Materials do not satisfy the soul or fill the heart with love. More cars, more houses, more income—more status. None of these things necessarily mean more happiness. Eventually, the pressure to acquire material wealth results in spiritual pain. And all too often, the response is to drug the pain.

The Chemically Dependent Male Adolescent

From a young age, too many men are socialized to "keep a stiff upper lip"—to demonstrate their manhood and so-called "strength" by refusing to show or even feel hurt, sad, or weak, even in the face of great pain or great failure. It comes as no surprise that even adolescent males have difficulty getting in touch with and expressing their emotions. They have learned to suppress them. Men are brave, strong, stoic. Chemically dependent male adolescents can get stuck in their adolescent notions and hang onto them into adulthood.

The Coaddicted Husband of an Addict

Similar to the coaddicted wife of an addict, a man who feels dependent upon his addicted mate may become dependent on the fact that she is addicted. The man's self-image becomes dependent upon his feelings of being his wife's keeper, caretaker, father, or guardian. She needs him and he is her *rescuer*. Occasionally, men in this situation follow their mates into actual chemical dependence. More often, the man becomes highly addicted to his role in the relationship and to his mate's addiction—a chemical dependence one step removed. He may remain addicted to his mate's addiction even if he ceases his own drug use. He may remain addicted to his mate even if she ceases her own drug use, as long as she does not upset the balance of power by changing, by outgrowing the need for a caretaker. If this sounds similar to the reverse situation described in the earlier section on women and drugs, it is because coaddiction has no bias or preference as to gender.

The Chemically Dependent Single Male

In my discussion of women's paths to chemical dependence, I commented that for women, the single or "unattached" life has gained greater respect and has become more alluring in recent years. For men, single life has been more socially acceptable, but it has nevertheless been a mixed blessing. In the case of men who use drugs, there is the potential among single men that they will "marry" a chemical—become addicted to drugs in place of having a close interpersonal relationship. On the other hand, just as their female counterparts, many young single men feel pressure to use drugs in order to "fit in with the crowd." Either way, young single men can be trapped into using drugs: with the crowd as a result of social pressure, without the crowd as a result of loneliness. Frequently, the chemically dependent single male is one who has carried adolescent chemical dependence into adulthood.

The Chemically Dependent Husband of a Social User

This situation is thought of as being more common than the reverse situation described in the earlier section on women and drugs. Some men begin drinking or drugging socially with their mates but are unable to stop at this level of use. They eventually develop an addiction to a chemical substance. Men in this situation have mates who do not become addicted but continue to use the problem substance socially. The women often defend their unhelpful social drugging and drinking behavior by saying, "I'm not going to give up my lifestyle just because he couldn't handle it and got hooked."

The Chemically Dependent Man Married to a Nonuser

Similar to some women, some men bring the drug-using behaviors that they developed while single into their married lives. Others respond to work, social and male ego pressures, or difficult marriages by "making friends with chemicals" while married. Wives of such men report feeling that their husbands had taken on lovers. Drugs can be demanding mistresses.

The Chemically Dependent Man Working in a Competitive System

Competition is stimulating. It brings out some of the best qualities in the participants. Unfortunately, it also can cause injury to self-esteem among losers and to peace of mind among all players. Our vigorous economic system is built upon competitive individualism. Men have built this system and must participate in it to survive. The drive to survive is whetted by the drive to achieve, to win. The pressure is great. It is not surprising that the male human organism drugs itself to cope with this pressure.

The Chemically Dependent Man Substituting Working for Healing

When the achievement-oriented man experiences a "drug problem," he may or may not realize what he is experiencing. In response to the vague sensation that something is wrong or to the stark realization that he is addicted, he dives deeper into an intense work schedule, putting his healing processes on the back burner. But working is no substitute for healing. The two are compatible, but workaholism tends to emerge as an avoidance behavior. Its victims think they are getting well when they are merely substituting or mixing together their addictions.

Experiencing the Buried Anguish of Not Achieving the American Dream

On some level, perhaps a subconscious one, the American ideal will always haunt American men. The anguish of not achieving this heavy personal and societal expectation—or not achieving as much of it as possible—is deeply rooted. Men have to work very hard to regain their trust in a world that seems to have caused them so much damage. Finding a place even to begin the renegotiation of trust is frightening. It's like scaling a very smooth, very high vertical cliff.

CHEMICAL DEPENDENCE AND GENDER IN THE WORKPLACE

Gender differences come, with their attending double standards, to the workplace. [2] Despite indications that women's rate of alcohol consumption is increasing, a long-term double standard continues to exist. Intoxicated women are viewed as more undesirable and less tolerable than intoxicated men. [3] Society's greater disapproval and denial of women alcoholics has resulted in a lower social awareness of women's drinking problems. Women often become "hidden drinkers," for they tend to drink at home and alone more often than men. Women who have trouble with alcohol and other drugs are frequently protected by other women and by men in the workplace. This so-called protection from discovery, stigma, and reprisal is achieved by ignoring or excusing a woman's symptoms. And because of society's intolerance of female addicts and alcoholics, women themselves are often afraid to admit that they have drug problems.

Gender Issues in Identification and Referral

It is, therefore, more difficult to identify female employees with drug problems during the early stages of their addiction. Early detection, however, is especially important for women because they are more likely than men to follow a pattern of "telescoped" development. Especially in the case of alcohol, it has been shown that drinking alcoholically will impair a woman's health more quickly than it will a man's. [4] Fortunately, since working women are more visible than many isolated, housebound women, earlier detection may be possible for them in the workplace. Although women may be more hesitant than men to acknowledge their chemical dependence problems, they are generally more willing than men to seek help for other personal (marital and family) problems. Routine, subtle questioning on the part of an employee assistance or human resource counselor often reveals the abuse of alcohol or other drugs. [5]

Workplace- or employer-sponsored counselors should explore women's general life crises with them and use these problems as smoother approaches to drinking and other drugging problems. This strategy may result in a higher entry into treatment of women who may not respond to coercion as readily as their male co-workers. Employee assistance and other counselors can play an important role in the identification and treatment of women alcoholics. They must, however, modify their outreach, intervention, and referral services, which were developed when men were the workplace majority and thus the overwhelming majority of chemically dependent people identified at work. This modification should be a programmatic expansion to better meet women's needs. Employee assistance programs should attempt to match treatment referrals with the specific needs of male and female employees. Child care and other family responsibilities must be taken into account. No man or woman is an island. Especially in the case of female employees, referral for treatment must take into account the employee's other full-time job: family management.

Sex-Role Socialization Pressure

The cultural norms by which we all live are norms which dictate sex roles as well as other cultural roles. The power hierarchies in our society and especially in our workplace are ordained and elaborated by traditional sex-role socialization. Social norms defining gender-based behavior are perpetuated in the work environment; they are reflected in the numbers of women who continue to assume traditional occupational roles.

One's maleness or femaleness carries with it both covert and overt directives regarding how powerful, competent, and autonomous or powerless, incompetent, and subordinate or dependent one is allowed and expected to be. Females who try to assume both male and female role expectations in and out of the workplace, by being an employee and a good wife and mother, experience enormous pressure to correct the socialized self. Again and again they clash with tradition and with their own brainwashing. Having to shift between vastly different functional capacities and the accompanying behaviors can indeed produce powerful desires to use drugs to help ease the pressure and smooth the shift. [6] A female drug user who is employed outside the home may drug herself more and more to rectify the extreme polarizations of behavior and self-experience that she does not comfortably juggle and maintain. The more women are likely to use drugs, the more likely they are to abuse drugs.

Woman's Work Is Never Done

The old adage that a woman's work is never done is more true now than ever before. Women's employment patterns and economic situations differ radically from those of men. Women continue to be concentrated in lower-paying jobs and in positions that are largely nonunionized. They are more likely to work part-time or intermittently, so that they often enjoy fewer health care and other benefits. If a woman is employed in a lower-paying position, she is also more likely to be without many of the conveniences that accompany higher earnings, from an automobile to a housekeeper to a dishwasher.

Confused Supervisory Roles

Those who work with chemically dependent and other drug-abusing men and women in workplace settings experience many gender-related pressures and confusions in their work. For example, confidentiality is the single largest reason cited for the underuse of employee assistance programs by both men and women. However, because a woman may be seen to be risking far greater loss than many of her male counterparts if her cover is blown, efforts to protect her, to deny or cover up her condition, and to keep it a secret may be doubled. [7] Supervisors risk being caught within a web of addictive denial that an addicted worker and his or her co-workers may attempt to spin around himself or herself. [8] This web may be more complex and/or less detectable when the addicted employee is a female. The roles assumed by supervisors acting upon the requirements of occupational intervention programs can be messy and undesirable when they take the form of watchdog, nursemaid, or ruthless threatener of a "poor and sick" alcoholic worker. These roles become all the more complicated if the supervisor and the worker are of the opposite sex.

In American business and industry the vast majority of men who go into treatment do so as a result of referrals emanating from managers and supervisors. For women, this is not the case; most are self-referred. [9] One implication of this fact is that males in a dominant position over females are not successful in confronting these females through the documentation of poor job performance which might begin the intervention process. The reasons offered to account for this lack of success are numerous and varied. An extreme explanation is that women are so underemployed, and there is so little use of their brainpower on the job, that it is relatively easy for them to be drugged day in and day out and still not turn in a markedly poor performance. Another explanation which has been tendered is that a male manager cannot adequately document deteriorating job performance when he never took that performance seriously in the first place. This view echoes the notion that women continue to be undervalued in society and in the workplace, and that, even if they are found to be in trouble with drugs they are not worth the time or money necessary to direct them into treatment. Yet another explanation has been offered by male managers I have interviewed: "Because female employees are protected from harassment and prejudice in the workplace by law, managers are loath to get into performance criticism of them."

It is extremely difficult for a manager or supervisor to come to grips with job deterioration in any employee, male or female. [10] Until job deterioration becomes flagrant, most look the other way, pretending not to see it or that it isn't so. Such is the nature of coaddiction, a term which describes the hampering of the detection and honest assessment of a person's drug use when one is involved with him or her in a relationship of any intimacy, including that of worker and boss. [11] Research indicates that the greatest period of supervisory cover-up of chemically dependent male workers occurs from the seventh through the eleventh year of their condition. [12] We must ask how much more engulfed by a chemically dependent person's denial system managers and supervisors are when there are gender-linked issues and roles clouding their already obscured perceptions about addiction.

What further complicates the manager's intervention is the observation that the addicted woman at work is more adept at hiding her condition than her male counterpart. [13] She may learn to manipulate the double stigma of being a woman and an addict. Some research findings suggest that male supervisors are less likely to confront any of their female subordinates because their female secretaries have in many cases become their "office wives." Extending this relationship to other female employees, male bosses may feel somewhat responsible for all of them. [14] This "chivalry" can lead to the male supervisor's feeling self-blame for the drugging behavior of a female subordinate, and thus to his being unwilling to admit that she may have a problem with alcohol or another drug. Thus the female employee would be more likely than the male to escape confrontation.

We don't have many data on whether or how much supervisors treat their subordinates differently according to gender. Perhaps the complex web of gender differences in the treatment of employee drug abuse reflects the encompassing complexities of workplace gender relations.

Supervisory training programs which include a discussion of gender issues are essential. Intraorganization campaigns which emphasize the value of self-referral and encourage the use of anonymous "hot lines" will encourage female and male employees to seek assistance on their own. The result may be an accumulation of referred cases which can generate momentum for the program on its own. Self-referrals can also perpetuate other self-referrals, as news about the availability, effectiveness, equity, and confidentiality of services is diffused through the workplace grapevine.

MEN AND WOMEN WHO FAIL TO THRIVE

Workplace training or counseling programs which focus on the pitfalls and rewards of worklife and male–female differences in the worklife experience can be of great help to employees. In the new era of what we like to call sexual equality, we see that women can achieve the same type of drive, stress, pressure, self-abuse, and addiction as men. This is all tied to the daze, the dream state in which women now can enroll along with men. Now women can and do fail at the American Dream just as men do. The tension between the drives to be the once socially acceptable "dependent" female and to become the economically powerful counterpart of the successful male generates addictive tendencies. If men fail at the American Dream, they risk dependence. If women fail at the new dream of independence, they risk falling back into dependence. Drug addiction is an obvious expression of dependence. It undermines the independence of the addicted person. Addiction drags everyone into a dependent state.

What, Me Worried?
Worklife Stress

Imagine signs posted around *your* workplace that say, "Caution: Working may be hazardous to your health." Assume, for a moment, that such signs are posted in all workplaces. Perhaps these imaginary signs target specific aspects of employee health, reading this way: "Warning: Working here may result in substance abuse and drug addiction, severe psychological stress, divorce, and various physical injuries and illnesses." Would you continue to work?

Chances are that you would stay on the job, being economically dependent upon the income derived from it. Employed people do not feel that they have much choice in the matter of work. This is something that they must do. This sense of "not having much choice" about whether or not to work, about the hours and days of the working week, about the commute required to get to and from work, and even about one's type of work is an inherent and ongoing source of stress for working people.

What is this thing we call work? There is a strong moral element behind the feeling that we must work. Work is something that we believe that people should do. In addition to being essential to economic survival, work is a socially approved use of human time. Work has traditionally been viewed as something which develops the capabilities, confidence, and self-esteem which serve as the basis for a stable family life and responsible citizenship. The capacity to obtain and hold a "good job" is the traditional test of participation in American society. Steady employment leads not only to purchasing power but to social status.

Most adults spend a significant portion of their lives, at least forty hours a week when employed full-time, in their workplace. Many never have the luxury of questioning the value of such activity, and many of those who dare to question merely make themselves very unhappy. There is an eerie security in our acceptance of or resignation to the modern social dictum that one must and should work.

Work is so taken for granted that we rarely think about its definition. Work has been described as both a right and a privilege. Its alternatives are usually viewed as being welfare and poverty. If we turn to the dictionary, we read that *work* is "exertion" or "effort to produce or accomplish something," and that *work* is synonymous with *labor*, *drudgery*, and *toil*. The dictionary may even go on to note that work is the opposite of play and/or rest.

Some people who enjoy their work will say that work is fun or that work is play. Very few call it restful, but I have even heard this said: "I can't wait to get back to work on Monday. It gets me away from the chaos and demands of my family life. I can relax and focus on one thing at a time in a quiet office away from home."

THE HIGH COST OF EMPLOYEES' MENTAL AND PHYSICAL HEALTH PROBLEMS

Although every employee's experience of work is different, there is an increasing appreciation of the fact that many employees either bring their own emotional problems to work or develop work-related mental health problems at work. Whether or not these take the form of chemical dependence, these problems can cost employers in terms of high absenteeism, tardiness, and turnover rates; wasted training costs; work slowdowns; comeback or defective work; and generally low productivity. The overwhelming majority of industrial accidents are attributed to personal factors. At least one-third of all employee absenteeism may be attributable to emotional problems. People are not machines or robots; they have feelings. This fact must be taken into account when we employ them in the workplace. Just as maintenance expenses are a given when machinery and robotics are used, mental health benefits and employee assistance expenses should be viewed as a given when people do the work. Industry's dependence on human productivity, while highly desirable, is very expensive.

Employers are paying for this predicament. The number of mental stress injuries being reported to workers' compensation boards is increasing rapidly. The National Council on Compensation Insurance reported that mental stress claims first appeared in the late 1970s and have increased on an annual basis. Today, the average stress claimant is approximately thirty-eight years old, while other claimants are about forty-one years of age. It is expected that this age gap will continue to widen. [1] Insurers and employers are wary of this age difference. This wariness may stem from the fact that while older workers are increasingly susceptible to physical injury and illness, younger workers are either increasingly prone to mental stress or are increasingly willing to point the finger at their working conditions as the cause of that stress and then to report stress as an on-the-job injury.

Technostress

The National Institute for Occupational Safety and Health has put psychological disorders on its list of leading work-related illnesses and has made one of its primary objectives to reduce stress in high-tech offices. [2] As this type of high-tech work-place becomes the typical workplace of the future, employee technostress will proliferate, and related claims may as well. Technostress illnesses represent an exceedingly expensive de-velopment for employers in the not-so-distant future.

Gender-Related Stress

There are other areas in which stressful problems experi-enced by employees on their jobs are costing employers. With an estimated 42% to 90% of the ever-growing female workforce experiencing verbal or physical conduct of a sexual nature which is directed at them while they are performing their duties in their workplaces, sexual harassment suits have proliferated. Related suits have reached the size of $200,000 in damages, paid by a corporation to an individual who has been sexually ha-rassed. [3]

General Mental Illness

Whatever the case may be, the overall cost of mental illness in the United States is growing at an alarming rate. Insurance companies are evidencing this trend. For example, hospital charges for treating mental illness totaled 9.5% of Metropolitan Life Insurance Company claims payments in 1985, up 3% from 1984. In the first three years of the 1980s, the economic cost of mental illness in this country more than tripled, according to the federal Alcohol, Drug Abuse and Mental Health Administra-tion. Metropolitan Life evidences this expense in its report, based on 1985 claims data, that the average cost of inpatient treatment for mental disorders was four times the average for all medical diagnoses, and that the average length of stay for inpa-tient treatment of mental disorders was four times that of all medical diagnoses. [4]

Mental health, while inextricably linked to physical health, is difficult to diagnose, and its onset and termination are often vague and almost impossible to pinpoint. These complicating factors make controlling the cost of mental health treatment all the more difficult. As a result, many employers are seeking cost control through prevention methods, such as health and fitness programs for existing employees and preemployment screening for emotional vulnerability in potential employees.

Chemical Dependence

Addiction treatment is an area that is costing employers and insurers an almost unfathomable amount in treatment dollars and in lost productivity. This cost was discussed in Chapters 2 and 10. In review, recall that drug and alcohol abuse costs employers over $100 billion a year in the form of absenteeism, accidents, turnover, waste, and health care expenditures. [5] Some one in six employees misuse alcohol and other drugs, and some 10% to 25% of all employees in the United States use drugs that are considered in some way harmful on the job. [6] Extensive employee drug and alcohol use escalates not only employers' expenditures on addiction treatment but also employers' general level of expenditure on health care costs. Employees who are addicted to drugs and/or alcohol cost employers a minimum of three times more than other employees in terms of their utilization of general sickness and accident benefits. [7]

Although its costs are somewhat more measurable, it is not only the addictive use of alcohol and drugs that affects employee productivity. For instance, recent studies of social drinking indicate that alcohol-related effects are not limited to alcoholics. A team of researchers that recently published its findings in the *American Journal of Public Health* (1987) reported that many social drinkers exhibit sober-state depression and decreased cognitive functioning. [8] While these symptoms increase as the amount of alcohol consumed increases, addiction to alcohol does not necessarily have to be present for productivity to be decreased among employees who drink alcohol. Unfortunately, the costs of social drinking are almost impossible to determine and nearly impossible to discuss. This is a highly controversial area, in which the rights of drinking and nondrinking employees are at risk and at odds. I will return to this issue in the next chapter.

A HISTORICAL PERSPECTIVE

Employee assistance programs began as industrial alcoholism programs. These programs were, in turn, preceded by informal arrangements between occupational physicians and members of Alcoholics Anonymous.

The phrase "employee assistance" was coined by the federal government when it funded the development of employee assistance programs in the early 1970s. At present, there are 9,000 to 12,000 employee assistance programs in the United States, representing a dramatic increase during this quarter of the century. [9] There are also many other current efforts on the part of employers to assist their employees. These programs either have not yet been labeled or have been given other names.

Although occupational alcoholism was the original focus of and inspiration for employee assistance, its scope has clearly broadened as a result of economic and social trends. Consider the simple extension of employee assistance from the treatment of alcohol problems to include the treatment of other drug problems.

Today, cocaine, marijuana, legal prescription and over-the-counter drugs, and even nicotine have been added to the list of drugs to which employees become addicted. Some workplaces fall prey to the drug use trends in the communities surrounding them. Other workplaces actually serve as breeding grounds for drug abuse and addiction. I recall consulting with a company in which an estimated 75% of all employees were using cocaine, at least one-third of these users doing so on the job. One male employee came to me privately, in tears: "I have no friends here at work, because I won't drink with that group and I won't coke (use cocaine) with this group. It's very lonely here. I'm a good worker but I hate coming to work." In another plant, I was brought in to interview employees about a suspected "drug problem." Three of the employees reported to me, anonymously despite a complete guarantee of their confidentiality, that they knew that "major drug deals" were being conducted on company grounds and that they knew "the guys who were doing it." They explained that they were not able to come forward and name the drug dealers because they had been threatened with death for talking. In these and many other situations, employee assistance must respond not only to the suffering inherent in alcohol and other drug addiction, but also to the needs of non-using employees who work in environments where addiction problems exist.

THE NEXT STEPS

Employee assistance must offer and already is offering drug-using and nonusing employees a range of services and training in the areas of health and mental health. These must go beyond mandated drug awareness training programs to include direct methods of stress reduction as well as educational programs aimed at improving the general mental health of employees, such as parenting and child care, smoking cessation, sexuality, AIDS prevention, loss and bereavement, and retirement classes. Employee assistance has already extended far beyond the problems of drug and alcohol addiction. As reported by the 1988 *Human Resources Yearbook,* the nationwide employee-assistance-program caseload consists of only an estimated 15% alcohol and other drug cases, while also carrying 40% family and marital cases, 20% emotional problems, and 25% other types of cases, including legal, financial, and physical cases. [10] Of course, many alcohol and drug problems are never reported to employee assistance programs.

Addressing the Needs of an Aging Workforce

In order to imagine how employee assistance aimed at reducing employee alcohol and drug use, as well as other problems, must evolve, consider the important demands that an aging workforce will place on employee assistance programs. As the median age of the American employee continues to increase, employee assistance must adapt to the needs of an older workforce. [11] Health education will become all the more critical: Older workers exhibit poorer health habits than their younger counterparts, in that they smoke more, exercise less, and practice prevention less. As employees retire at older ages, employee assistance must adapt to the needs of a workforce that spans more years. Older workers exhibit their own special morale problems while offering their own special wisdom in their working environment. Relationships between age groups in the workplace will become increasingly important. Expanded retirement counseling will also be in demand.

Recognizing New Occupational Hazards

Consider the pressure that new occupational hazards will place on employee assistance. As we continue to manufacture new products, there will be new occupational hazards in their production. Employee assistance will be faced with growing concerns among employees about the health-threatening chemical exposure that they face on their jobs. These present an emerging form of work-related mental stress that we must be prepared to address. As employees learn that many working environments contain hazards to their physical health, they also learn that all too often these hazards go undetected for years. For example, the electronics and computer industry was heralded as a clean industry for years until Silicon Valley and other high-tech-concentration areas found contaminants in the water supply that had seeped out of storage from clean industry tanks. During the mid-1970s in California, it was found that the occupational illness rate for semiconductor workers was about three times that for employees in general manufacturing. [12] This type of experience affects employee mental health as employees wonder what other as-yet-unrecognized hazards they face on a daily basis. This sort of diminished morale takes a bite out of productivity.

We have learned that many employees who work with certain workplace chemicals actually experience highs and lows similar to those experienced by drug users. Thus, the costly effects of diminished capacity on the job under the influence of drugs and alcohol may also be present in cases of exposure to mind-altering workplace chemicals.

The Future of Employee Assistance

These are but some of the newer areas for employee assistance. Whether they offer a limited or a broad range of services, companies are reporting that the longer their employee assistance programs are in place, the greater are their benefit-to-cost ratios. Many companies calculate that the programs are highly cost-effective, returning from three to twenty dollars for each dollar spent on the program. Yet, there are numerous additional effects that are hard to quantify. The increased well-being of employees and their families and communities will remain a good outcome that can never be fully measured. This will continue to be true long into the future, when we have established worksites and entire company towns on the sea, under the sea, at space stations, and even on the moon. Employee assistance programs can serve as one, if not the major, catchment area for chemical dependence and other health and mental health problems of the population at large, especially when these programs are expanded to include families as well as employees.

Employee assistance programs must evolve rapidly in order to keep up with employees' needs in our rapidly changing organizational, technical, emotional, and economic environments. Prevention and education programs must be offered by employee assistance in order to avert large-scale and ever-increasing demands for addiction, mental health, and physical health treatment. Employee assistance must be the bridge between employee productivity and employee well-being, vigilantly balancing these oppositional *and* synergistic conditions.

The Choicepoint
Undrugging Ourselves

We are at a critical choicepoint in human evolution. We squirm with discomfort, in faint recognition of this landmark, and then we look away, denial being so soothing. Population, urbanization, institutionalization, mechanization, globalization, and other modern pressures are bringing about a profound change in the life of the individual. Depersonalization and dehumanization are encroaching upon us. Even if she or he does not see it or believe it, the individual human is receding in the face of the technological collective. More than ever before, we are members of a large species which swarms the globe. We are soldiers, drones in the army of change. We are the new working-class heroes. We each do our part to help build the mirage of progress, to manifest what we believe is the human destiny. We participate, we cooperate, because this gives our lives meaning. We are good at taking orders, especially implicit ones which are difficult to question. As we become increasingly committed to our individual roles in the development of an increasingly global social order, we must be certain to remain highly conscious, to recognize the subtle trade-offs that we are making. Many of the desired outcomes of modernization are beneficial; however, we must ask ourselves if we are willing to pay their price.

It is important to pay attention at all times, to shake off our daze, and never to look away. In this way we will be able to override the specific evolutionary developments which make it increasingly difficult to pay and to want to pay attention. Consider some of the undesirable futures depicted by science fiction writers. How close have we already come to these fictionally depicted means of mind and social control? In Yevgeny Ivanovich Zamyatin's book, *We*, workers live in glass houses, have numbers rather than names, wear identical uniforms, eat chemical foods, and have their sex rationed by the government. The "single state" depicted in the anti-Utopian *We* uses an operation resembling a lobotomy on workers to control them. In our culture, we are not subjected to surgical lobotomies; however, we do use drugs, television, and our denial mechanisms to lie to and "control" ourselves and our feelings. In George Orwell's *1984*, torture and brainwashing are relied upon to keep the masses in line. In our nonfictional 1980s and 1990s, we don't need to use torture when we are so adept at cultural brainwashing. Aldous Huxley's *Brave New World* depends upon artificial biological selection and drugs to control the masses. In our real-life brave new world, we are close to performing conception in a jar, and genetic engineering is upon us. But, the most shocking is that our government does not need to drug us. We willingly do this to ourselves. Social control is most expedient when the subjects participate voluntarily and, better yet, when they do so unbeknownst to themselves.

The atrocities of *Brave New World* are not restricted entirely to fiction. Only centuries ago, in the early 1500s, Spanish conquistadores conquered the Inca empire of what is now called South America. In so doing, they assumed control over the Incas' coca leaves. They changed the use of the coca leaf, which is the source of the modern drug cocaine, from a cherished right to a form of social control. The Spaniards gave coca quite liberally to the Indians in order to enslave them. Under the influence of coca, the Indians were able to work harder, longer, with less food, and with less awareness of their misery. [1] Similar to what happens in fictional accounts of futuristic controlled societies, in this culture of the past, tucked away neatly in history, the Indians were drugged by their "employers" to work.

We tell ourselves that the use of drugs for social control cannot happen now; we have come too far. Yet, drugs have been used and are being used to control people in modern times. During the 1970s, I worked in an institution for homeless and disturbed children and adolescents which, along with many of its competitor institutions, placed over 90% of all children admitted, whether exhibiting psychological problems or not, on psychoactive drugs, and 50% of them on Thorazine and Mellaril. Young staff, myself included, in training, but uncredentialed, were expected to administer these pills between 4 P.M. and 8 A.M. and on weekends and holidays. Some staff, having failed to distribute the pills, took the leftovers home and used them. Others blatantly refused to feed the pills to the children, convinced that the children were being needlessly drugged, and lost their jobs. These staff felt that drugs were being abused by those who prescribed them to children who did not need them, in order to control them and hire fewer people to care for them. The economic and often inhumane aspects of prescribed psychoactives for incarcerated persons are obvious: short of chains, bars, and straitjackets, drugs are thought to be the least expensive way to manage a large number of seemingly unmanageable people.

Let's take this examination of people management—crowd control—a step further. The administration of drugs is less expensive and seemingly less immoral than the use of chains, bars, straitjackets, and extra staff. If the people who are being controlled will willingly drug themselves or engage in some activity that dazes their minds, it will not even be necessary to hire the staff to administer the drugs. (If we stretch the definition of drugs to include television, we see how common it is to control institutionalized youths and adults with this voluntarily ingested audiovisual tranquilizer.)

Although we are outraged by the fictional *Brave New World* concept of compulsory mass psychoactive medication in a controlled society, we calmly acquiesce to massive self-medication in our free society. We do not merely acquiesce; we insist upon trying to convince ourselves that the "drug problem" is small— that it affects only a small portion of the population—and that we are not a part of it. We tell ourselves that some drugs are acceptable while others are not. We tell ourselves that some drugs are drugs while others are not. If we are this unclear and this dishonest about alcohol, nicotine, tranquilizers, and caffeine—and sugar-, caffeine-, and stimulant-laced colas, candies, weight-loss capsules, and stay-awake pills, then we are bound to be in a deep state of denial about supposed nondrugs which drug us, such as television, computers, work, and the biggest drug of all, money. We are living in such a daze, such a largely benevolent stupor, that we do not recognize how drugged, how dulled, our minds and our senses are. We do not realize how numb and dronelike, even mechanical, we are becoming. We do not realize this, but we feel it deeply.

SHADOWBOXING DRUG ABUSE

And so we shadowbox with drug abuse, for want of greater contact with the real struggle in which we are engaged. We focus on employee drug abuse because it is dangerous and because it is expensive. This is a topic fraught with paradox, double standard, and hypocrisy. Working people at different levels of the corporate hierarchy are subjected to different rules regarding drug use. They are offered different benefit levels if they need treatment for addiction. Working-class heroes are, apparently, not viewed as having been created equal. And even if all workers and their drug use were treated equally, there would remain other inconsistencies. The boundaries of the drug problem would remain vague. These and many other questions would remain difficult to answer fairly and clearly:

- Where does the worksite end?
- Where does the workday end?
- Where do the effects of drug use begin and end?
- Which drug problems respond better to abstinence than to controlled use?
- Does a drug problem begin when someone becomes addicted, or does it begin when someone uses the drug irresponsibly? Are these problems different types of problems?
- Is there an acceptable level of use? Why is there an acceptable level of use for some drugs but not for others?

As is true of all complex social problems, an optimum solution to the ill-defined problem of drug abuse is difficult to formulate. In the preceding chapters we have, therefore, taken a journey into a dark corner of the American workplace, the corner where some working-class heroes work under the influence of some drugs. We have estimated, and have analyzed various methods of estimating, the size of the problem—the number of employees who occupy that dark corner (Chapters 2, 5, and 6). We have reviewed their physical, behavioral, and job performance symptoms (Chapter 3). We have scrutinized the individual treatment of these symptoms when and if they translate into outright addiction (Chapter 10). We have analyzed some of the problems of bringing about recovery from addiction in the workplace (Chapter 12).

We have also journeyed out of the dark corner, in hopes of gaining some perspective and shedding some light on the situation, into the dimension of denial, the world of explicit and implicit lies, in which many work organizations operate (Chapters 4 and 7). In this dimension of denial, energy which would otherwise directly support the manufacturing of the company product is siphoned off to support an elaborate denial system. It is as if the company is engaged in two businesses: the primary business that it advertises and the secondary business of denying and hiding its problems.

Somewhere amid all of the fanfare about the laudable goal of a drug-free workplace, a few quiet truths are emerging. One truth is that drug use, abuse, and addiction will linger on, perhaps in a steady state, perhaps in oscillation. The balance of use, abuse, and addiction may vary. The types of drugs which are preferred may shift. Still, the workforce will reflect, if not magnify, the proportions of drug use, abuse, and addiction that exist in the surrounding society. Employers must therefore be prepared to grapple with employee drug use, abuse, and addiction on a permanent basis.

Moreover, employers must dare to repeat out loud what so many of them feel compelled to ask only in silence, "Is there an acceptable level of drug use?" (Chapter 8). This is an honest question which deserves an honest answer. Tackling this question and defining exactly what it would mean if the answer were "yes" helps to shift us out of the dangerous dimension of denial. If all employers fire all drug-using, -abusing, and -addicted employees, we will have a significant portion of the workforce out of work, or we will have these employees resurfacing in other workplaces. I have observed the resurfacing of such employees within geographical areas and industries. It appears that many employers have decided to recycle the "drug problem" rather than to treat it. Employers must face this situation with open eyes. They must assume some responsibility for the deterioration of workforce ecology.

Drug testing is not enough. Employers will, quite logically, continue to feel compelled to identify drug-using employees (Chapter 6) in the name of workplace, consumer, and public safety. Most of all, they will feel compelled to identify employee drug use for the sake of their economic survival. However, employers will not discover and prevent all employee drug use. Working under the influence is here to stay.

Health benefits and carefully managed care for employees must weigh cost-effectiveness against treatment effectiveness. It is true that the most expensive addiction treatment is not necessarily the most effective. However, indiscriminately cutting costs on care only serves to recycle the problem. The former is throwing money at chemical dependence; the latter is denying its severity.

The drug-free workplace policy poses a beautiful model for us to aim at. I am, nevertheless, concerned about whether such a policy is realistic and whether such a policy holds us in the dangerous dimension of denial. As long as companies' drug-free workplace policies permit some drugs to be used in the workplace while prohibiting the use of others, they are not *drug-free* workplace policies. Why design a policy which undermines itself? It would be more direct to design *controlled-drug-use policies* for *controlled-using organizations*. This might be a more honest, achievable, and manageable proposition. As long as companies' drug-free workplace policies purport to make their ultimate goal a workplace entirely free of drugs, companies are explicitly denying that portions of the population will continue to be drug-using, drug-abusing, and drug-addicted, and that they will have some of this subpopulation in their employ. Companies are also explicitly denying that they actually condone particular levels and forms of drug use (Chapter 8).

The state-of-the-art workplace drug policy remains nascent (Chapter 9). It is necessary to reexamine the roles of the smallest companies and the middle-sized and largest corporations in society. As long as working may be hazardous to the health of employees (Chapter 13), employers must assume some responsibility for the mental and physical well-being of their workers. Certainly, this involves the provision of health benefits and employee assistance services, which many employers are already providing. It also involves closely examining these benefits and services for their quality. We can no longer throw benefits, services, and other interventions such as law enforcement at social problems and expect them to go away. We have learned too much from the War on Poverty of the 1960s and the War on Drugs of the 1980s. Only effective efforts will have a positive effect. We have had enough ineffective addiction treatment (Chapter 10) to know that "any old" treatment is not the answer and that the treatment of addicted individuals must be responsive to individual differences (Chapter 10). We must also understand that good addiction treatment is labor-intensive and that downtime (and television time) in treatment is not treatment. This means that effective treatment will cost more than warehousing and "dry-out" types of treatment.

We must also dare to question the whole notion of individualized treatment. I prefer to see addicted employees treated in the workplace. I prefer that we treat the "drug problem" in the workplace. And I do not mean behind closed doors. And I do not mean that only some employees be involved. Our separation from what we call the drug problem is a denial of our coinvolvement.

The very dimension of denial in which we live and work is a drug, a drug to which we are all addicted. It is in this dimension that we all continue to work dazed. It is in this dimension that drugs not only pervade the workplace, drugs *are* the workplace: Our jobs in the primary business of the workplace (the production of the company product) and our roles in the secondary business of the workplace (the production of company denial) become our drugs.

This does not mean that we should not have jobs, or that we should not work hard at these jobs. It does mean that we must radically restructure worklife and radically redefine "job," and that we must reform and make explicit the secondary business of our companies. Where do we begin? We begin by making admissions regarding the anatomy of our drug-using organizations. This means that:

- We must admit that companies are drug-using organizations rather than organizations that have some drug-using members.
- We must see that companies are controlled-use organizations and that they respond negatively to uncontrolled use or, better stated, to employee drug use which they do not control.
- We must carefully and painstakingly ask employers to notice under what conditions they prefer that their employees work controllably dazed; for example, is a certain degree of mindlessness useful in assembly lines, data entry houses, factory maintenance, farm labor, board meetings, exposure to toxic chemicals, and sales of undesirable and unhealthy products.
- We must recognize that companies choose not to admit to the above and therefore sustain an elaborate web of denial.
- The acceptance rather than the denial of the possibility of present and future employee drug use is essential. An atmosphere of acceptance will not encourage employee drug use; however, it will encourage the open admission of such use and open communication about such use.
- Acceptable use must be clearly and explicitly defined.
- Specific levels of specific drugs in the bodies of employees engaged in specific occupations can be defined; however, more regular tests of general fine and gross motor coordination, reaction time, mental organization, and task performance must be administered to provide regular monitoring (but not policing) of potential job performance problems. Checking in at work must take on a new dimension. Fitness for duty must become an issue larger than whether or not drugs are present in an employee's system. We must come to see that drug use is only one of many behaviors that affect job performance. Even if there were no drug use, there would still be performance problems at work.

The workplace performance of individuals must be addressed first by examining the performance of companies in society. After all, *society is the workplace of the company*. Here are a few philosophical suggestions:

- Companies are the mainstay of the economy.
- Companies are critical building blocks of society: Changing companies will, therefore, change society.
- Companies must be people-changing organizations in that they not only sell their products to consumers but sell their goals to their employees and the consumers of their products.
- People-changing is a deep and multilevel process with ethical ramifications and must be treated as such.
- People-changing organizations must be run by people who are changing.
- Change must be sold to all participants in the organizational system.
- Selling change involves selling methods of change, energy for change, and a belief in change. This requires the development of excellent communication skills in the workplace and in the marketplace. Clear definitions of job performance and product quality must be communicated to everyone involved.
- Employers should view themselves as competing for employees, as competing to sell employees on their organizations and the change processes within their organizations.

CONSUMER MONITORING

Although employers and employees have been the focus of this book, consumers have a great deal of opportunity to encourage change in the workplaces which produce the goods and services that they consume. Unfortunately, consumers feel relatively powerless when they must purchase something that they need or believe that they need. However, if each of us, as often as is humanly possible, demands to speak to the pilot of our airplane and to know whether the pilot has used a drug in the past seventy-two hours and, if so, which one; refuses to go under anesthesia without a discussion with our anesthesiologist and surgeon regarding their daily drug uses and states of mind; refuses to send our children to school until we make the bus drivers' and teachers' drug-using behaviors a matter of public record and continuous discussion; visits the factories where our medicines are manufactured and interviews its employees; and refuses to eat in a restaurant without meeting the cook and assessing for ourselves whether he or she is working dazed—*we will have more say in the quality of whatever it is we purchase than we do now.* And if we learn to examine ourselves for indications that we are working dazed as a result of drugs or mind-drugging activities, we will be more likely to recognize these indications in others. Awareness is the best defense. Awareness is our responsibility.

BRAVE NEW WORKPLACE

The bravest new workplaces will invite such consumer examination. Workplaces are treated like temples in the religion of commerce and money, but there is nothing very spiritual about them. Instead, we find that many companies are a spiritual wasteland full of dazed workers who work at jobs that have little or no meaning to them because they feel that they have no choice. Why not work dazed? Why not self-administer social control on a voluntary basis?

The bravest new workplaces will stop focusing on the "drug problem" as the actual problem, for it is a problem far greater than drug use that we are facing. This is the problem of the evolution of the human species. Because the prime of life is spent in the workplace, the workplace is one, if not the main, catchment area for the growing malaise of the species.

SYNAPTIC RIGHTS

Our malaise is one of decreasing spiritual and intellectual freedom. Our mental territories are being subtly but powerfully restricted—jailed by invisible bars. Does an individual have a right to the biochemical control of his or her own biology? Does he or she have a right to choose the mental chemistry which dictates his or her thoughts? I hope so.

What does it mean to our individual human minds when we relinquish the right to choose our own mental chemistries? To answer this question we must first understand something about mental chemistry.

The functioning of the brain is based upon the activity at the "synapse" (the gap between brain cells) where the electrical impulse within a cell triggers the release of a neurotransmitter which triggers electrical activity in the next cell. Theory holds that when an individual takes a drug—say, a tranquilizer or a stimulant—its metabolite (see Chapter 6) binds with receptors in the brain and deceives the body by telling it that there is a sufficient or even overabundant amount of its natural (in-body) counterpart. The natural production of the natural counterpart eventually decreases or ceases. When the artificial neurotransmitter is withdrawn, the shortage of natural neurotransmitter is felt, and withdrawal symptoms appear. It has been suggested that prolonged use of drugs may produce a chronic or permanent imbalance in some natural neurotransmitters. It has also been suggested that some addicts self-medicate with drugs in response to natural, preexisting biochemical deficiencies. This deficiency may be the physiological basis of an addictive personality. When we say that someone is addicted to a feeling such as stress, we may be referring to the body's ability to change its mental chemistry without drugs and to become addicted to particular states of mind.

Whatever the individual's motivation for or method of tampering with the synapse, which is the site of the crucial conducting of messages from one brain cell to the next, the synapse remains her or his own. And any social regulation of this very private, molecular, inner transaction may be viewed as a transgression. The individual should have freedom of choice between using only her or his internal and natural neurotransmitters and using other external and artificial chemicals—drugs—at her or his synapses. The individual should retain control over her or his own state of mind.

At what point should this individual choice be regulated by outsiders? When the welfare of the outsiders is threatened by this choice. How should this choice be regulated by outsiders? Several earlier civilizations chose to make drug use a sacred right, a spiritual privilege. Today, we are confused about our motivations for drug use. Nevertheless, as long as the privilege of drug use is abused—and working on the job under a dangerous level of influence *is* abuse—outside regulation is, quite sadly for the entire human species, necessary.

Notes

CHAPTER 1

1. I further specify these requirements in Chapter 9. See U.S. Congress (1988), 41 U.S.C., Sec. 701 et seq., "Drug Free Workplace Act of 1988," which became effective March 18, 1989; and National Institute on Drug Abuse (1990), "A New Horizon: Drug Free Workplace Goals Can Help Eliminate the Problem of Drugs," *Employee Assistance*, Vol. 2, No. 8, March, pp. 16, 23; see also Department of Alcohol and Drug Programs (1989), *ADP Research and Activity Memorandum*, Vol. 8, No. 5, December. Sacramento, CA: State of California, Health and Welfare Agency, p. 3.
2. National Institute on Drug Abuse (1990), ibid., pp. 16, 23.

CHAPTER 2

1. Shedler, J. and J. Black (1990), "Adolescent Drug Use and Psychological Health," *American Psychologist*, Vol. 45, No. 5, pp. 612–630.
2. Parachini, A. (1988), "Grim Report on Mental Illness," *San Francisco Chronicle*, November 2, p. A9.
3. Williams, G. D. et al. (1989), "Population Projections Using DSM-III Criteria: Alcohol Abuse and Dependence, 1990–2000," *Alcohol Health and Research World*, Vol. 13, No. 4, p. 366 of 366–370.
4. Ibid.
5. National Institute of Justice (1990), "DUF: 1988 Drug Use Forecasting Annual Report," *Research in Action*. Washington, DC: U.S. Department of Justice, U.S. Government, pp. 10–11.

6. Ibid., p. 10.
7. Whitman, D. (1990), "The Streets Are Filled with Coke," *U.S. News,* March 5, pp. 24–26: and National Institute on Drug Abuse (1989–1990), "AIDS Research," *NIDA Notes.* Washington, DC: U.S. Department of Health and Human Services, ADAMHA, pp. 16–17.
8. Associated Press (1989), "Ice Drug Now Used at Work, Officials Say," *San Francisco Chronicle,* October 25, p. B7.
9. Browne, A. (1986), "Drug and Alcohol Use among Employees: Critical Issues," *Employee Assistance Quarterly,* Vol. 2, No. 1, pp. 11–22.
10. Ibid.; American Public Health Association (1987), "APHA Petitions OSHA to Ban Smoking in the Workplace," *The Nation's Health,* July, pp. 1, 13; Association of Labor-Management Administrators and Consultants on Alcoholism (1988), "Where There's Smoke," *Santa Clara Valley ALMACA Newsletter,* November–December, pp. 1–3; Conally, Gregory (1988), excerpt from testimony on behalf of the American Public Health Association in July 1988 before the U.S. Congress Subcommittee on Health and Environment in "Tobacco and the Drug Laws," *The Nation's Health,* September, p. 7; Fielding, J. E. (1986), "Banning Worksite Smoking," *American Journal of Public Health,* Vol. 76, No. 8, pp. 957–959; Kozlowski, L. T. (1979), "Psychosocial Influences on Cigarette Smoking," in N. A. Krasner (Editor), *Research Monograph Series 26: The Behavioral Aspects of Smoking.* Washington, DC: National Institute on Drug Abuse, U. S. Government #017-024-00947-4, August.
11. Castro, Janice (1986), "Battling the Enemy Within: Companies Fight to Drive Illegal Drugs Out of the Workplace," *Time,* March 17, p. 53.
12. Wall Street Journal (1989), "Firm Debates Hard Line on Alcoholics," *Wall Street Journal,* April 13, p. 16.
13. NIDA (1989), *Drugs in the Workplace,* Research Monograph, Series 91. Washington, DC: U.S. Department of Health and Human Services.
14. Scanlon, W. F. (1986), *Alcoholism and Drug Abuse in the Workplace.* New York: Praeger, pp. 5–10; also Ruffenach, G. (1988), "Health Insurance Premiums to Soar in '89," *Wall Street Journal,* October 25, p. B1.
15. Castro (1986), op. cit., p. 53.
16. Chambers, Carl D. and Richard D. Heckman (1972), *Employee Drug Abuse.* Boston: Cahners Books; Levy, Stephen J. (1983), *Managing the*

"Drugs" in Your Life. San Francisco: McGraw-Hill; Brady, John C., II, (1985), "Substance Abuse and Treatment in Silicon Valley—A Cost Analysis, July." Milpitas, CA: Psychology Management Systems; Browne, (1986), op. cit.; Carey, P. C. (1985), "By Work Obsessed," San Jose Mercury News, February 18, p. 10; and NIDA (1989), op. cit.

17. Castro (1986), op. cit., p. 53.
18. Ibid.
19. Ibid.
20. Brady, J. C. (1985), op. cit.
21. Levy (1983), op. cit.
22. Browne (1985), op. cit.
23. Associated Press (1989), op. cit.
24. Levy (1983) op. cit.
25. Ibid.
26. Ibid.
27. Ibid.
28. California Nonsmokers' Rights Foundation (1985), "A Smokefree Workplace: An Employer's Guide to Nonsmoking Policies." Berkeley, CA: Nonsmokers' Rights Foundation; and Bureau of Business Practice (1986), "Company Smoking Policy Manual," Employee Relations and Human Resources Bulletin, August 21, Report No. 1622, Section III. Waterford, CT: Bureau of Business Practice, Prentice-Hall.
29. Orr, M. (1972), "Business and the Compulsive Drinker," Addictions, Vol. 19, pp. 39–43.
30. Browne, Angela Christine (1988), "A Survey Regarding Coworker Drug Abuse as Reported by Employed Persons in Treatment for Drug Addiction." Emeryville, CA: METATECH, unpublished.
31. Browne (1988), ibid.
32. Kaufman, Herbert (1971). The Limits of Organizational Change. Birmingham, AL: University of Alabama Press. See also Wilson Shaef, Anne and Diane Fassel (1988), The Addictive Organization. San Francisco, CA: Harper & Row.
33. Chambers and Heckman (1972), op. cit.
34. Holder, H. D. (1989), "Prevention of Alcohol Related Problems," Alcohol Health and Research World, Vol. 13, No. 4, p. 339 of 339–342; and National Institute on Alcohol Abuse and Alcoholism (1987), Sixth Report to the U.S. Congress on Alcohol and Health. DHHS Pub.

No. (ADM) 87-1519. Washington, DC: U.S. Government Printing Office.

35. Levy (1985), op. cit.
36. Ibid.
37. Ibid.
38. Bureau of Business Practice (1983), "Drugs in the Workplace: Solutions for Business and Industry." Waterford, CT: Bureau of Business Practice, Inc., Employee Relations Bulletin.

CHAPTER 5

1. Negri, S. (1990), in Business Section, *The Arizona Republic*, May 12, pp. D-1, D-6.

CHAPTER 6

1. Blenkey, N. and R. Mottley (1989), "Exxon Valdez: America's Ship of Shame," *Marine Log*, May, pp. 20–23.
2. Ibid., p. 21.
3. Schneider, E. (1978), "Aftermath of the Amoco Cadiz," *Oceans*, July, p. 58.
4. National Transportation Safety Board (1989), *Aircraft Accident Report. Trans-Colorado Airlines, Inc. Flight 2286; Fairchild Colorado, January 19, 1988*. Washington, DC: National Transportation Safety Board, U.S. Government, No. NTSB/AAR-89/01, pp. v, 2, 14–15, 20–21, 29, 34.
5. "Fighting Drugs in the Workplace" (1989), *Inc.*, January, p. 107.
6. "Test Workers for Drugs?" (1987), *Industry Week*, December 14, p. 17.
7. Lee, C. (1988), "Testing Makes a Comeback," *Training*, December 4, p. 52.
8. Gifford, B. R. (Editor) (1989), *Test Policy and the Politics of Opportunity Allocation*. Boston: Kluwer Academic Publishers, and National Commission on Testing and Public Policy, p. 3.
9. Finkle, B. S. (1989), "Technological Issues Associated with Monitor-

ing Drug Use in the Workplace," in Walsh, J. M. and S. W. Gust (Editors), *Workplace Drug Abuse Policy Consideration and Experience in the Business Community.* Washington, DC: National Institute on Drug Abuse, p. 11.

10. Finkle (1989), op. cit., p. 11.
11. Bureau of Labor Statistics (1989), "Survey of Employer Antidrug Programs," *Report 760.* Washington, DC: U.S. Department of Labor.
12. Schachter, J. (1990), "Many Job Seekers Flunk Drug Tests," *San Francisco Chronicle,* May 24, p. A3.
13. Ibid.
14. Ibid.
15. Ibid.
16. Ibid.
17. State of California Department of Alcohol and Drug Programs (1989), *ADP Research Activity Memorandum,* Vol. 8, No. 5. Sacramento: State of California Health and Welfare Agency, December, p. 5.
18. Ibid., p. 4.
19. Mazura, A. C., J. E. Tilson, and K. M. Cochran (1989), *Drug Testing in the Workplace.* Washington, DC: Bureau of National Affairs, p. 151.
20. Ibid., p. 84.
21. Ibid., p. 70.
22. State of California Department of Alcohol and Drug Programs (1989), op. cit., p. 5.
23. Alder, R. A. (1989), "Civil Liberties and Ethical Concerns," in Walsh, J. M. and S. W. Gust (Editors), *Workplace Drug Abuse Policy Consideration and Experience in the Business Community.* Washington, DC: National Institute on Drug Abuse, p. 309.
24. Finkle (1989), op. cit., p. 12.
25. Ibid., p. 13.
26. Mazura, A. C., J. E. Tilson, and K. M. Cochran (1989), "Legal Considerations: An Overview," in Mazura, Tilson, and Cochran, op. cit., p. 14.
27. Ibid.
28. Dawsey, D. (1990), "Top LAPD Officials Agree to Submit to Random Drug Tests," *Los Angeles Times,* April 14, p. 3.
29. Ibid.
30. Mazura, Tilson, and Cochran (1989), op. cit., p. 18.

31. Chiang, H. (1990), "Major Setback for Drug Tests by Employers," *San Francisco Chronicle*, March 14, pp. A1, A18.
32. Ibid.
33. Ibid.
34. Kasten, B. J. (1987), "Controlling Drugs and Alcohol in the Workplace," *1987 Functional Committee Meetings, International Bridge, Tunnel and Turnpike Association*, Washington, DC, p. 206.

CHAPTER 9

1. U.S. Congress (1988), Drug Free Workplace Act of 1988, 41 U.S. Congress, Sec. 701 et seq.
2. Bowen, O. R. (1986), in the introductory letter to National Institute on Drug Abuse, *Interdisciplinary Approaches to the Problem of Drug Abuse in the Workplace: Consensus Summary.* Washington, DC: Alcohol, Drug Abuse and Mental Health Administration, U.S. Department of Health and Human Services, DHHS Publ. No. (ADM) 86-1477, p. i.

CHAPTER 10

1. Ruffenach, G. (1988), "Health Insurance Premiums to Soar in '89," *Wall Street Journal*, October 25, p. B1.
2. Association of Labor-Management Administrators and Consultants on Alcoholism (1988), "EAP Tax-Credit Bill Introduced in Senate," *ALMACAN*, August, p. 10; Danforth, Senator John C. (1988), "Tax Credit for Employee Assistance Programs," Introduction of S. 2594, *Congressional Record*, June 29, p. S8805.
3. Ruffenach (1988), op. cit., p. B1.
4. Levin, B. L., J. H. Glasser, and C. L. Jaffee, Jr. (1988), "National Trends in Coverage and Utilization of Mental Health, Alcohol and Substance Abuse Services within Managed Care Systems," *American Journal of Public Health*, September, Vol. 78, No. 9, pp. 1222–3; Penzer, W. N. (1987), "Toward Sustaining Quality Mental Health Services," *EAP Digest*, March–April, pp. 35–40.

5. Casey, T. J. and H. M. Seigel (1982), "Health Care Cost Containment: Compensation and Benefits," *Personnel Journal*, June, pp. 410–411.

6. Graves, E. and C. Lovato (1981), "Utilization of Short Stay Hospitals in the Treatment of Mental Disorders, 1974–78," *Advance Data No. 70*, National Center for Health Statistics, DHHS No. (PHS) 81-1250, May 22.

7. Ruffenach, (1988), op. cit., p. B1; Graves and Lovato (1981), op. cit.

8. Edwards, G. and S. Guthrie (1966), "A Comparison of Inpatient and Outpatient Treatment of Alcohol Dependence," *Lancet*, February 26, pp. 467–468; Edwards, G. and S. Guthrie (1967), "A Controlled Trial of Inpatient and Outpatient Treatment of Alcohol Dependency," *Lancet*, March 11, pp. 555–559; Longabaugh, R. et al. (1983), "Cost-Effectiveness of Alcoholism Treatment in Partial vs. Inpatient Settings," *Journal of Studies on Alcohol*, Vol. 44, No. 6, pp. 1049–1071; McLachlan, J. F. C. and R. L. Stein (1982), "Evaluation of a Day Clinic for Alcoholics," *Journal of Studies on Alcohol*, Vol. 43, No. 3, pp. 261–273; Miller, W. R. and R. K. Hester (1986a), "Inpatient Alcoholism Treatment: Who Benefits?" *American Psychologist*, Vol. 41, No. 7, pp. 794–805; Miller, W. R. and R. K. Hester (1986b), "The Effectiveness of Alcoholism Treatment: What Research Reveals," in Miller, W. and N. Heather (Editors), *Treating Addictive Behaviors: Processes of Change*. New York: Plenum, 1986, pp. 121–174.

9. Babow, I. (1975), "The Treatment Monopoly in Alcoholism and Drug Dependence: A Sociological Critique," *Journal of Drug Issues*, Vol. 5, pp. 120–128; Moore, R. A. (1977), "Ten Years of Inpatient Programs for Alcoholic Patients," *American Journal of Psychiatry*, Vol. 134, p. 542.

10. These data are age-adjusted. American Hospital Association (1988), "1987 Annual Survey," *Annual Survey Data: Hospital Statistics*. Chicago: American Hospital Association; American Hospital Association (1979), "1978 Annual Survey," *Annual Survey Data: Hospital Statistics*. Chicago: American Hospital Association.

11. American Hospital Association (1988), op. cit.; American Hospital Association (1979), op. cit.

12. American Hospital Association (1979), op. cit.

13. American Hospital Association (1984), "1983 Annual Survey," *An-*

nual Survey Data: Hospital Statistics. Chicago: American Hospital Association.

14. Office of Technology Assessment (1983), *The Effectiveness and Costs of Alcoholism Treatment* (OTA-HCS-22). Washington, DC: U.S. Government Printing Office.

15. Mansdorf, I. J. (1988), "Managed Mental Health Care: The Silver Lining for Professionals," *Register Report*, Vol. 15, No. 1, November–December, p. 4; McClellan, K. (1989), "The Benefits of an EAP," in E. Danto and R. McConoghy (Editors), *New Concepts in Employee Assistance Programs: Designing Tomorrow's EAP Today.* New York: Prentice-Hall.

16. Gove, W. R. (1979), "Sex, Mental Status and Psychiatric Treatment: A Research Note," *Social Forces*, Vol. 58, pp. 54–61; Smeade, V. S., D. Smithey-Willis, and R. J. Smead (1982), "Utility of Sex, Marital Status, Race and Age in Targeting Populations for Mental Health Services," *Psychological Reports*, Vol. 50, No. 3, pp. 843–55; Taube, C. H., H. Goldman, B. Burns, et al. (1988), "High Users of Outpatient Mental Health Services, I: Definition and Characteristics," *American Journal of Psychiatry*, Vol. 145, No. 1, pp. 19–24; Tudor, W., J. F. Tudor, and W. R. Gove (1977), "The Effect of Sex Role Differences on the Social Control of Mental Illness," *Journal of Health and Social Behavior*, Vol. 18, pp. 98–112.

17. Veroff, J. et al. (1981), *Mental Health in America: Patterns of Help-Seeking, 1957–1976.* New York: Basic Books.

18. Watts, C. A., R. Scheffler, and N. P. Jewell (1986), "Demand for Outpatient Mental Health Services in a Heavily Insured Population: The Case of the Blue Cross and Blue Shield Association, FEHBP," *Health Services Research*, Vol. 21, No. 2, pp. 267–290. For a counterargument, see Taube, C., H. Goldman, B. Burns, et al. (1988), op. cit. For a detailed look at use "differentials," see Wells, K. B. et al. (1982), *Cost Sharing and the Demand for Ambulatory Mental Health Services*, RAND Report R-2960-HHS, September 1982.

19. Tudor, Tudor, and Gove (1977), op. cit., pp. 98–112; Rushing, W. A. (1979), "Marital Status and Mental Disorder: Evidence in Favor of a Behavioral Model," *Social Forces*, Vol. 58, pp. 32–38.

20. National Institute of Mental Health (1987), *Mental Health.* Bethesda, MD: NIMH.

21. Office of Disease Prevention and Health Promotion (1987), *Preven-*

tion Fact Book. Washington, DC: U.S. Department of Health and Human Services, Public Health Service.

22. Stinson, F. S. et al. (1986–87), "Alcohol-Related Morbidity, 1974–1984," *Alcohol Health and Research World,* Vol. 11, No. 2, pp. 56–61.

23. Beckman, L. J. and H. Amaro (1983), *Barriers to Treatment among Anglo Women Alcoholics.* Los Angeles: University of California Alcohol and Drug Research Center.

24. Gomberg, E. S. and V. Franks (Editors) (1979), "Problems with Alcohol and Other Drugs," in *Gender and Disordered Behavior: Sex Differences in Psychopathology.* New York: Brunner/Mazel.

25. Mulford, H. A. (1977), "Women and Men Problem Drinkers: Sex Differences in Patients Served by Iowa's Community Alcoholism Centers," *Journal of Studies on Alcohol,* Vol. 38, pp. 1624–1639.

26. Gomberg and Franks (1979), op. cit.

27. National Institute on Alcohol and Alcoholism Treatment (1977), *Women in Treatment for Alcoholism: A Profile.* Bethesda, MD: NIAAA, Analysis and Evaluation Branch, February.

28. Barrera, M. (1982), "Raza Populations," in L. Snowden (Editor) (1982), *Reaching the Underserved: Mental Health Needs of Neglected Populations.* Beverly Hills, CA: Sage Publications; Broman, C. L. (1978), "Race Differences in Professional Help Seeking," *American Journal of Community Psychology,* Vol. 15, pp. 473–489; Kahn, M. W. and E. Heiman (1978), "Factors Associated with Length of Treatment in Barrio Neighborhood Mental Health Service," *International Journal of Social Psychiatry,* Vol. 24, pp. 259–262; Wong, F. T. L. (1986), "Counseling and Psychotherapy with Asian-Americans: Review of the Literature," *Journal of Counseling Psychology,* Vol. 33, No. 2, pp. 196–206; Liu, W. (1985), *Research Priorities Development for Pacific/Asian Americans.* Rockville, MD: NIMH Contract No. 84MO5259301D, March 29.

29. Scheffler, R. M. and A. Browne Miller (1989a), "Differences in Mental Health Service Utilization among Ethnic Subpopulations," *International Journal of Law and Psychiatry,* July–August, pp. 43–49.

30. Ibid.

31. Scheffler, R. M. and A. Browne Miller (1989b), "Demand Analysis of Mental Health Services Use among Ethnic Subpopulations," *Inquiry,* Summer, Vol. 26, pp. 202–215.

32. Scheffler and Miller (1989a, 1989b), op. cit.

33. Mayo, J. A. (1974), "Utilization of a Community Mental Health Center by Blacks," *Journal of Nervous and Mental Disease*, Vol. 158, pp. 202–207.

34. Flaherty, J. A. and R. Meaer (1980), "Measuring Racial Bias in Inpatient Treatment," *American Journal of Psychiatry*, Vol. 137, January, pp. 679–682.

35. Snowden, L. R. (1986), "Minority Mental Health Services Research: A Systematic Approach," prepared for Minority Research Branch Institutes of Mental Health, NIMH Contract No. 65501D, October.

36. Snowden, L. R. (1988), "NIMH Surveys of Research on Ethnic Minority Groups: Review and Extension," prepared for Minority Research Branch Institutes of Mental Health, NIMH Contract No. 88MO30499503D, June 30.

37. Good, R. (1984), In-house memorandum, unpublished. San Francisco: Bechtel Corp.

38. Miller and Hester (1986a, 1986b), op. cit.; Miller, W. R. and R. K. Hester (1980), "Treating the Problem Drinker: Modern Approaches," in W. R. Miller (Editor), *The Addictive Behaviors*. Oxford: Pergamon Press, pp. 11–14.

39. Miller and Hester (1986b), op. cit.

40. Edwards and Guthrie (1966, 1967), op. cit.; Longabaugh, R. et al. (1983), op. cit.; McLachlan and Stein (1982), op. cit.; Miller and Hester (1986b), op. cit., pp. 11–14.

41. McLachlan and Stein (1982), op. cit.; Penk, W. E., H. L. Charles, and T. A. Van Hoose (1978), "Comparative Effectiveness of Day Hospital and Inpatient Psychiatric Treatment," *Journal of Consulting and Clinical Psychology*, Vol. 46, No. 1, pp. 94–101.

42. Mosher, V. et al. (1975), "Comparison of Outcome in a 9-Day and 30-Day Alcoholism Treatment Program," *Journal of Studies on Alcohol*, Vol. 36, No. 9, pp. 1277–1281; Page, R. D. and L. H. Schaub (1979), "Efficacy of a Three Versus a Five Week Alcohol Treatment Program," *The International Journal of Addictions*, Vol. 14, pp. 697–714.

43. Ruffenach (1988), op. cit., p. B1.

44. Coile, R. C. (1990), "Managed Care Poised to Dominate Health," *GPS Provider*, Vol. 2, No. 1. Washington, DC: General Psychological Services, May, p. 3.

45. Ibid.

46. Ibid.
47. Miller and Hester (1986a, 1986b), op. cit.; Sobell, L. C. and M. B. Sobell (1981), "Outcome Criteria and Assessment of Alcohol Treatment Efficacy," *Evaluation of the Alcoholic: Implications for Research, Theory and Treatment, Alcohol and Health Monograph No. 5.* Rockville, MD: Alcoholism, Drug Abuse, and Mental Health Administration.
48. National Academy of Sciences (1990), "News from the Institute of Medicine." Washington, DC: National Academy of Sciences, March 12. See also Institute of Medicine (1990), *Broadening Base of Treatment for Alcohol Problems.* Washington, DC: National Academy Press.

CHAPTER 11

1. Browne Miller, A. (1988), "The Chemical Family Affair," *Employee Assistance Quarterly,* Vol. 4, No. 1, pp. 87–95.
2. Googins, B. and N. Kurtz (1981), "Discriminating Participating and Nonparticipating Supervisors in Occupational Alcoholism Programs," *Journal of Drug Issues,* Spring, pp. 26–35.
3. Waring, M. (1975). "The Impact of Specialized Training in Alcoholism on Management-Level Professionals," *Journal of Studies on Alcohol,* Vol. 36, No. 3, pp. 37–43.
4. Trice, H. and P. Roman (1978), *Spirits and Demons at Work: Alcohol and Other Drugs on the Job,* 2nd ed. New York: Cornell University.
5. Ibid.; Kaden, S. (1977) "Compassion or Cover-Up: The Alcoholic Employee," *Personnel Journal,* July, p. 33.
6. Barger, M. (1985–1986), "Is There a Conspiracy to Deny Alcoholism," *Employee Assistance Quarterly,* Vol. 1, No. 2, Winter, pp. 46–52.
7. Trice and Roman (1978), op. cit.
8. Googins and Kurtz (1981), op. cit.
9. Zemke, R. (1983), "Should Supervisors Be Counselors?" *Training/HRD,* March, pp. 48–50; Googins and Kurtz (1981), op. cit.
10. Stern, B. (Director, Merritt-Peralta Institute for Drug Treatment) (1988), personal interview, November.
11. Axelrod, S. and S. Wetzler (1989), "Factors Associated with Better

Compliance with Psychiatric Aftercare," *Hospital and Community Psychiatry*, Vol. 40, No. 4, pp. 397–401.

12. Axelrod and Wetzler (1989), op. cit., pp. 400–401.
13. Miller, W. R. and R. K. Hester (1986a), "Inpatient Alcoholism Treatment: Who Benefits?" *American Psychologist*, Vol. 41, No. 7, pp. 794–805; Miller, W. R. and R. K. Hester (1986b), "The Effectiveness of Alcoholism Treatment: What Research Reveals" in Miller, W. and N. Heather (Editors), *Treating Addictive Behaviors: Processes of Change*. New York: Plenum, pp. 121–174. Miller, W. R. and R. K. Hester (1980), "Treating the Problem Drinker: Modern Approaches," in W. R. Miller (Editor), *The Addictive Behaviors*. Oxford: Pergamon Press, pp. 11–14.
14. Axelrod and Wetzler (1989), op. cit., pp. 400–401.
15. Klinger, E. and W. M. Cox (1986), "Motivational Predictors of Alcoholic's Responses to Inpatient Treatment," *Advances in Alcohol and Substance Abuse*, Vol. 6, No. 1, pp. 35–45.
16. Brownell, K. D., G. A. Marlatt, E. Lichtenstein, and G. T. Wilson (1986), "Understanding and Preventing Relapse," *American Psychologist*, July, Vol. 41, No. 7, pp. 765–782.

CHAPTER 12

1. Trice, H. M. and J. M. Beyer (1980), "Women Employees and Job-Based Alcoholism Programs," in Cristen, C. E. (Editor), *Alcoholism in Women*. Dubuque, IA: Kendall/Hunt, p. 74.
2. For an interesting report on the development of gender differences in boys and girls, and on the effects of gender upon relationships, see Maccoby, E. (1990), "Gender and Relationships," *American Psychologist*, Vol. 45, No. 4, pp. 513–520.
3. Gomberg, E. S. (1974), "Women and Alcoholism," in Franks, A. and R. Burtle (Editors), *Women in Therapy*. New York: Brunner/Mazel, pp. 169–189.
4. Merkin, A. C. (1977), "Career on the Rocks: The Woman Alcoholic in the Workplace," *Woman's Work*, Vol. 3, No. 3, pp. 15–17, 28; see also McCrady, Barbara S. (1984), "Women and Alcoholism," in Blechman, E. (Editor), *Behavior Modification with Women*. New York: Guilford Press, pp. 428–449.

5. Blume, S. B. (1980), "Diagnosis, Casefinding and Treatment of Alcohol Problems in Women," in Cristen, C. E. (Editor), *Alcoholism in Women*. Dubuque, IA: Kendall/Hunt, pp. 122–141; and Merkin (1977), op. cit.
6. Beckman, L. J. and S. C. Wilsack (Editors) (1984), *Alcohol Problems and Women*. New York: Guilford Press.
7. Trice, H. and J. Beyer (1979), "Women Employees and Job-Based Alcoholism Programs," *Journal of Drug Issues*, Vol. 3, pp. 371–385.
8. Googins, B. and N. Kurtz (1980), "Factors Inhibiting Supervisory Referrals to Occupational Alcoholism Programs," *Journal of Studies on Alcohol*, Vol. 41, No. 11, pp. 1196–1207.
9. Beckman and Wilsack (1984), op. cit.
10. Googins and Kurtz (1980), op. cit.
11. See, for example, Beckman and Wilsack (1984), op. cit.
12. Weiss, R. M. (1980), *Dealing with Alcoholism in the Workplace*. New York: The Conference Board.
13. Trice, H. and T. Beyer (1981), "A Retrospective Study of Similarities and Differences between Male and Female Employees in a Job-Based Alcoholism Program from 1965–1977," *Journal of Drug Issues*, Vol. 2, pp. 233–262.
14. Trice and Beyer (1981), op. cit.

CHAPTER 13

1. King, R. (1985), "Stress Claims Are Making Business Jumpy," *Business Week*, October 14, p. 152.
2. Ibid., p. 154.
3. See Institute of Industrial Relations (1980), *Labor Center Reporter*. Berkeley, CA: Center for Labor Research and Education, No. 23, October; Human Resource Bulletin (1986), "Sexual Harassment in the Work Place," *Research Institute Recommendations*, Vol. 37, No. 31, Sec. 2, pp. 1–6; and "Sexual Harassment: A Victim's Profile," *Employee Relations and Human Resource Bulletin*, August 7, pp. 7–8. See also Fukami, A. (1990), "Sexual Harassment in Japan," *San Francisco Chronicle: This World* section, June 3, p. 18, for a note about *sekuhara*, or sexual harassment in Japan. *Sekuhara* has recently become a national buzzword in Japan, where women find themselves treated as

if they are sex objects because they are present in the workplace. Japan is viewed as being about fifteen years behind the United States in dealing with the issue of sexual harassment in the workplace.

4. Wojcik, J. (1986), "Cost of Treating Mental Illness Soars," *Business Insurance*, September 29, p. 64.
5. Voorhees, L. A. and R. B. Maddux (1987), *Job Performance and Chemical Dependency: A Practical Guide for Managers and Supervisors*. Los Altos, CA: Crisp Publications, p. iii.
6. Ibid., pp. iii, 4.
7. Ibid., p. 4.
8. Parker, D. et al. (1987), "Alcohol Use and Depression Symptoms Among Employed Men and Women," *American Journal of Public Health*, June, Vol. 77, No. 6, pp. 704–707.
9. Tuthill, M. (1982), "Joining the War on Drug Abuse," *Nation's Business*, Vol. 70, No. 6, pp. 64–66; and Human Resources Yearbook (1987), *Human Resources Yearbook*. Englewood Cliffs, NJ: Prentice-Hall.
10. Norbuck, C. (Editor) (1988), *Human Resources Yearbook: 1988 Edition*, Section 5.4. Englewood Cliffs, NJ: Prentice-Hall.
11. Knowles, D. (1984), "Middle-Aged and Older Workers: An Industry Perspective," *The Aging Employee*. New York: Human Sciences Press.
12. Barney, C. (1985a), "Toxic Chemicals Jar Industry," *Electronics Week*, March 18, pp. 32–43; and Barney, Clifford (1985b), "Most of U.S. Cool on Toxics," *Electronics Week*, March 25, pp. 26–29.

CHAPTER 14

1. Brecher, M. (1972), *Licit and Illicit Drugs*, The Consumers Union Report. Boston: Little, Brown, pp. 269–271.

Directory of Assistance for Employees and Employers

I have included in this directory a sampling of the many valuable services and agencies which can be of assistance to individuals and organizations in addressing drug use, abuse, and addiction among employees. The items in the sections of this directory are intended to serve as examples of the many excellent resources that are available rather than as a complete list. Check your local directory or contact organizations in this directory to find external employee assistance and managed care providers.

HOTLINES

Drug Free Workplace Helpline
1-800-843-4971

The National Institute on Drug Abuse (NIDA) has established a toll-free telephone helpline to assist employers in working toward a drug-free workplace. The line operates from 9 A.M. to 8 P.M., Eastern Standard Time. Consultation is provided in the areas of company policy, employee education, drug testing, and employee assistance program start-up.

Drug Abuse Information and Treatment Referral Line
1-800-662-HELP

NIDA also operates a toll-free information line to help individuals who need drug-related information and who may need help finding treatment.

PREVENTION, EDUCATION, AND CONSULTING SERVICES

Angela Browne Miller, M.S.W., M.P.H., Ph.D.
Metasome Corporate Consulting
98 Main Street, Suite 315
Tiburon, CA 94920
1-415-526-4324

Metasome Corporate Consulting offers nationwide services in the areas of employee drug awareness training, employee assistance program development, Substance Abuse Organizational Indicator Mapping,© workplace drug policy development, work–family programs, and other methods and techniques discussed in this book.

Leonard J. Donk, M.A., Ph.D., Vice President
    for Corporate Development
Behaviordyne, Inc.
994 San Antonio Road
Palo Alto, CA 94303
1-800-62-SCORE

The Behaviordyne Group is composed of computer and behavioral scientists dedicated to the application of sophisticated, leading-edge technologies to individual, group, and organizational analysis and behavioral prediction, including addictive behaviors. Computerized scoring and interpretation of proven standardized instrumentation are applied to cutting-edge psychological screening.

Robert Dupont, M.D.
Bensinger, Dupont, and Associates
6191 Executive Boulevard
Rockville, MD 20852
1-301-881-8210

Management consulting regarding drugs and alcohol in the workplace is provided.

Les Francis, Conference Chairman
Drug-Free Workplace Conference
90 West Montgomery Avenue, Suite 313
Rockville, MD 20850
1-703-762-3003

Directs Drug-Free Workplace Conferences and Expositions in various locations.

Richard Hagberg, Ph.D., Inc.
Executive Development Counseling
1307 South Mary Street, Suite 209
Sunnyvale, CA 94087
1-408-738-3868
FAX 1-408-738-3347

Executive Development Counseling works with upper management on an individual basis to save rather than terminate the employee.

Daryl Inaba, Pharm.D.
Director, Haight-Ashbury Medical Clinic Drug Programs
409 Clayton Street
San Francisco, CA 94117
1-415-565-1905

Dr. Inaba offers consultation on the pharmacology and toxicology of common street drugs of abuse.

MODEL EMPLOYEE ASSISTANCE AND WORKPLACE PROGRAMS

Manuel Perez, Director
Tim Mayo, Program Manager
Santa Cruz County Employee Assistance Services
Alto Counseling Center
271 Water Street
Santa Cruz, CA 95060
1-408-423-2003
1-408-728-2233

This organization has developed an innovative model of county-based employee assistance services for small businesses that do not have internal employee assistance programs. In so doing they fill the community "EAP-lack gap." This program offers outpatient treatment, assessment and referral, training, and consultation, all in Spanish as well as English. Fees to employers and employees are based on ability to pay.

Unlike the community-based program listed above, the model programs listed below are workplace-based.

Employee Assistance Program
Westinghouse Electric
Process Control Division
2000 Beta Drive
Ohare Township
Pittsburgh, PA 15238
1-412-963-4085
1-412-244-2000

Live for Life Program
Johnson & Johnson Corporation
Johnson & Johnson Plaza, WH-6G38
New Brunswick, NJ 08933
1-201-524-3140

Baking Industry and Teamster Labor Conference
1111 14th Street NW, Suite 300
Washington, DC 20005
1-202-296-5800

Employee Assistance
General Motors
3044 General Motors Boulevard
Detroit, MI 48202
1-313-556-4425

Policy for the Use or Possession of Illegal Drugs
Goodyear Tire & Rubber Co.
1144 East Market Street
Akron, OH 44316
1-216-796-4140

Employee Assistance Services
Wells Fargo Bank
343 Sansome Street
San Francisco, CA 94163
1-415-395-3033

Corporate EAP
Union Carbide, D-3
Danbury, CT 06817
1-203-794-5606

Employee Assistance Program
Lockheed-California Company
P.O. Box 551
Burbank, CA 91520
1-818-847-7303

Training and Associate Relations
Toyota Motor Sales USA, Inc.
19001 South Western Avenue
Torrance, CA 90509
1-213-618-4911

Employee Assistance Program
County of Ventura
950 County Square Drive, Suite 200
Ventura, CA 93009
1-805-658-2136

Navy Drug and Alcohol Drug Abuse Treatment Program
Navy Drug and Alcohol Drug Abuse Prevention and Control
  Division
Naval Military Personnel Command (NMPC-63)
Washington, DC 20370
1-202-694-8008

Drug-Alcohol and Safety and Health: Policies and Programs
AFL-CIO
Building and Construction Trades Department
815 16th Street NW, Suite 603
Washington, DC 20006-4189
1-202-347-1461

EEI Guide to Effective Drug and Alcohol Fitness for
  Development
Edison Electric Institute
1111 19th Street NW
Washington, DC 20036
1-202-508-5425

International Business Machines
2000 Purchase Street
Purchase, NY 10577
1-800-999-9426

EMPLOYEE ASSISTANCE ASSOCIATIONS AND ASSOCIATION PRESIDENTS

Employee Assistance Professionals Association (EAPA)
National Headquarters
4601 North Fairfax Drive, Suite 1001
Arlington, VA 22207
1-703-522-6272

Daniel Lanier, D.S.W., President of EAPA
c/o UAW-GM, Human Resources Center
2630 Featherstone Road
Auburn Hills, MI 48057
1-313-377-6503

Employee Assistance Society of North America (EASNA)
National Headquarters
PO Box 3909
Oak Park, IL 60303
1-708-383-6668

Keith McClellan, President of EASNA
c/o Multi Resource Centers
24725 West 12 Mile, Suite 310
Southfield, MI 48034
1-313-352-6000

TREATMENT PROGRAMS

Amity, Inc.
P.O. Box 60520
Tucson, AZ 85751-6520
1-602-749-5980

Betty Ford Center
39000 Bob Hope Drive
Rancho Mirage, CA 92270
1-619-773-4100

Cokenders Alcohol and Drug Program
1240 Powell Street, 2nd floor
Emeryville, CA 94608
1-415-652-1772
1-800-331-7001

Daytop Village
54 West 40th Street
New York, NY 10018
1-212-354-6000

Hazeldon Institute
Box 11
Center City, MN 55012
1-612-257-4010

Parkside Medical Services Corporation
205 West Touhy Avenue
Park Ridge, IL 60068-5881
1-708-698-4700
1-800-221-6364

Public Information Office
Phoenix House Foundation
164 West 74th Street
New York, NY 10023
1-212-595-5810

Second Genesis, Inc.
4720 Montgomery Lane, Suite 502
Bethesda, MD 20814
1-301-656-1545

Sierra Tucson
16500 North Lago del Oro Parkway
Tucson, AZ 85737
1-602-624-4000

Therapeutic Communities of America
P.O. Box 6037
Washington, DC 20005
1-202-265-9596

TREATMENT CONSULTING, CASE MANAGEMENT, AND GENERAL PSYCHOLOGICAL SERVICES

Jim Guinan, Ph.D.
Psychological Services
6010 Garden Street
Maumee, OH 43537
1-419-865-9615

Melissa Lawler, M.A.
927 East Westfield Blvd., Suite B
Indianapolis, IN 46220
1-317-255-7009

Raymond Lovett, L.C.S.W.
Psychological Services
2400 Pennsylvania Avenue NW, #215
Washington, DC 20037
1-202-965-3222

Richard Louis Miller, Ph.D.
Executive Psychological Services
2 Kenyon Avenue
Kensington, CA 94708
1-415-526-2334

Bruce Schell, Ph.D.
3301 Harden Street
Columbia, SC 29203
1-803-765-6116

David Stewart, M.Div.
1925 Pickens Street
Columbia, SC 29201
1-803-771-0243
Message with Answering Service: 1-803-256-1408

TESTING AND PHARMACEUTICAL INFORMATION AND SERVICES

Information

American Association of Clinical Chemistry (AACC)
2029 K Street NW, 7th floor
Washington, DC 20006
1-202-857-0717

Pharmaceutical Manufacturers Association (PMA)
1100 15th Street NW, Suite 900
Washington, DC 20005
1-202-835-3400

Services

Abbott Laboratories
1 Abbott Park Road
AP6C, #2MH
Abbott Park, IL 60064
1-708-937-9785

American BioTest Laboratories, Inc.
3350 Scott Boulevard, Building 15
Santa Clara, CA 95054
1-800-344-5525

American Medical Laboratories
11091 Main Street
Fairfax, VA 22030
1-703-691-9100

Roche Biomedical Laboratories
1912 Alexander Drive
P.O. Box 13973
Research Triangle Park, NC 27709
1-800-533-0567

RELEVANT LEGAL INFORMATION AND LEGAL SERVICES

American Bar Association (ABA) Advisory Commission
on Youth, Alcohol, and Drug Problems
American Bar Association
1800 M Street NW
Washington, DC 20036
1-202-331-2200
1-312-988-5613 (Family Law Section of ABA)

American Prosecutors Research Institute
Center for Local Prosecution of Drug Offenses
1033 North Fairfax Street, Suite 200
Alexandria, VA 22314
1-804-549-4253

Drug Enforcement Administration
1405 Eye Street NW
Washington, DC 20537
1-202-307-1000

National Organization on Legal Problems of Education
3601 Southwest 29th Street, Suite 223
Topeka, KS 66614
1-913-273-3550

Patton, Boggs, and Blow
2550 M Street NW
Washington, DC 20037
Attn.: Martha Kendrick, J.D.
1-202-457-6000

Schacter, Kristoff, Ross, Sprague, and Curiale
505 Montgomery Street, 14th floor
San Francisco, CA 94111
1-415-391-3333

Washington Legal Foundation Courtwatch
1705 N Street NW
Washington, DC 20036
1-202-857-0240

SELF-HELP ORGANIZATIONS AND CLEARINGHOUSES

Self-Help (Support) Groups

Adult Children of Alcoholics
P.O. Box 35623
Los Angeles, CA 90035
1-213-534-1815

Alcoholics Anonymous
Box 459
Grand Central Station
New York, NY 10163
Use local phone listings in many cities.

American Atheist Addiction Recovery Groups
Box 6120
Denver, CO 80206
1-303-758-6686
1-512-458-3731

Cocaine Anonymous
P.O. Box 1367
Culver City, CA 90232
1-213-839-1141

Jewish Alcohol and Chemical Dependent Persons
   and Significant Others
197 East Broadway, Room M-7
New York, NY 10002
1-212-473-4747

Marijuana Anonymous
135 South Cypress
Orange, CA 92666
1-213-964-2370

Men for Sobriety*
Box 618
Quakertown, PA 18951
1-215-536-8026

Narcotics Anonymous
P.O. Box 9999
Van Nuys, CA 91409
1-818-780-3951

National Association for Children of
   Alcoholics
31706 Coast Highway, Suite 201
South Laguna, CA 92677
1-714-499-3889

*Men for Sobriety and Women for Sobriety are separate gender-oriented and
mental-health-oriented organizations, administered through one office.

Rational Recovery Systems
Box 800
Lotus, CA 95651
1-916-621-2667
1-916-621-4374

Secular Organizations for Sobriety
also Save OurSelves
Box 15781
North Hollywood, CA 91615
1-919-980-8851

The Society Catholic Orientation
7601 Wayzata Boulevard
Minneapolis, MN 55426
1-612-546-6209

Women for Sobriety
Box 618
Quakertown, PA 18951
1-215-536-8026

Regional Clearinghouses in the United States

Regional clearinghouses refer callers to local self-help groups
that offer support for people facing a variety of illnesses and life
problems, including addictions. If an appropriate support group
exists in your area, the clearinghouse will know about it. If no
appropriate group exists, clearinghouse staff members can help
you start one.

Federal

National Clearinghouse for Alcohol and
    Drug Information
5600 Fishers Lane
Rockville, MD 20852
1-301-468-2600

National Council on Alcoholism
12 West 21st Street
New York, NY 10010
1-212-206-6770

National Institute on Drug Abuse (NIDA)
U.S. Department of Health and Human Services
5600 Fishers Lane
Rockville, MD 20857
1-301-443-6245

U.S. Department of Education
Drug-Free Schools and Communities
400 Maryland Avenue SW
Washington, DC 20202
1-202-401-0709

California

Adult Children of Alcoholics
Central Service Board
P.O. Box 3216
Torrance, CA 90505
1-213-534-1815

Bay Area Self-Help Center
Mental Health Association
2398 Pine Street
San Francisco, CA 94115
1-415-921-4401

California Self-Help Center
UCLA Psychology Department
405 Hilgard Avenue
Los Angeles, CA 90024
1-213-825-1799
1-800-222-LINK (in California only)

Central Valley Self-Help Center
Mental Health Association
P.O. Box 343
Merced, CA 95341
1-209-723-8861

Families Anonymous, Inc.
P.O. Box 528
Van Nuys, CA 91408
1-818-989-7841

Nar-Anon Family Group Headquarters, Inc.
World Service Office
P.O. Box 2562
Palos Verdes Peninsula, CA 90274
1-213-547-5800

Narcotics Anonymous
World Service Office
P.O. Box 9999
Van Nuys, CA 91409
1-818-780-3951

Northern Region Self-Help Center
Mental Health Association
8912 Volunteer Lane
Sacramento, CA 95825-3221
1-916-368-3100

Southern Region Self-Help Center
Mental Health Association of San Diego
3958 Third Avenue
San Diego, CA 92103
1-619-692-8880

Connecticut

Connecticut Self-Help/Mutual Support Network
Consultation Center
19 Howe Street
New Haven, CT 06511
1-203-789-7645

District of Columbia

Self-Help Clearinghouse of Greater Washington
Mental Health Association of Northern Virginia
100 North Washington Street, Suite 232
Falls Church, VA 22046
1-703-536-4100
(serves Washington, DC; northern Virginia; and southern
  Maryland)

Illinois

Self-Help Center
1600 Dodge Avenue, Suite S-122
Evanston, IL 60201
1-312-328-0470

Self-Help Center
Family Service of Champaign County
405 South State Street
Champaign, IL 61820
1-217-352-0092

Kansas

Self-Help Network
Campus Box 34
Wichita State University
Wichita, KS 67208-1595
1-316-689-3170

Massachusetts

Massachusetts Clearinghouse of Mutual Help Groups
Massachusetts Cooperative Extension
University of Massachusetts
113 Skinner Hall
Amherst, MA 01003
1-413-545-2313

Michigan

Center for Self-Help
Riverwood Center
1485 Highway M-139
Benton Harbor, MI 49022
1-616-925-0594

Michigan Self-Help Clearinghouse
109 West Michigan Avenue, Suite 900
Lansing, MI 48933
1-517-484-7373
1-800-752-5858 (in Michigan only)

Minnesota

Minnesota Mutual Help Resource Center
Wilder Foundation Community Care Unit
919 Lafond Avenue
Saint Paul, MN 55104
1-612-642-4060

Missouri

Support Group Clearinghouse
Kansas City Association for Mental Health
1020 East 63rd Street
Kansas City, MO 64110
1-816-561-HELP

Nebraska

Self-Help Information Services
1601 Euclid Avenue
Lincoln, NE 68502
1-402-476-9668

New Jersey

New Jersey Self-Help Clearinghouse
Saint Clare's-Riverside Medical Center
Denville, NJ 07834
1-201-625-9565
TDD (Telecommunications Device for the Deaf) 1-201-625-9053
1-800-FOR-MASH
(1-800-367-6274 in New Jersey only)

New York

Al-Anon Family Group Headquarters
P.O. Box 862
Midtown Station
New York, NY 10018-0862
1-212-302-7240

Alcoholics Anonymous
Box 459
Grand Central Station
New York, NY 10163
1-212-473-6200

Brooklyn Self-Help Clearinghouse
Heights Hills Mental Health Service
30 Third Avenue
Brooklyn, NY 11217
1-718-834-7341
1-718-834-7332

Long Island Self-Help Clearinghouse
New York Institute of Technology
Central Islip Campus
Central Islip, NY 11722
1-516-348-3030

New York City Self-Help Clearinghouse, Inc.
P.O. Box 022812
Brooklyn, NY 11202
1-718-596-6000

New York State Self-Help Clearinghouse
New York Council on Children and Families
Empire State Plaza, Tower 2
Albany, NY 12224
1-518-474-6293

Westchester Self-Help Clearinghouse
Westchester Community College
Academics Arts Building
75 Grasslands Road
Valhalla, NY 10595
1-914-347-3620

Oregon

Northwest Regional Self-Help Clearinghouse
718 West Burnside Street
Portland, OR 97209
1-503-222-5555

Pennsylvania

Self-Help Group Network of the Pittsburgh Area
710 1/2 South Avenue
Wilkensburg, PA 15221
1-412-247-5400

Self-Help Information Network Exchange (SHINE)
c/o Voluntary Action Center
2125 North Washington Avenue
Park Plaza, Lower Level
Scranton, PA 18503
1-717-961-1234

Rhode Island

Support Group Helpline
Rhode Island Department of Health
Cannon Building, Davis Street
Providence, RI 02908
1-401-277-2223

South Carolina

Midland Area Support Group Network
Lexington Medical Center
2720 Sunset Boulevard
West Columbia, SC 29169
1-803-791-9227

Tennessee

Support Group Clearinghouse
Mental Health Association of Knox County
6712 Kingston Pike, #203
Knoxville, TN 37919
1-614-584-6736

Texas

Dallas Self-Help Clearinghouse
Mental Health Association of Dallas County
2500 Maple Avenue
Dallas, TX 75201-1998
1-214-871-2420

Greater San Antonio Self-Help Clearinghouse
Mental Health in Greater San Antonio
1407 North Main Street
San Antonio, TX 78212
1-512-222-1571

Self-Help Clearinghouse
Mental Health Association in Houston and Harris County
2211 Norfolk Street, Suite 810
Houston, TX 77098
1-713-523-8963

Tarrant County Self-Help Clearinghouse
Mental Health Association of Tarrant County
3136 West 4th Street
Fort Worth, TX 76107-2113
1-817-335-5405

Texas Self-Help Clearinghouse
Mental Health Association in Texas
1111 West 24th Street
Austin, TX 78705
1-512-454-3706

Vermont

Vermont Self-Help Clearinghouse
c/o Parents Assistance Line
103 South Main Street
Waterbury, VT 05676
1-802-241-2249
1-800-442-5356 (in Vermont only)

National Information Centers in the United States

These three centers maintain current listings of self-help groups
throughout the country. The New Jersey clearinghouse pub-
lishes *The Self-Help Sourcebook,* a national directory of support
groups, which is available for $9.

National Self-Help Clearinghouse
City University of New York Graduate Center, Room 1206A
33 West 42nd Street, Room 629-N
New York, NY 10036
1-212-840-1259

Self-Help Center
1600 Dodge Avenue, Suite S-122
Evanston, IL 60201
1-312-328-0470

Self-Help Clearinghouse
Saint Clare's-Riverside Medical Center
Denville, NJ 07834
1-201-625-9565
TDD 1-201-625-9053

Regional Clearinghouses in Canada

Canadian Council on Social Development
(Conseil Canadien de Development Social)
P.O. Box 3505, Station C
Ottawa, Ontario, Canada K1Y 4G1
1-613-728-1865

Family Life Education Council
233 12th Avenue SW
Calgary, Alberta, Canada T2R 0G9
1-403-262-1117

Camac.-Centre d'Aide Mutuelle, Inc.
CP 535, Succ. Desjardins
Montreal, Quebec, Canada H5B 1B6
1-514-341-1440

Self-Help Development Unit
410 Cumberland Avenue North
Saskatoon, Saskatchewan, Canada S7M 1M6
1-306-652-7817

Self-Help Clearinghouse of Metropolitan Toronto
40 Orchard View Blvd., Suite 215
Toronto, Ontario, Canada M4R 1B9
1-416-487-4355

Self-Help Collaboration Project
United Way of the Lower Mainland
1625 West 8th Avenue
Vancouver, British Columbia, Canada V6J 1T9
1-604-731-7781

Winnipeg Self-Help Resource Clearinghouse
NorWest Co-op and Health Center
103-61 Tyndall Avenue
Winnipeg, Manitoba, Canada R2X 2T4
1-204-589-5500
1-204-633-5955

STATE, TERRITORY, AND PROVINCE SUBSTANCE-ABUSE AUTHORITIES

These agencies can direct you to chemical dependence treatment programs and information in your state.

Department of Mental Health Community Programs
Division of Mental Illness and Substance Abuse
200 Interstate Park Drive
P.O. Box 3710
Montgomery, AL 36193
1-205-271-9209

Department of Health and Social Services
Office of Alcoholism and Drug Abuse
Pouch H-05-F
Juneau, AK 99811
1-907-586-6201

Arizona Department of Health Services
Office of Community Behavioral Health
701 East Jefferson Street, Suite 400A
Phoenix, AZ 85034
1-602-255-1152

Arkansas Office on Alcohol and Drug Abuse Prevention
1515 West 7th Street, Suite 300
Little Rock, AR 72201
1-501-371-2603

Department of Alcohol and Drug Abuse
111 Capitol Mall, Suite 450
Sacramento, CA 95814
1-916-445-0834

Colorado Department of Health
Alcohol and Drug Abuse Division
4210 East 11th Avenue
Denver, CO 80220
1-303-331-8201

Connecticut Alcohol and Drug Abuse Commission
999 Asylum Avenue
Hartford, CT 06105
1-203-566-4145

Bureau of Alcoholism and Drug Abuse
1901 North Dupont Highway
New Castle, DE 19720
1-302-421-6106

Department of Human Services
Office of Health Planning and Development
1875 Connecticut Avenue NW, Suite 836
Washington, DC 20009
1-202-673-7481

Department of Health and Rehabilitative Services
Alcohol and Drug Abuse Program
1317 Winewood Blvd.
Tallahassee, FL 32301
1-904-488-0900

Georgia Department of Human Resources
Division of Mental Health and Mental Retardation
Alcohol and Drug Section
878 Peachtree Street NE, Suite 318
Atlanta, GA 30309
1-404-894-6352

Government of Guam
Department of Mental Health and Substance Abuse
P.O. Box 8896
Tamuning, GU 96911
1-671-477-9704

Department of Health
Mental Health Division
Alcohol and Drug Abuse Branch
1250 Punchbowl Street
P.O. Box 3378
Honolulu, HI 96801
1-808-548-4280

Department of Health and Welfare
Bureau of Substance Abuse and Social Services
450 West State Street
Boise, ID 83720
1-208-334-6800

Illinois Department of Alcoholism and Substance Abuse
100 West Randolph Street, Suite 5-600
Chicago, IL 60601
1-312-917-3840

State of Indiana Department of Mental Health
Division of Addiction Services
117 East Washington Street
Indianapolis, IN 46204
1-317-232-7816

Iowa Department of Public Health
Division of Substance Abuse and Health Promotion
Lucas State Office Building
321 East 12th Street, 4th floor
Des Moines, IA 50319
1-515-281-3641

Alcohol and Drug Abuse Services
Biddle Building
2700 West 6th Street
Topeka, KS 66606
1-913-296-3925

Department of Mental Health/Mental Retardation Services
Division of Substance Abuse
275 East Main Street
Health Services Building, 1st floor
Frankfort, KY 40621
1-502-564-2880

Office of Prevention and Recovery from Alcohol and Drug
  Abuse
2744-B Wooddale Blvd.
P.O. Box 53129
Baton Rouge, LA 70892
1-504-922-0730

Office of Alcohol and Drug Abuse
Prevention Bureau of Rehabilitation
State House, Station 11
Augusta, ME 04333
1-207-289-2781

State of Maryland
Addiction Services Administration
Herbert O'Connor Building
201 West Preston Street
Baltimore, MD 21201
1-301-225-6926

Massachusetts Division of Substance Abuse Services
50 Tremont Street
Boston, MA 02111
1-617-727-1960

Michigan Department of Public Health
Office of Substance Abuse Services
3500 North Logan Street
P.O. Box 30035
Lansing, MI 48909
1-517-373-8600

Department of Human Services
Chemical Dependency Program Division
Space Center Building, 2nd floor
444 Lafayette Road
Saint Paul, MN 55155
1-612-296-3991

Mississippi Department of Mental Health
Division of Alcohol and Drug Abuse
1500 Woolfolk State Office Building
Jackson, MS 39201
1-601-359-1297

Missouri Department of Mental Health
Division of Alcohol and Drug Abuse
1915 South Ridge Drive
P.O. Box 687
Jefferson City, MO 65102
1-314-751-4942

State of Montana Department of Institutions
Alcohol and Drug Abuse Division
1539 11th Avenue
Helena, MT 59620
1-406-444-2827

Nebraska Department of Public Institutions
Division on Alcoholism and Drug Abuse
801 West Van Dorn Street
P.O. Box 94728
Lincoln, NE 68509
1-402-471-2851/5583

Department of Human Resources
Bureau of Alcohol and Drug Abuse
505 East King Street
Carson City, NV 89710
1-702-885-4790

New Hampshire Office of Alcohol and Drug Abuse Prevention
Health and Welfare Building
Hazen Drive
Concord, NH 03301
1-603-271-4627

New Jersey Division of Narcotic and Drug Abuse Control
129 East Hanover Street, CN 362
Trenton, NJ 08625
1-609-292-5760

Behavioral Health Services Division
Substance Abuse Bureau
725 Saint Michaels Drive
P.O. Box 968
Santa Fe, NM 87504
1-505-827-0117

New York Division of Substance Abuse Services
Executive Park South
Box 8200
Albany, NY 12203
1-518-457-7629

Division of Mental Health/Mental Retardation Services
Alcohol and Drug Abuse Section
325 North Salisbury Street
Albermarle Building, Room 1100
Raleigh, NC 27611
1-919-733-4670

North Dakota Department of Human Services
Division of Alcoholism and Drug Abuse
State Capitol/Judicial Wing
Bismarck, ND 58505
1-701-224-2769

Bureau of Drug Abuse
30 East Broad Street, Room 295A
Columbus, OH 43215
1-614-466-7893

Oklahoma Department of Mental Health
Alcohol and Drug Programs
4545 North Lincoln Blvd.
P.O. Box 53277
Capitol Station
Oklahoma City, OK 73152
1-405-521-0044

Office of Alcohol and Drug Abuse Programs
301 Public Service Building
Salem, OR 97310
1-503-378-2163

Pennsylvania Department of Health
Commonwealth and Forster Avenues
P.O. Box 90
Harrisburg, PA 17108
1-717-787-9857

Puerto Rico Department of Addiction Control Services
P.O. Box B-Y
Rio Piedras Station
Rio Piedras, PR 00928
1-809-764-3795

Department of Mental Health/Mental Retardation and
    Hospitals Division of Substance Abuse
Substance Abuse Administration Building
Cranston, RI 02920
1-401-464-2091

South Carolina Commission on Alcohol and Drug Abuse
3700 Forest Drive
Landmark East, Suite 300
Columbia, SC 29204
1-803-734-9520

South Dakota Division of Alcohol and Drug Abuse
Joe Foss Building, Room 125
523 East Capitol Street
Pierre, SD 57501
1-605-773-3123

Tennessee Department of Mental Health/Mental Retardation
Alcohol and Drug Abuse Services
706 Church Street, 4th floor
Nashville, TN 37219
1-615-741-1921

Department of Health Services
Office of the High Commissioner
HICOM Headquarters
Saipan, Mariana Islands, TT 96950
1-615-741-1921

Texas Commission on Alcohol and Drug Abuse
1705 Guadalupe Street
Austin, TX 78701
1-512-463-5510

Utah State Division of Alcoholism and Drugs
150 West North Temple
P.O. Box 45500
Salt Lake City, UT 84145
1-801-538-3939

Office of Alcohol and Drug Abuse Programs
State Office Building
103 South Main Street
Waterbury, VT 05676
1-802-241-2170

Virginia Department of Mental Health/Mental Retardation
Office of Substance Abuse Services
109 Governor Street
P.O. Box 1797
Richmond, VA 23214
1-804-786-3906

Virgin Islands Division of Mental Health,
   Alcohol and Drug Dependency
P.O. Box 7309
St. Thomas, VI 00801
1-809-773-1992

Washington Department of Social and Health Services
Bureau of Alcoholism and Substance Abuse Office
Building 44W
Olympia, WA 98504
1-206-753-5866

Department of Health
Division of Alcoholism and Drug Abuse
1800 Washington Street East
Building 3, Room 451
Charleston, WV 25305
1-304-348-2276

Office of Alcohol and Other Drug Abuse
1 West Wilson Street
P.O. Box 7851
Madison, WI 53707
1-608-266-3442

Canadian Provincial Agencies

These agencies can direct you to chemical dependency treatment programs and services in your province.

Alberta

Alberta Alcoholism and Drug Abuse Commission
10909 Jasper Avenue, 7th floor
Edmonton, Alberta, Canada T5J 3M9
1-403-427-7301

British Columbia

Ministry of Labour and Consumer Services
Alcohol and Drug Programs
818 Fort Street
Victoria, British Columbia, Canada V8W 1H8
1-604-387-5870

Manitoba

The Alcoholism Foundation of Manitoba
1031 Portage Avenue
Winnipeg, Manitoba, Canada R3G 0R9
1-204-944-6200

New Brunswick

Alcoholism and Drug Dependency Commission
of New Brunswick
65 Church Street
P.O. Box 6000
Fredericton, New Brunswick, Canada E3B 5H1
1-506-453-2136

Newfoundland

The Alcohol and Drug Dependency Commission
of Newfoundland and Labrador
120 Torbay Road, 1st floor
Saint John's, Newfoundland, Canada A1A 2G8
1-709-737-3600

Northwest Territories

Alcohol and Drug Services
Department of Social Services
Government of Northwest Territories
Yellowknife, Northwest Territories, Canada X1A 2L9
1-403-873-7155

Nova Scotia

Nova Scotia Commission on Drug Dependency
5676 Spring Garden Road, Suite 314
Halifax, Nova Scotia, Canada B3J 1H1
1-902-424-4270

Ontario

Addiction Research Foundation
33 Russell Street
Toronto, Ontario, Canada M5S 2S1
1-416-595-6000

Prince Edward Island

Addiction Services of Prince Edward Island
P.O. Box 37
Charlottetown, Prince Edward Island, Canada C1A 7K2
1-902-892-4265

Quebec

Ministry of Social Affairs
1075 Chemin Ste. Foy
Quebec City, Quebec, Canada G1S 2M1
1-418-643-6042

Saskatchewan

Saskatchewan Alcoholism Commission
Hamilton Street, 3rd floor
Regina, Saskatchewan, Canada S4P 3V7
1-306-565-4085

Yukon

Alcohol and Drug Services
Department of Human Resources
Government of Yukon
P.O. Box 2703
Whitehorse, Yukon, Canada Y1A 2C6
1-403-667-5777

PUBLICATIONS AND PUBLISHERS

These are just some of the many valuable publications and publishers on the topics of drug use, abuse, and addiction, and workplace mental health.

Alcohol and Drug Abuse in the Workplace: Complete Resource Guide and *The New Drug-Free Workplace Act: Complete Guide for Federal Contractors and Grantees*
Bureau of National Affairs, Inc.
1231 25th Street NW
Washington, DC 20037
1-202-452-4200

Drug Abuse: The Workplace Issues
Don Bohl
American Management Association Membership
    Publications Division
135 West 50th Street
New York, NY 10020
1-212-903-8070

Employee Assistance Quarterly
Haworth Press, Inc.
10 Alice Street
Binghamton, NY 13904-1580
1-800-342-9678

GPS Provider
General Psychological Services, Inc.
1730 Rhode Island Avenue NW, Suite 1204
Washington, DC 20036
1-202-331-7792

The National Report on Substance Abuse
Buraff Publications
Washington, DC 20036
1-202-862-0990

NIDA Capsules
Press Office of National Institute on Drug Abuse
5600 Fishers Lane
Rockville, MD 20857
1-301-443-6245
1-800-729-6686

Substance Abuse Report
Business Research Publications
817 Broadway, 3rd floor
New York, NY 10003
1-212-673-4700

Comp Care Publications (request publication list)
2415 Annapolis Lane
Minneapolis, MN 55441
1-612-559-4800
1-800-328-3330

Coronet/MTI Film & Video (request film and video list)
108 Wilmot Road
Deerfield, IL 60015
1-800-621-2131

Drug Enforcement Administration (request publication list)
700 Army Navy Drive
Arlington, VA 22202
1-202-289-1780

Hazeldon Education Materials (request publication list)
Box 176
Center City, MN 55012
1-800-462-7700
1-612-257-4010

Parkside Publications (request publication list)
205 West Touhy Avenue
Park Ridge, IL 60068-5881
1-708-698-4700
1-800-221-6364

Stevens Publishing Corporation (request magazine list)
225 North New Road
P.O. Box 2573
Waco, TX 76702-2573
1-817-776-9000

Index